MUSLIMS UNDER SIKH RULE IN THE NINETEENTH CENTURY

Islamic South Asia Series
Series Editor Ruby Lal, Emory University

Advisory Board
Iftikhar Dadi, Cornell University
Stephen F. Dale, Ohio State University
Rukhsana David, Kinnaird College for Women
Michael Fisher, Oberlin College
Marcus Fraser, Fitzwilliam Museum
Ebba Koch, University of Vienna
David Lewis, London School of Economics
Francis Robinson, Royal Holloway, University of London
Ron Sela, Indiana University Bloomington
Willem van Schendel, University of Amsterdam

Titles
Sexual and Gender Diversity in the Muslim World: History, Law and Vernacular Knowledge, Vanja Hamzic
The Architecture of a Deccan Sultanate: Courtly Practice and Royal Authority in Late Medieval India, Pushkar Sohoni
Sufi Shrines and the Pakistani State: The End of Religious Pluralism, Umber Bin Ibad
The Hindu Sufis of South Asia: Partition, Shrine Culture and the Sindhis in India, Michel Boivin
Islamic Sermons and Public Piety in Bangladesh: The Poetics of Popular Preaching, Max Stille
The Mosques of Colonial South Asia: A Social and Legal History of Muslim Worship, Sana Haroon
The Language of the Taj Mahal: Islam, Prayer and the Religion of Shah Jahan, Michael D. Calabria
Muslims under Sikh Rule in the Nineteenth Century, Robina Yasmin

MUSLIMS UNDER SIKH RULE IN THE NINETEENTH CENTURY

Maharaja Ranjit Singh and Religious Tolerance

Robina Yasmin

I.B. TAURIS
LONDON · NEW YORK · OXFORD · NEW DELHI · SYDNEY

I.B. TAURIS
Bloomsbury Publishing Plc
50 Bedford Square, London, WC1B 3DP, UK
1385 Broadway, New York, NY 10018, USA
29 Earlsfort Terrace, Dublin 2, Ireland

BLOOMSBURY, I.B. TAURIS and the I.B. Tauris logo are trademarks of Bloomsbury Publishing Plc

First published in Great Britain 2022
This paperback edition published 2023

Copyright © Robina Yasmin, 2022

Robina Yasmin has asserted her right under the Copyright, Designs and Patents Act, 1988, to be identified as Author of this work.

For legal purposes the Acknowledgements on p. vi constitute an extension of this copyright page.

Series design by Adriana Brioso
Cover image: Maharajah Ranjit Singh in the Bazaar.
(© The Ashmolean Museum/Alamy Stock Photo)

All rights reserved. No part of this publication may be reproduced or transmitted in any form or by any means, electronic or mechanical, including photocopying, recording, or any information storage or retrieval system, without prior permission in writing from the publishers.

Bloomsbury Publishing Plc does not have any control over, or responsibility for, any third-party websites referred to or in this book. All internet addresses given in this book were correct at the time of going to press. The author and publisher regret any inconvenience caused if addresses have changed or sites have ceased to exist, but can accept no responsibility for any such changes.

A catalogue record for this book is available from the British Library.

A catalog record for this book is available from the Library of Congress.

ISBN:	HB:	978-0-7556-4032-4
	PB:	978-0-7556-4036-2
	ePDF:	978-0-7556-4033-1
	eBook:	978-0-7556-4034-8

Series: Library of Islamic South Asia

Typeset by RefineCatch Limited, Bungay, Suffolk

To find out more about our authors and books visit www.bloomsbury.com and sign up for our newsletters.

CONTENTS

Acknowledgements	vi
Introduction	1
Chapter 1 SIKH−MUSLIM RELATIONS: A HISTORICAL PERSPECTIVE	15
Chapter 2 CONQUESTS OF MAHARAJA RANJIT SINGH: TREATMENT OF THE FALLEN MUSLIM RULERS AND POPULATION	39
Chapter 3 STATE POLICIES TOWARDS MUSLIMS: REALITY OR FAÇADE	63
Chapter 4 *SARKAR-E-KHALSA*: STATUS AND ROLE OF HINDU, MUSLIM AND EUROPEAN COURTIERS	89
Chapter 5 SIKH−MUSLIM RELATIONS IN THE POST-RANJIT SINGH PERIOD (1839−49)	111
Conclusion	127
Glossary	133
Notes	137
Bibliography	171
Index	185

ACKNOWLEDGEMENTS

First of all, I am thankful to Allah, the Most Merciful and the Most Beneficent, for giving me much-needed strength and perseverance to undertake this research work. I owe a great deal to my teacher, Prof. Dr. Muhammad Iqbal Chawla, who has been a constant source of guidance, support and inspiration throughout the development and refinement of this study.

In every academic endeavour, special people, through chance or circumstance, become part of the fabric of the story. Likewise, the efforts of many sincere and knowledgeable teachers and friends went into the creation of this work. Collectively, they contributed priceless comments that clearly improved the quality of the final product. I am also greatly indebted to the staff of the Directorate of Punjab Archives, British Library London, and the library of the Department of History and Pakistan Studies, University of the Punjab, for their unconditional support and valuable time. Completion of my research work would have not been possible without their support. Very special thanks go to Prof. Francis Robinson of Royal Holloway, University of London, UK, who despite all his engagements and constraints guided me throughout this work. He further honed my exploratory skills and gave me much-needed confidence and skills to undertake this research. I am also grateful to Fakir Saifuddin of the Fakir Khana family, Lahore, who not only provided me with the primary documents of his family but also guided me at every stage of this writing.

Finally, I am grateful to my entire family, including my husband, sons and parents, who believed in me and supported me with their love and prayed throughout this study; particularly to my five-year-old son, whom I left behind in Pakistan when he needed me the most, go my deepest thanks and love.

Robina Shoeb

INTRODUCTION

The aim of this book is to offer an understanding of the socio-economic, political and religious condition of the Muslims under Sikh rule in the Punjab, 1799–1849. Its main purpose is to review the relationship between the Muslims and the Sikhs during this period, so that a larger picture of their relationship can be viewed from a new perspective. This relationship went through several phases, with many ups and downs, but was especially tense during the endgame of the British Raj in India. Muslims and Sikhs fought each other and caused severe damage to life and property on the eve of the partition of India and the division of the Punjab in 1947, leaving a permanent legacy of rift between the two. The real causes of the dispute between Sikhs and Muslims are still an enigma, and historians have not paid sufficient attention to the relationship between them. In fact, one school of thought, mostly Sikh historians, hold the Muslims – especially the Mughal rulers – responsible for killing and mistreating the Sikh Gurus; while the other group, mostly Muslim historians, consider that the Sikh rule in the Punjab was nothing but the establishment of a Sikh Raj in which Muslim life, property and existence were dishonoured. There is no end to this blame game, although the historiography of the Muslim era and the Sikh period reveals some irrefutable truths about the treatment of minorities during these times.

This book focuses on the condition of the Muslims during the Sikh rule in the Punjab. The underlying hypothesis is that the Sikh rule, especially under Ranjit Singh, took a secular approach and that his successors followed his policies; however, in a number of places the Sikh administration and policies did maltreat the Muslims on religious grounds, and hence the existence of Islam as a religion and faith was seen to be in peril. This perception subsequently had serious religious, socio-economic and political implications for the relations between Sikhs and Muslims. What were the exigencies and dynamics that prompted such policies? In light of the available narratives, the story of the Muslims' condition under Sikh rule has become so complicated and bleak that no clear picture can be drawn. Therefore, a re-examination is long overdue. Through primary and secondary sources, which had not previously been completely explored by historians, a clearer picture of the key factors governing Sikh–Muslim relationships can be drawn.

After the death of Aurangzeb Alamgir in 1707, the centrifugal forces in the subcontinent became powerful and many provinces and princely states became semi-independent. The province of Punjab was one of these. As a result, towards the end of the eighteenth century, Sikhs became politically strong and succeeded in establishing their own rule in the Punjab.

There is controversy among historians about the policies under the Sikh rule of the Punjab regarding Muslims, especially about Ranjit Singh's rule. While most Sikh historians have appreciated the policies of Ranjit Singh, the British and Muslims have criticized the Maharaja for his anti-Muslim policies and have quoted various atrocities inflicted on the Muslims. Therefore, there is a clear need to analyse the Sikh regime without any bias or bigotry.

In exploring the condition of the Muslims, the current study will make an unbiased and independent evaluation of Sikh rule and its policies towards Muslims. By comprehensively reviewing the existing literature and artefacts, and interviewing academics, researchers and others, the study will try to find evidence to appraise the policies of the Sikh regime vis-à-vis the Muslims. It will make a suitable contribution to the existing literature and help to explain the current dynamics of the relationship between Muslims and Sikhs.

The personality and polity of Maharaja Ranjit Singh has been the subject of great controversy among historians. Writers such as Cunningham[1] and Kohli[2] point to some very 'high and noble' motives, which mainly drove his passion for the creation of a grand kingdom that subsequently proved to be a great source of pride for the Sikhs and posterity. Other scholars such as Prinsep[3] and Sinha[4] term his polity a farce, which was only a 'jigsaw block' in his overall grand military and political scheme.

By and large, kingdoms are created and sustained through strength of arms and armies. However, the basic norm to measure a ruler's greatness should be the manner in which the ruler 'wields his authority. To what end does he use his power, for the furtherance of his personal ambitions or for the welfare of his subjects through the projection of eternal values of truth, goodness, equity, justice, and freedom?'[5]

Both Eric Bentley[6] and J. B. Macaulay[7] lament history being made a mere record of the 'court and camp of royal intrigues and state rivalry, of pageants or processions or chivalric encounters'. Bentley believes that 'history does not lie in laws, Senate Houses or battle-fields but in the tide of thought and action – the world of existence that brightens, glooms, blossoms and fades'. He adds that 'what gives meaning to history is not merely the exploits and aggressive enterprises of the conquerors and kings, but how the victorious sword is used during the time of peace'. In line with this principle, by exploring the condition of Muslims under a Sikh ruler, the current study attempts to capture the real ethos of the Sikh kingdom under the legendary Maharaja Ranjit Singh.

In tracing the origins of the hostility between Muslims and Sikhs, Jean-Marie Lafont[8] observes that Sikhism grew at a time when Hinduism and Islam were intensifying their 'orthodoxies and were evolving under the influence of Bhaktis and Sufis'. He further observes that a pleasant and healthy relationship existed between Sikhs and early Mughal emperors including Babur, Humayun and Akbar. Unlike their ancestors, later Mughal emperors, including Jahangir, Shahjahan and Alamgir, were more 'orthodox Islamists' due largely to their personal beliefs and education. Moreover, with continued incursions from Central Asia, Iran and Afghanistan to exploit the riches of India, sociopolitical and fiscal pressure increased on non-Muslims. A saying was very common in the then Punjab that 'What we eat and drink is ours, the rest is Ahmed Shah's'.[9] This necessitated Mughal power keeping open the Punjab plains at any cost to get constant reinforcements during their conquest of the Deccan and war against Maratha. Prince Khusroo's rebellion against his father Jahangir in early 1606 can also been seen as a struggle between orthodox and liberal Islam. Mughal enmity further intensified when Guru Arjun sided with Khusroo against Jahangir, resulting in the Guru being called to Lahore and executed, but matters did not stop there. Guru Har Gobind was reportedly kept in prison for more than ten years. As a result, Guru Gobind Singh declared 'he is of the *Khalsa* who combats in the van, who mounts the war horse, who is ever waging battle and who is continually armed'.[10] This background adequately explains the worsening relations between Sikhs and Muslims, including Mughals and Afghans, in the Punjab from Guru Arjun's execution in 1606 to the fall of Lahore in 1799.

Filled with such unpleasant memories of Afghan conquests and later Mughal orthodoxy, it seems likely that the Sikh rulers must have been full of revenge and revulsion for Muslims. In a similar vein, as a likely consequence Muslims might have been maltreated in the Ranjit Singh era.[11] Some incidents are referred to time and again in support of this argument. For example, in 1810 Ranjit Singh without any justification exacted Rs. 10,000 from the people of Uchkal Imam, the shrine of a Muslim saint. In 1813 he extorted the Koh-e-Noor diamond from Shah Shuja, ex-monarch of Kabul.[12] There is more, similar evidence to prove ill-treatment of Muslims under Ranjit Singh.

From the other side, considerable evidence exists to contradict this view. Historians such as Lepel Griffin,[13] W. G. Osborne[14] and Jean-Marie Lafont[15] hold that Ranjit Singh was a benevolent ruler for all religions and faiths. His policies were largely free from bigotry or any kind of narrowness or racial superiority. Ranjit Singh was definitely a voracious warrior, but his sword hardly shed any blood during times of peace. Although he did subjugate Lahore, Peshawar, Kashmir and other Muslim areas, he always refrained from barbarism and looting. When Peshawar fell, he issued clear directions against plundering and looting of the city.[16] The city of Lahore returned to normal life soon after its conquest. Ranjit Singh assured Lahorites safety against plunder in order to resume their economic life without fear. He did not declare Sikhism to be the state religion, nor did he make any conscious effort to propagate his religion.[17] He bestowed few special privileges on Sikhs and never undertook deliberate efforts to limit the opportunities for non-Sikhs. All Sikhs, Muslims and Hindus enjoyed special status in his court. Historians report a number of events in support of this. Sonehri Masjid in the Kashmiri Bazar of Lahore, formerly in the possession of non-Muslims, was restored to the Muslims. The tombs of Hazrat Data Ganj Bukhsh and Moj-e-Darya were repaired at state expense. Ranjit Singh paid a handsome price to a Muslim calligraphist who had transcribed the Holy Quran but could not find a buyer for his lifelong hard work.

According to Griffin, Ranjit Singh was so completely a product of the Sikh theocracy and so embodied the spirit of the *Khalsa* that no account of his character and career would be complete without having an understanding of the religious system of the Sikhs.[18] A deep discussion is required to explore this aspect of the persona of Maharaja Ranjit Singh.

In light of the above divergent, conflicting arguments and evidence, it is imperative to formally and in detail explore the condition of the Muslims under Maharaja Ranjit Singh and subsequent Sikh rulers to objectively assess the regime of Sikhs in the Punjab. Although both arguments are well founded and reasonably supported by the evidence, given the history of constrained relations between Muslims and Sikhs, maltreatment of Muslims seems theoretically quite logical and obvious. However, contrary to this logical corollary, many historians have portrayed Ranjit Singh as a benevolent ruler. While focusing on the position of Muslims under his rule, the current study will attempt to find answers to the following questions:

- What impact did the orthodoxies of later Mughal emperors and Afghan incursions have on Sikh–Muslim relations?
- What were the real dynamics that governed the personality and polity of Ranjit Singh?
- Was the spirit of forbearance and moderation displayed by Ranjit Singh real or a facade?
- What were the administrative, political, socio-economic and religious policies of Ranjit Singh?
- What was the role and status of Muslim nobles in the court of Ranjit Singh in shaping state policies?

A large body of literature holds that Ranjit Singh was an enlightened and moderate ruler who looked at everyone with 'one eye'. His policies and administration were fair, temperate and equitable for all faiths, including Islam. However, a number of historians, both Sikh and non-Sikh, believe that Ranjit Singh's tolerant policies were based on political and administrative expediency. Thus, the picture remains unclear about the Sikh regime's policy towards the Muslims. A brief review of the literature follows.

W. G. Osborne[19] presents an in-depth account of everyday proceedings at the Maharaja's court. However, the author mentions hardly anything that reflects upon maltreatment of Muslims. Instead, the book presents a detailed description of the personality of Fakir Azizuddin who had a significant influence over Ranjit Singh. Fakir Azizuddin's special status at court, in fact, signifies a positive relationship between Muslims and the Sikh rulers.

Sohan Lal Suri's *Umdat-ut-Tawarikh* contains information on many matters during the reign of Ranjit Singh.[20] There are frequent references to the movements, events and charities supported by the Maharaja, his participation in festivals, and his treatment of those who served him. All the happenings in the Lahore *Darbar* (court), his interest in the army and in administration, his revenue policy, and even small events, are also discussed. Detailed descriptions of his alms to the poor and needy, Sikhs and non-Sikhs alike, and to different institutions reflect his catholicity and generosity. This book is a good source of information for the period; of its five volumes, volumes 2 and 3 are concerned with the court of Ranjit Singh.

In his exhaustive narrative of the Sikh regime, Lepel Griffin[21] objectively touches upon the crucial subject of the condition of Muslims. He devotes a whole chapter to his subject's personality, his habits and his behaviour towards his enemies and friends, claiming that although passionate he was never violent. He treated the Muslim khans wisely and successfully earned their support to strengthen his position in the western areas. His practical policies won over the family of Nawab Muzaffar Khan of Multan and many other Muslim *sardars*. Griffin further explains that although the Muslims were the enemies of the Sikhs, even then the trustworthy ministers of Ranjit Singh were Muslims. The prime minister and foreign minister of his Cis-Sutlej states were Syed Muhammad Hassan and Syed Muhammad Hussain respectively, and he always held the services of the Fakir brothers in high esteem. Even in other states under Ranjit Singh's sway, Muslims served in very high official positions, while the Nawabs of Multan were famous for their wisdom and influence during Ranjit Singh's reign. Some renowned Muslims also enjoyed high status in the army and administration.

S. M. Latif[22] traces the history of the Punjab from remotest antiquity to the present. He believes that Ranjit Singh's zenith owes much to his mother-in-law Sadakaur. Ranjit Singh grew up in an odd and carefree fashion, with little interest in learning. The author reports that the Muslims of Lahore invited him to invade their city and free the Lahorites from the tyranny of three Sikh Rajas. No plunder or looting followed the fall of Lahore, under the directions of Ranjit Singh, and during his regime Muslims were freely allowed to practise Islam. In fact, Qazi Nizamuddin was appointed to settle the matrimonial affairs of the Muslims of Lahore and the Fakir brothers were given high positions at court. However, Latif observes that Ranjit Singh did not strictly abide by his promises and pledges; he would change his stance as and when required, in order to accomplish his designs. While Ranjit Singh did not allow his army to plunder Lahore or Peshawar, Jhang enjoyed no such amnesty. Latif also mentions several occasions when Muslim monuments were damaged, such as the tomb and mosque of Shah Sharaf in digging a ditch around the city. This shows that the Maharaja's tolerance and benevolence were just political pragmatism and met the needs of the time; his cruelty or maltreatment of Muslims was not out of religious bias, but rather a craving for more and more power and wealth.

Kanaya Lal[23] offers a sad saga of the Ranjit Singh period. He also narrates an incident wherein *Akali* Sikhs attacked the Muharram procession in Amritsar, led by Muslim soldiers accompanying the English ambassador. However, the Muslim soldiers, trained in European warfare, bravely defended the procession and forced the *Akali* Sikhs to flee. Ranjit Singh immediately reached the scene of the fighting and pacified the soldiers and the ambassador; terming the incident a mistake and a misunderstanding. While this shows his shrewd mind, it also supports the viewpoint of Surjit Hans[24] that his tolerance was no more than a political gimmick.

Hans's argument that the Maharaja, on account of his minority status, had to strengthen his bonds with the Hindus and pacify the Muslims seems tenable. In this context it seems that Ranjit Singh's policies towards the Muslims were related to some consideration of pacification of the majority community.

W. L. M'Gregor's two-volume book describes all the events from the time of the first Guru, Nanak, until the last Maharaja of the Punjab, Dilip Singh.[25] He outlines the life of each Guru and points out the reasons behind their murders and the causes of Sikh–Muslim enmity. He also explains how the Sikh *misls* (Sikh confederacy) were formed, followed by the rise of Ranjit Singh, describing in detail the habits of the Sikh ruler and his behaviour towards the other communities. He further describes the character of his *darbar* and different ministers. The second volume deals with matters after the death of Ranjit Singh, the race for succession and the British involvement in the Punjab.

A. F. M. Abdul Ali[26] read a paper at the eighth meeting of the Indian Historical Records Commission held at Lahore in November 1925. He compared the behaviour of Ranjit Singh in his conquests in Multan and Afghan territories with that of Napoleon, in how they treated the defeated local people. Both, indeed, encouraged their troops while at war. The writer illustrates the Maharaja's curiosity for other religions and sheds light on his family tree and possessions.

H. S. Bhatia and S. R. Bakshi[27] present a detailed account of the Maharaja, his wars, conquests and consolidations, court and camps and state policies. They offer a realistic description of the polity and economy of the Punjab under the Sikh regime. The book also presents an exciting exposé of Ranjit Singh's habits, virtues, vices and so forth. While discussing his early life, they observe that there is a very sharp difference of judgement between Indian and European writers regarding the religious views and outlook of Ranjit Singh. They further observe that he was 'neither a bigot nor a vain religious dreamer'. Although he used *Khalsa* fervour against Muslims, he understood that this policy would be harmful for his own political designs. Therefore, he preferred to refrain from interfering with the people's religions. In line with this policy, he made efforts to check the fanatical tendencies of *Akalis* (order of Sikhs) and also entrusted some responsible positions to Muslims such as Fakir Azizuddin, Fakir Nuruddin and Fakir Imamuddin. They also present a detailed narrative of the treatment by Maharaja Ranjit Singh of Shah Shuja and the extortion of the Koh-e-Noor diamond. Indeed, this unlikely and uncustomary treatment exposed the Maharaja to adverse comment.

Ikram Ali Malik[28] comprehensively covers the history of the Punjab from the early *Mahabharata* to the modern day. While presenting various views, the book seems a little confusing at times. In defending Ranjit Singh's secularism, it also presents numerous cruelties meted out to the Muslims during the Sikh regime. The author reports that Ranjit Singh bestowed great blessings and status on Muslim *sardars* (chiefs) such as the Fakir family, the famous artillery expert Elahi Bukhsh and the Qazian family. Separate courts were established for Muslims. Ikram writes that annexation of Muslim states was never followed by any cruelty and plunder during the regime of Ranjit Singh. Instead, he conferred estates upon the Muslim *sardars* of annexed states. This lends support to the view that he was a bias-free ruler. However, Ikram also quotes incidents that utterly contradict this view, such as damaging the holy places of Muslims in order to build the *Darbar Sahib* (most sacred place for Sikhs) in Amritsar; the Badshahi mosque was turned into stables. The author also agrees that the ill-treatment of Shah Shuja at the hands of Ranjit Singh was due largely to his lust for money and not out of religious bigotry. He concludes that Muslims by and large enjoyed a good life during Ranjit Singh's regime. Their mistreatment was mainly due to the fanaticism of Ranjit Singh's officials. Personally, he had no bias against Muslims, but he seems to have had a confused and dual personality. Ikram reports that at times he went to any lengths to support Muslims, from building mosques and celebrating the Muharram and Eid festivals to buying a priceless piece of the Holy Quran. However, at other times, the same Ranjit Singh is seen extorting the Koh-e-Noor and turning the Badshahi mosque into an animal pound.

Fakir Syed Waheeduddin,[29] a descendant of the famous Fakir family who served the Sikh monarch with great dedication and devotion, has written about the life and achievements of Ranjit Singh. His work is based on archival material in the possession of the Fakir family, and resolves some of the mysteries surrounding the Maharaja's personal life and policy towards other religions. According to the Fakir, Ranjit Singh had a profound reverence for all that was holy and spiritual, irrespective of what religion it pertained to. He paid regular visits to *Harmandir Sahib* (the Golden Temple) on special occasions, but his visits to the shrines of Muslim saints and Hindu temples were as much acts of faith as those to the Golden Temple. He donated liberally to the religious places of all sects in the Punjab and participated in the religious festivals of both Hindus and Muslims; thus, he was the first Sikh to be a secular king of the Punjab. The Fakir offers a personal account of the Maharaja's rule of justice, his secular politics, his conquests and empire building and his wise relations with the other religions. Nevertheless, the chronicle fails to determine the cause of the fall of Sikh rule, although the author seems to be very positive throughout his book that it needs to be examined critically.

A. Nadeem observes that Ranjit Singh's era, apart from its military might, affluence and glorious conquests, was a time of religious tolerance, reconciliation and nation building.[30] It was during his rule that people were raised to commanding positions in the administration as well the army, regardless of their faith. Certain Muslim historians have painted a possibly biased picture of his disrespect for the Muslim faith and deliberate desecration of Muslim holy places. It is true that mosques were used as ammunition dumps and stables, but the fact is that history is stained with cases of religious places being abused.

G. S. Dhillon reports that Ranjit Singh gave complete freedom of expression and worship to all his subjects.[31] He further observes that under Ranjit Singh, talent was the main ladder to high positions and not religion, caste or class. He maintained a balance among various religions while rewarding courtiers and officials. Dhillon further documents that Ranjit Singh was very generous in his endowments to Hindu and Muslim places of worship. He bestowed generous grants on Muslim scholars and paid due respect to the Sufis and saints of his kingdom. The minority status of the Sikh ruler was no handicap in commanding allegiance from his Muslim and Hindu subjects. Dhillon reports that 'during his reign, there were no outbursts of communal fanaticism, no forced conversions, no attempts at bloody revenge, no language tensions, no second-class citizens, no repression, no bloodshed, no executions and no tortures'.

Jean-Marie Lafont presents a very impressive and lucid catalogue of the life and times of Ranjit Singh on the occasion of the bicentenary celebrations of the Maharaja in Amritsar in 2001.[32] Soon after his accession to the throne of Lahore, he appointed a Muslim, Imam Bukhsh, as *Kotwal* (police officer) of Lahore, also taking due care to preserve the Muslim places of worship. Teaching institutions of various religious groups, including Muslims, were also maintained with the help of state grants and estates. Like many other authors, Lafont also mentions the restoration of the Sonehri Mosque to the Muslims, confirming that Ranjit Singh was a shrewd, tolerant and bias-free king.

Fauja Singh and A. C. Arora's book on Maharaja Ranjit Singh, his politics, society and the economy, is a compilation of articles written by many famous writers, including Grewal, Kirpal Singh, Indu Banga and Bina Parsad, about the ruler of the Punjab, describing his different qualities and the nature of the administration of the Lahore *Darbar*.[33]

G. S. Chhabra discusses every event relating to the lives of the Gurus and their deaths, and describes the causes of Sikh–Muslim enmity and its effects on both communities.[34] The rise of Ranjit Singh, his character, his revenue system, his military policy, and his relations with his subjects are all discussed in detail, as are the reasons for the failure of the Sikh regime, the invasion of the British and the various conspiracies. This is a very useful book for the knowledge it imparts on the whole of Sikh history.

Fauja Singh gives a detailed study of the organization and establishment of the Sikh army during the period of Ranjit Singh.[35] It was the first attempt to examine the character of the military system of the Sikh rulers of the Punjab, which among other things hastened the end of Indian independence and the establishment of British rule. This book also throws light on the fact that the military policy of Ranjit Singh turned his old, badly organized army into a new, efficient one under the supervision of French officers. This strategy affected the army's organization, recruitment, pay and allowances, and moral discipline, all discussed here in detail, along with the reasons for the failure of the Sikh army in fighting the British.

Khushwant Singh's book on Ranjit Singh is a classic biography.[36] From the status of petty chieftain, Ranjit Singh rose to become the most powerful Indian ruler of his time. His empire extended from Tibet to the deserts of Sindh and from the Khyber Pass to Sutlej. His army was one of the most powerful of the time in India and was the first Indian force in a thousand years to stem the tides of invasion from the northwest frontiers of India. In this classic work, Khushwant Singh presents Ranjit Singh as he really was, including his weaknesses and strengths. Based on Persian, Punjabi and English sources and drawing upon the diaries and accounts of European travellers including Moorcroft, Sir Alexander Burne, Masson, Fane and Emily Eden, it presents a lively portrait of one of the most colourful characters in Indian history.

J. S. Grewal, in the series *New Cambridge History of India,* in some respects marks a radical change in the style of the Cambridge histories.[37] His work falls into four well-marked periods: from its beginning with the mission of Guru Nanak to the death of Guru Gobind Singh in 1708; the rise of Banda Bairagi to the annexation of the Punjab by the British in 1849; the near-century of colonial rule up to 1947; and the four decades following independence.

Fakir Syed Aijazuddin, another member of the famous Fakir family, writes a very informative book covering the period of Ranjit Singh.[38] Although the author belongs to the Fakir family, he relies on information not only from his own family documents but also from other sources, especially British writers. It gives us the real picture of the Lahore *Darbar* and the character of Ranjit Singh. The writer not only describes the influence of his ancestors but also their faithfulness towards the Maharaja.

K. S. Duggal portrays the emergence of the phenomenon that was Ranjit Singh in its historical setting, tracing in detail the evolution of the Sikh commonwealth from the time of Guru Nanak.[39] Under the Gurus, the basic Sikh tenets and institutions were built. The fights of the Sikhs under Banda Bairagi against the Mughal rulers, the establishment of the Sikh *misls*, their fights with the Muslim ruler Ahmad Shah Abdali and the rise of Ranjit Singh, as well as the establishment of the Punjabi rule, are all described in a straightforward manner. The author intelligently explores the personality of Ranjit Singh, who was not a common character but was possessed of powers of mind rarely encountered either in the East or in the Western world. The author highlights his generosity, his liberal outlook and his equal treatment of his entire people, no matter who or which religion they belonged to. He also highlights the ruler's affection for art and education. In fact, this book is a tribute to the great leader's love and care for his people without any discrimination of race or creed, also correcting several faulty perspectives of European writers concerning the personality and character of the Maharaja.

Rajinder Singh presents the life story of Ranjit Singh from his early conquests up to his death.[40] The author tries to dispel the mist that hangs over the personality of this great ruler, as he considers the literature to be very blurred, controversial and sometimes uninteresting, and from which no clear image of the man emerges.

Maharaja Ranjit Singh and His Times is a collection by J. S. Grewal and Indu Banga, both renowned historians of the Punjab.[41] The title of the book comes directly from the subject of a seminar organized by the Guru Nanak Dev University for the 200-year celebrations of the Maharaja. The papers cover a wide range of themes from politics and government, art and literature, historiography and the agrarian system, to military, economic and social structures during the reign of Ranjit Singh.

The biography by Patwant Singh and Jyoti M. Rai covers not only the entire range of Ranjit Singh's military achievements but also his just and humane rule.[42] It discusses his daily routine, his likes and dislikes, and his everyday dealings with his people. It also discusses his relations with different women in his life and their influence on him, and the courtiers in his *darbar* whom he treated with equality no matter to which religion they belonged. The writers have drawn on many sources concerning the period, both primary and secondary, in order to answer the questions they pose. They argue that Ranjit Singh included more non-Sikhs in his cabinet than any other ruler in the subcontinent.

J. S. Grewal's other book examines the philosophy of the Sikh Gurus.[43] There are thirty essays, nearly all based on contemporary evidence, each making a few basic points, and not necessarily offering a direct discussion of the broad theme. There are overlaps too in terms of the information given in each chapter. In the first part of the book, which consists of six chapters, the ideology of Guru Nanak is discussed. Guru Nanak looked upon the contemporary systems of religious belief and practices in terms of three traditions: the Brahmanical, the Ascetical and the Islamic. The second part is made up of eleven chapters, all directly or indirectly related to the *Khalsa*. The third part comprises eight essays on Sikh polity. The organization of the Sikh *misls* as a unity of the Sikhs is discussed from the viewpoint of several historians. The last chapter on the Sikh Raj and Sikh social order is based on the contemporary evidence of the Gurbilas literature, Rahitnamas, and chronicles in Persian, the Gurmukhi and early British writers.

Indu Banga covers the period of Sikh rule in the Punjab during the late eighteenth and early nineteenth centuries.[44] Following a brief explanation of the political and official developments of the period that affected the agrarian system, the emphasis of this study is on the *sardars*, the chiefs, the *jagirdars* (holders of *jagirs*), the *dharmarth* (charity) grantees, the poor, land income, revenue management and land occupancy. The book is marked by many long footnotes to support the proof of a point – helpful for readers who have a special interest in this subject.

Amrinder Singh starts with the success story of Ranjit Singh and ends with the annexation of the Punjab in 1849, covering almost all of Ranjit Singh's reign and the activities of the Lahore *Darbar*.[45] It discusses the intrigues after the death of Ranjit Singh, which became the main cause of the decline of the *darbar*. A detailed discussion of the Sikh wars and the annexation of the Punjab occupies a large part of the book.

J. S. Grewal writes on the political-administrative organization, agrarian and town economy and the social order during Ranjit Singh's times.[46] This book has no references or notes but it does take into account the known existing sources and historical research. In fact there is hardly any statement that does not come from a reliable source, and a vital understanding of Ranjit Singh emerges from this pragmatic evidence.

Purnima Dhavan explores the formation of the Sikh community, comprising Sikh peasants, scholars and chiefs, over the course of the eighteenth century – a crucial time for Sikh political development.[47] Dhavan challenges the popular thinking that attributes the formation of the *Khalsa*'s rites and practices to the Tenth Guru, Gobind Singh. By doing so, she argues that the emergence of the *Khalsa* and promotion of martial practices among the Sikhs cannot be understood in separation from the mobilization of the peasant populations. This emphasis on the agency of the peasant communities allows Dhavan to uncover a range of outlooks and exchanges that, in due course, created a complex *Khalsa* narrative. She places the *Khalsa*'s distinguishing cultural practices within the broader context of the military labour market that was significant in constructing new identities. Her complex engagement with primary sources in both Punjabi and Persian illustrates how these new identities, communities and practices were transformed by negotiations, collaborations and debates among Sikh society.

Jaspal Kaur Singh reviews the constructs and depictions of Sikh men and women in existing literature in light of the importance that is attached to violence as essential to Sikh identity.[48] The author is interested in how Sikh males and females develop their identities within the Indian state and diaspora. Through an examination of Indian literature, she attempts to understand how violence, being a pre-established necessary characteristic for Sikh men, shapes their identity, as well as the feminization of baptized and turbaned Sikh men. She also explores how Sikh women, whose experiences have largely been either erased or overlooked, are represented in Indian literature and culture. Some have been altogether removed through honour killings while others have been characterized as invisible and minimized within the literature. This book examines the instrumental part that violence has played at crucial points in Sikh history: Mughal rule, colonization by the British, partition of India in 1947, anti-Sikh riots in India in 1984, and the September 11 attacks in the United States in 2001.

Dalvir Singh Pannu masterfully captures Sikh heritage in a book that encompasses eighty-four sites, each of which is described in rich detail.[49] This comprehensive work is the result of several years of research and fieldwork. The author carries out a thorough investigation that includes exhaustive analysis and verification from myriad sources. This facilitates readers' understanding of Sikh history by employing critical thinking and first-hand sources. His book is an excellent attempt at presenting valuable insights on the deep histories of these sites and at protecting their splendour.

Mohammad Sheikh's biography of Ranjit Singh notes that he was barely 21 years old when he became the first Maharaja of the Sikhs in 1801.[50] In the years that followed, he surfaced as a key personality in Punjabi history. He was faced with many challenges, not just limited to difficult geography, high levels of diversity in populations and external threats. However, he still proved himself capable in uniting the Sikhs and exercising formidable power. After his death in 1839, his empire suffered greatly and finally in 1845, the Sikhs endured a harsh defeat at the hands of the British, with the East India Company gaining control. It was Ranjit Singh's charisma and strong leadership that served as the backbone of the Sikh empire and kept it robust and sound in the face of various dangers. His policies, aiming for equality and harmony among the faiths, were strange and uncommon for that time. Muhammad Sheikh's account brings to light Ranjit Singh's far-reaching vision and extraordinary military and leadership skills, which gained him immense reputation and success as a political leader.

In 1801, Ranjit Singh became Maharaja of Punjab at 21 years of age. Sarbpreet Singh's book offers an intriguing re-creation of his vivid court and breathes new life into the king's turbulent but powerful rule.[51] One of the key figures who inhabited his court was Akali Phoola Singh, an unrestrained Sikh militant leader who attained a great many noteworthy conquests for the king, yet never fully yielded to his authority. Then there was the young Bibi Moran, a Muslim dancing girl and courtesan, who went on to become the king's favourite. The other individual who has been emphasized in this book is the foreigner Josiah Harlan, a Quaker from Philadelphia, who proceeded to become the Maharaja's trusted advisor and governor, only to be disgraced when he displayed excessive greed and pride. Other foreigners included the French officers Jean-Baptiste Ventura and Jean-François Allard, who formed and commanded the king's French divisions and simultaneously achieved exalted positions in the armies. The author also examines Ranjit Singh's multifarious relationship with his mother-in-law, Mata Sada Kaur, who is argued to be the force behind his rise to kingship, and the progress of the Dogra brothers, who started out as modest soldiers and went on to become extremely influential, high-ranked members of his court. All these stories aim to introduce a more intricate side to the king through his connections and relationships with these different personalities. This is an enlightening and personalized account of Maharaja Ranjit Singh, one which paints a more humane picture of him and dives into those shades of his personality that are commonly overlooked in history.

The above review of literature clearly shows a research gap. Not a single historian has thoroughly probed the matter of Sikh–Muslim relations in the Punjab, and their calculations are diverse and contradictory. My research uncovered abundant source material which has not yet been consulted thoroughly by the previous writers. The Punjab Archives, Lahore; the National Documentation Centre, Islamabad; the Punjab Public Library, Lahore; and the Central Library of the University of the Punjab, Lahore, provided both published and unpublished material about the Sikh Regime, 1799–1849. The Punjab Archives in particular is an invaluable source of information, with a wide range of rare books, magazines, articles and other sources of information and evidence. The Fakir Khana Library is another rich source of information and evidence which helped to complete my study. I also visited England to explore the British Library and the library of Royal Holloway, University of London, along with the Royal Asiatic Society Library and the British Museum. These institutions are rich in primary and secondary sources and made an important and timely contribution to my research.

The topic is a historical one, therefore primary and secondary material are the main sources of information; to interpret them, a descriptive and analytical approach has been adopted. Moreover, oral and alternative sources have also been used to investigate the larger picture of Sikh–Muslim relationships.

Following this introduction, which outlines the main thesis and structure of the present study, the book consists of five chapters along with the conclusion, glossary and bibliography. The first chapter describes the historical background of Sikh–Muslim relations. Indeed, it is of great importance to understand these relations from a historical perspective, as a reappraisal will reveal that some political and interest groups, including the orthodox Muslims and Hindu elites, considered friendship between Sikhs and Muslims as a threat to their own positions and the status quo. These 'interest groups' deliberately created circumstances that eventually developed into unfortunate conflicts between the two communities. The chapter argues that it was not religious prejudice that governed Sikh–Muslim relations but other factors, including political and economic issues, that shaped the uncertain relations between the two communities.

The second chapter describes the conquests of Ranjit Singh and his treatment of rulers and the common people of the fallen states. In fact, Ranjit Singh emerged on the scene of the subcontinent when the whole of the Punjab was politically, socially and even economically at its lowest ebb. The result was ever-increasing sociopolitical unrest and uncertainty, a weakening state, poor social services, and an acute sense of insecurity. Frustrated by the existing rulers, people not only welcomed Ranjit Singh, but supported him against their own rulers and rajas. This chapter explores how Ranjit Singh subdued and captured different parts of the Punjab, and investigates how he treated the Muslim rulers while subjugating or capturing their states.

The third chapter analyses various state policies towards Muslims, including the administrative, education, economic, revenue and judicial systems of the *Khalsa* government. To the present day, religious freedom, equal access to education and economic opportunities, dispensation of fair justice, and security of life and property are the mainstay of any benevolent state; a minority, however, would always like to keep its religious identity intact and still have access to all the facilities that other citizens enjoy. This chapter explores this aspect of Ranjit Singh and the *Khalsa* state.

The fourth chapter concerns the role and status of the Muslim nobles, throwing light on the strength, composition and workings of the *darbar* of Maharaja Ranjit Singh. *Khalsa* state machinery included Hindus, Muslims and Sikhs alike with no discrimination. The chapter explores how the Maharaja cared only for the greatness of the state and the welfare of the people, and makes the case for his policies being driven by a secular approach and not by a bigoted or myopic approach based on religion.

The fifth chapter attempts to understand Sikh–Muslim relations during the post-Ranjit Singh period. It is especially important to investigate how the Sikh state adopted a communal policy, particularly towards the Muslim community, during this period and how the Muslims reacted to the declining power of the Sikh rule in the Punjab. This chapter discusses the causes of the downfall of the Sikh rulers, the main political developments, the Sikh state policy towards Muslims and the response of the Muslims to these developments.

Finally, the conclusion presents the results of the study.

Chapter 1

SIKH–MUSLIM RELATIONS: A HISTORICAL PERSPECTIVE

The Muslim Mughal Empire and Sikhism grew side by side in South Asia. While Zahir-ud-Din Muhammad Babar was laying the foundations of the Mughal Empire in 1526, Guru Nanak, the founder of Sikhism, was expounding a new religious philosophy. Broadly speaking, both religions, Islam and Sikhism, believe in monotheism, equality, tolerance and love for mankind. These similarities provided a very strong basis of alliance between the two religions and therefore this note of 'tolerance and religious co-existence' of Sikhism was well received by the people, saints and many sages among Sikhs and Muslims alike. The Mughal emperors by and large showed great generosity to the majority of Sikh Gurus. However, despite the similarities in the religions and the benevolence of the Mughal emperors, Sikh–Muslim relations underwent many changes. In practice, political expediencies and economic imperatives largely kept the two communities estranged and alienated. From Babar to Akbar the relations between Sikhs and Muslims remained friendly, but after the death of Arjun in 1605 they began to weaken. The circumstances that wove together the very relationship between the two communities remained obscured beneath the thick layers of intrigue of the Mughal rulers, courtiers and opportunists. For a number of reasons, Sikh Gurus were martyred during this period, which resulted in strong hostility by the Sikhs against the Mughal rulers. However, once Ranjit Singh came to power, he tried to address the tense Sikh–Muslim relations that he had inherited. These events and conflicts later played a major role in deciding the fate and condition of Muslims under Sikh rulers. Therefore, it is of great importance to understand Sikh–Muslim relations in the Punjab from a historical perspective. Many historians have written about them and analysed the details, nature and development of their estrangement, but they have built their arguments largely on religious differences – they have not rigorously analysed religious affinity. There were more similarities than dissimilarities in the religious beliefs, and therefore religion cannot be considered as the main cause of friction; nevertheless, a narrative gradually developed when both the Muslims and Sikhs developed their own versions on a religious basis. A reappraisal of the background of Sikh–Muslim relations will reveal that some political and interest groups, including the orthodox Muslims and Hindu elites, considered friendship between Sikhs and Muslims as a great threat to their positions and the status quo. These 'interest groups' deliberately created circumstances that eventually developed into unfortunate conflicts between the two communities. Therefore, I argue that it was not religious prejudice that governed Sikh–Muslim relations but other factors, including political and economic issues, that shaped the uncertain relations between the two communities.

Sikh–Muslim Relations – Common Grounds for Alliance

Various studies have already indicated many similarities of religious belief and ideas between Islam and Sikhism. Khawaja Hassan Nizami, in his famous work *Sikh Quam Aur Uske Bani Ke Nisbat Musalmano Ki Muhabbat Amez Rai* (*Muslims' Views Filled with Love for the Sikh Community and its Founder*), draws out many similarities and bonds between Islam and Sikhism, and between Muslims and Sikhs.[1]

Teachings and beliefs of the Sikh religion are recognized by others to have a clear bent towards Muslims and Islam.[2] Available evidence suggests that Muslims and Sikhs share common perceptions, contexts and, at times, beliefs. Both religions believe in unity, equality, tolerance and love for mankind. In line with and motivated by these beliefs, Guru Nanak laid down the basis of a new religion created out of the 'wedlock of Hinduism and Islam':[3]

> Some are called Hindus others are Muslims, members of sects such as Shia or Sunni. Let it be known that mankind is one, that all men belong to a single humanity ... so too with God, whom Hindu and Muslim distinguish with differing names. Let none be misled, for God is but one; he who denies this is duped and deluded. There is no difference between a temple and a mosque, nor between the prayers of a Hindu or a Muslim. Though differences seem to mark and distinguish, all men in reality are the same. Gods and demons, celestial beings, men called Muslims and others called Hindus – such differences are trivial, inconsequential, the outward results of locality and dress. Allah is the same as the God of the Hindus, Puran and Qur'an is one and the same ...[4]

Guru Gobind Singh reiterated these beliefs in the following lines:

> Recognize all mankind, whether Hindus or Muslims, as one. The same Lord is the Creator and nourisher of all, Recognize no distinction among them: The temple and the mosque, the Hindu and the Muslim prayer, Men are all one![5]

Sikhism and Islam have more similarities than dissimilarities. The concept of God in both religions is the same, and particularly that He is the only God. Both religions value humanity and denounce egocentric living. Both religions prohibit renunciation of the world and social obligations, unlike Hinduism. Both require their followers to perform their familial and social duties along with religious ones. Sikhism condemns blind and inhuman rituals, as does Islam. Like Islam, Sikhism preaches equality for all races and sexes.[6]

These similarities provided a very sound and strong basis of alliance between the two religions. The new philosophy of life and religion was welcomed by many downtrodden and deprived sections of society.[7] However, mere similarities and commonalities between Sikhs and Muslims hardly establish clear evidence of robust links between the two. Political expediency, economic imperatives and social systems largely kept both communities estranged most of the time.[8] While the common people and the Sufis shared beliefs and a social ethos, political and power lords found Sikhism a threat against the state.[9] Available evidence suggests that Muslims were also attracted to the egalitarian and monotheistic ideology of the Sikh Gurus.[10] In fact, many Muslims also endangered or sacrificed their lives to save this common egalitarian and monotheistic ideology. Therefore, it was not primarily religion that governed Sikh–Muslim relations but the political, social and economic realities that characterized the relationship.[11]

Hargobind Singh, the sixth Guru, declared it mandatory for all Sikhs to wear a turban and carry two swords at all times: one against the government and one to protect their religion. He laid down the foundations of the *Akal Takht*[12] and had it built twelve feet higher than the Mughal *Takht* as a sign of superiority. Every decree, political as well as religious, was given from the *Takht* (throne).[13] Taigh Bahadur, the ninth Guru, expanded Sikhism to all parts of India and established the city of Anandpur. He fell victim to Hindu conspiracies that led to his murder by the Mughal Emperor Aurangzeb. After Guru Taigh Bahadur, his son Guru Gobind laid down the foundations of the Sikh *Khalsa* Army in 1699. He also assigned a special cap as well as five signs, namely:

1. *Kacha*: an undergarment reminding one to live a virtuous life.
2. *Kara*: an iron or steel bracelet worn on the forearm to inspire one to do good things; also used in self-defence.
3. *Karpan*: a sword to defend oneself and to protect other people regardless of religion, race or creed.
4. *Kanga*: a wooden comb, a symbol of cleanliness to keep one's body and soul clean.
5. *Kais*: uncut hair as a symbol of acceptance of form as God intended it to be.

These Five Ks or *Panj Kakar* are the five articles of faith that *Khalsa* Sikhs still wear at all times as commanded by the tenth Sikh Guru, Gobind Singh. During his lifetime Guru Gobind Singh also established the *Khalsa* order, meaning 'pure soldier'. He thought that the *Khalsa* should uphold the highest Sikh virtues of commitment, dedication and social consciousness, and the term is applied to those Sikhs who have undergone the Sikh baptism ceremony, who strictly follow the Sikh Code of Conduct and Conventions and wear the prescribed physical articles of faith, most noticeably the uncut hair (required to be covered with a turban for men) and the ceremonial sword.[14]

Harmiandir Sahib (the Golden Temple) is the most significant religious centre for Sikhs, situated at Amritsar. It is the inspirational and historical centre of Sikhism, although it is not a mandatory place of pilgrimage or worship. All places where the scripture, *Sri Guru Granth Sahib*, is installed are considered equally holy for Sikhs.

Genesis of Sikhism – Sociopolitical Context

Sikand identifies four theories to explain the genesis of the Sikh religion.[15] The first is that God sent the Guru Nanak to create a new religion clearly different from existing religions. However, Sikand lends little support to this approach, as Nanak Sahib never wanted to add 'another sect to the bewildering variety of narrow and divisive religious orthodoxies' which all his life he opposed. The second theory defines Sikhism as a 'reformist movement' to save Hinduism from Muslims, while the third suggests that it evolved under the influence of Muslim Sufis. Nizami has very comprehensively highlighted this relationship between Sikhism and Islam.[16] Pincott[17] and Hughes[18] also report the very strong influence of Islamic teachings on the Sikh Gurus including Baba Nanak Sahib. The fourth belief is that Sikhism drew heavily on both Islamic mysticism and Hindu Bhaktism. Most believe that Sikhism is an 'egalitarian religio-philosophical faith'.[19] Without tracing the historical perspective and framework under which Sikhism developed in South Asia, an objective and meaningful discourse cannot be held on relations between Muslims and Sikhs.

Sikhism was born out of Hinduism and Islam but gradually took its own shape and form. Guru Nanak was born at a time of religious reform movements in northern India, when both Islam and Hinduism were passing through a crucial time in the history of the subcontinent.[20] Both were intensifying their 'orthodoxies', and religious intolerance, social injustice and political persecution were the landmarks of that time.

It is of great importance to understand why and under what circumstances Sikhism was born. At the time of Guru Nanak, the religious situation in India was unsatisfactory; religion was no longer the source of human salvation or a means to seek eternal happiness, but had become a source of subjugation and a means to acquire power. Hindus were caught up in the vicious circle of the caste system, and Muslims in their various sects. While Hindu *pandits* (learned Brahmins) were demeaning the masses with inhuman rituals, the Muslim scholars were destroying the very spirit and ethos of Islamic teaching with their intolerance. Muslim sultans and Hindu rajas were more concerned with the accumulation of wealth and the acquisition of political power than with the wellbeing of their poor. The result was disillusionment and alienation from the existing religious and social systems that denied freedom and justice to the common man. Therefore, the stage was set to welcome a redeemer who believed in love and the equality of mankind, and who was free from the traces of ego, greed and bigotry. This was the political condition in India at the time of Guru Nanak.

At the same time, the Indian subcontinent was going through a crucial phase characterized by confusion and uncertainty. While the Lodhi Dynasty (1451–1526) was decaying fast, the Mughal Empire was being established under Babar.

The subcontinent was merely a collection of small and large fiefdoms and kingdoms with no sense of unity or nationalism. At the same time, the revival and reformation movements of the Middle Ages were gaining ground in other parts of the globe.[21] A number of great personalities and ideas were touching the hearts and souls of ordinary people. Around this time, too, Columbus[22] discovered the New World and Vasco da Gama[23] reached India by the sea route around Africa. European art and culture were reborn with the great works of Michelangelo,[24] Raphael[25] and Leonardo.[26] This was also the time when Martin Luther,[27] Huldreich Zwingli[28] and John Calvin[29] were leading movements for the reformation of the Catholic Church. In a similar vein, the Indian subcontinent was witnessing the Bhakti movement and Sufism. Both movements aimed at removing with the caste system, religious intolerance and social injustice.[30] They emphasized morality, purity of heart and love for mankind.

The birth of Baba Guru Nanak and Sikhism coincided with this religious and social reawakening in the subcontinent and further afield. Guru Nanak's social and religious philosophy was, indeed, an opportune and timely response to the emerging milieu in the subcontinent. He was well aware of the teachings of Islam.[31] In fact, Sikhs and Muslims shared many common canons of religious and social doctrines and seemed natural allies. Some Muslims claimed Guru Nanak to be a Muslim because many of his *shalouks* (a form of Punjabi poetry) mention Allah and the prophets. He described the greatness of God in many of his verses and redefined Allah in his own conception of God, very much according to the Islamic faith.[32] His respect for the Holy Quran is at its highest when he declares that no other book can be more important.[33]

The Guru *Granth Sahib* is the sacred book of the Sikhs. The word *Granth* is a Sanskrit word meaning book, treatise, code or section. The *Granth Sahib* contains the compositions of six of the ten Sikh Gurus: Guru Nanak, Guru Angad, Guru Amar Das, Guru Ram Das, Guru Arjun and Guru Tegh Bahadar. The *Granth Sahib* is also called the *Adi Granth*, which means the original book. Guru Arjun dictated and Bhai Das[34] wrote down the *Adi Granth*, which was completed in 1604. It includes the writings and sayings of many Hindu and Muslim saints such as Namdev,[35] Ramananda,[36] Sur Das,[37] Kabir,[38] Baba Farid[39] and Mian Mir.[40,41]

In fact, from the *shalouks* in the *Granth Sahib* and the teachings of Baba Nanak, it would appear that Baba Nanak was a Muslim. His teachings and beliefs seem very similar to those of Sufi Islam.[42] It is argued that references to Hindu mythological figures and mystical concepts in the *Granth Sahib* and in Baba Nanak's teachings were simply to contextualize his Islamic ideals from the local perspective.[43]

Sila Khan,[44] the latest exponent of this view, goes a step further. Based on close inspection of Nazria Ismaili and Sikh records and traditions, she argues that Baba Nanak was an Ismaili Shia Muslim under *taqiyya* (disguise), to protect Sikhism from the Sunni Muslim rulers. She finds this to be consistent with the teachings of Ismaili missionaries of the period.[45]

In addition to Sila Khan's exploration, many Punjabi Muslims consider Baba Nanak to be actually a Muslim. His respect and love are evident from this saying:

Baba Nanak Shah Faqir Hindu da Guru Muslaman da Pir (Baba Nanak Shah, Guru of the Hindus and *Pir* of the Muslims).[46] Duggal further observes that in line with Muslim mystical tradition, many Muslims considered Baba Nanak as *waliullah*, a friend of God.[47]

Such was the attachment and sense of belonging that at the time of Guru Nanak's demise, Muslims and Sikhs fought to claim the right to perform his final rituals.[48] His concept of monotheism, equality among all human beings, purity of heart as a measure of eminence and love for 'His' mankind very much corresponded to the Islamic concept of religion and way of life.[49]

However, according to some Muslim historians, Sikhism was inspired by Hindu customs and beliefs, and the concept of Guru and the avatar are very much related to each other;[50] on the other hand, some Muslims believe that Guru Nanak's model of inspiration was as the last prophet of Muhammad (PBUH).[51]

Given that Guru Nanak's philosophy and Sikhism grew during a period of great reformers, philosophers and ideologies in the subcontinent and elsewhere,[52] it would not be too far-fetched to say that his teachings were the logical conclusion of the Sufi and Bhakti movements in the subcontinent,[53] and that Sikhism was a synthesis of Hindu Bhaktism and Muslim Sufism.[54] Under the influence of such saints and social philosophers as Ramananda, Tulsi Das, Kabir, Baba Farid and Mian Mir, these movements had prepared the Hindustani mind to accept newer ideas and philosophies of life.[55] They were heterodox in nature and hence denounced social injustice, religious intolerance, superstition and prejudice against women.[56] These were the woes of the common Hindustani who was looking for a saviour. Guru Nanak's religious and social doctrine deeply embedded in humanism immediately touched the hearts of many, especially in the rural Punjab.[57]

There were ten Gurus who introduced, preached and practised the Sikh religion; in fact, Sikhism is an amalgamation of their sayings, teachings and practices. An overview of these follows.

A Brief Introduction of Sikh Gurus

Baba Guru Nanak was born in 1469 in Talwandi, now called Nankana Sahib, near Lahore.[58] A poet and musician, he was also a practical thinker. He was sent to receive his early education from a *pathshala*, a Hindu religious school. Very soon, he started asking his teachers unacceptable questions about some of the Hindu rituals,[59] and was expelled from the *pathshala*. He was then sent to a Muslim teacher to learn Arabic and Persian,[60] but did not stop asking questions. Most of his questions were about the Oneness of God, which his teachers frequently found difficult to answer. The rebellious act of refusing to wear the sacred thread of Hindu traditions proved to be a turning point in the life of Guru Nanak.[61]

He embarked upon an extended journey across the subcontinent, the first of four major journeys during his lifetime, which changed his life completely. He travelled to many places of various religions and met diverse religious leaders.[62] His journey helped him better understand the concept of the Oneness of God. In his philosophical work, which was directed towards humanity, he borrowed many views and visions from Hindu as well as Muslim Sufi writers. The writings and wisdom of such saints as Baba Farid-ud-Din Ganj Shakar and Bhagat Kabir Das were also part of his work. He actually aimed to bring together the Hindu and Muslim points of view and craft a new domain, based upon the Oneness of God and humanity.[63]

Baba Nanak wrote poetry, mostly in his mother tongue, Punjabi, utilizing *shabat, shalouks, dhora, kaafi, alania*[64] and other types of folklore for his expression and teachings.[65] The main aim behind all of his teachings remained the same: promoting equality of humankind and the Oneness of God. He continued to promote through his writings and scriptures the Oneness of God, and the fact that He (God) had no children, no family and no partners.[66] He criticized many Hindu rituals and teachings, especially the Brahman caste system and every religious aspect that supported the caste or creed system. His writings are clearly reflective of his teachings and knowledge, underpinning fairness, equality and love for mankind. He also vehemently opposed gender discrimination and advocated equal rights for women and men. The *Adhi Granth* recurrently highlights the subject of women and their equality.[67]

Baba Nanak was an extraordinary social reformer with an immense power of observation and analysis. He had witnessed the woes of poverty and the caste system and the wretched lives of women, and had the courage to challenge superstitions, conventions and stereotypes. Hindu by birth and also taught by a Muslim teacher, he had a clear leaning towards an egalitarian way of life. As a young boy, he would spend all his money on the poor people.[68] He never took an interest in his father's business and preferred spending time with religious people.[69] Dissatisfied with his life, he left home to search for the truth of life and eternal happiness.[70] He came to the conclusion that 'There is no Hindu, there is no Mussulman'. Love for God and equality of all human beings became the mainstay of his religious and social way of life, in opposition to religious intolerance and social stratification on the basis of caste, sex and religion.[71] In his last writing, he says:[72]

> There is one God. Eternal Truth is His name.
> Maker of all things,
> All-pervading.
> Without fear and without hate,
> timeless and formless.
> Beyond birth and death.
> Self-enlightened.
> By the grace of the Guru He is known.

For Guru Nanak, God's blessing lies in His love and care for mankind.[73] Empirical and spiritual or mundane and sublime, together they make life.[74] He believed that mankind's salvation lies in total submission and love for God – in his own words, 'By walking according to the commandments of God or by accepting His will'.[75] He passed on his enlightened leadership of this new religion not to his sons but to one of his followers named Lahna, whom he later renamed Angad.[76]

Bhai Lahna, renamed Angad,[77] was born in Matti di Sarai, a small village in the Ferozpur district, in March 1504.[78] He was a Hindu and a believer in Durga, and every year visited the temple of Jwalamukhi.[79] One day he heard the hymns of Guru Nanak from a devotee and was deeply impressed by the thoughts expressed in them. When he met Guru Nanak he was so influenced by his teachings that he threw away the dancing bells around him and became a follower.[80] After his succession, on the advice of Guru Nanak he left Kartar Pur to secure himself from the Guru's family. He went to Khadur, Amritsar, and concealed himself for more than six months.[81] Emerging from this seclusion, he started preaching the mission of Guru Nanak. He took special steps to popularize the institution by establishing a *guru da langar* (free kitchen of the Guru).[82] This was basically run through the contributions of the followers of the Sikh Gurus.[83]

Guru Angad laid the foundations of a new script, *Gurmukhi*. On his death Guru Amar Das succeeded him.[84]

Guru Amar Das was born in 1479 at Basarka in Amritsar.[85] He went to meet Guru Angad and bowed down at his feet. He started living in Khadur in a very peaceful environment – listening to the hymns every day and eating food from the *langar*.[86] For his devotion and wisdom he was chosen as the successor to Guru Angad. Amar Das made his headquarters at Goindwal in the district of Taran Taran[87] in the Punjab. He built a *bowli* (well), spending a large sum of money in Goindwal. Amar Das also separated the Udassis[88] from the regular Sikhs.[89]

Guru Amar Das introduced many changes that tended to break the close affiliations of the Sikhs with the Hindus. He also fixed the first day of Baisakhi[90] as the festival for the Sikhs. He introduced new forms of ceremonials for births and deaths, in which the recitation of the hymns of the Gurus replaced the chanting of the Sanskrit *shalouks*. He also preached the seclusion of women, encouraged inter-caste marriages and the remarriage of widows. He forbade the practice of *suttee* (a Hindu ritual in which a widow is burnt with her husband's body after his death).[91] Guru Amar Das established many Sikh educational institutes to promote the teachings of Sikhism, engaging many Hindus as well as Muslims.[92] He built the Holy Tank at Amritsar on land given by Akbar to his daughter Bibi Bhani.[93]

Guru Amar Das died in 1574 and instead of making his sons his successors, he appointed his son-in-law as the next Guru, namely Ram Das, who became the fourth Guru of the Sikh religion.[94]

Guru Ram Das's real name was Jetha. He was born in 1534 in Lahore.[95] He had a religious mind and through his devotion he earned the perfect confidence of Guru Amar Das.[96] He is said to have deputized on behalf of Amar Das at the court of Akbar.[97] On the advice of Amar Das he moved to the land granted to him by Akbar, where he constructed the city of Amritsar.[98]

Another development of great significance took place during the pontification of Guru Ram Das: the succession, which had been purely conferred on merit with no concern for family relationship, now became hereditary. Instead of choosing a person from outside his family, Ram Das appointed his son Arjun Dev as his successor. Guru Ram Das died in 1581.[99]

Born in 1563 at Goindwal, Arjun Dev was the youngest of the three sons of Guru Ram Das. From an early age he loved privacy and humility. He was just 18 years old when he succeeded his father.[100] At Amritsar, Guru Arjun Dev constructed the *Harmandir Sahib* (Golden Temple),[101] whose foundation stone was laid by the Muslim Sufi Saint Mian Mir. The *Granth* was completed and was placed in the temple by him.[102]

After the death of Akbar, Mughal–Sikh relations began to deteriorate, and the Guru was imprisoned and tortured on the orders of the next emperor, Jahangir (1605–27).[103]

Guru Hargobind was born in 1595 at Wadali in Amritsar.[104] He was made Guru on the death of his father when he was just 11 years old.[105] The young Guru did his best to fulfil Guru Arjun's wish and rapidly assembled a solid army of more than 500 men around him. He asked the people to bring him gifts of horses and weapons. This was a new approach, with far-reaching significance, and it established the basis of Sikh organization in the coming years. Hargobind fortified the city of Amritsar by building a fort, Lohgarh, and a mutual gathering place for the Sikhs called *Akal Takht*.[106]

Hargobind had three wives, with whom he had five sons. The eldest wife, Gurdittah, died during his lifetime, but he had great affection for Gurdittah's son, Har Rai.[107] After appointing Har Rai as his successor, Guru Hargobind died in 1644.[108]

Guru Har Rai was born in 1630, and at the time of his succession he was only 14 years old.[109] During the War of Succession between Aurangzeb (1658–1707) and Dara Shikoh, he sided with the latter. However, on Prince Dara Shikoh's defeat, the Sikhs returned to their home place. When Aurangzeb won the throne and imprisoned his father Shah Jehan, Har Rai started taking an interest in affairs of the state. Aurangzeb invited him to come to court, and the Guru sent his elder son Ram Rai with a letter to the Mughal emperor affirming his loyalty to the new king. The Emperor Aurangzeb, who considered Har Rai a *fakir* (religious-minded person, mendicant), treated Har Rai with honour and regard.[110]

The eighth Guru Har Krishen, born in 1656, succeeded his father at the age of 5.[111] Suffering from smallpox, his condition became serious and he was asked to appoint the next Guru. Har Krishen simply uttered the name of the place, Baba Bakala, where Guru Tegh Bahadur was residing.[112] He died in 1664 at the age of 8.[113]

Guru Tegh Bahadur was the fifth and youngest son of Guru Hargobind, born in Amritsar in 1621.[114] He received his early education from Bhai Buddha, who was considered to be the wisest among the Sikhs. He studied history, Punjabi and mathematics. He was also trained in warlike activities.[115] After the death of his father he, along with his mother and wife Gujri, spent the next twenty years in complete isolation. When Guru Har Krishen died, of the twenty-two claimants to the Sikh religious leadership living in Baba Bakala, Tegh Bahadur was found to be the true one.[116] He founded the town of Anand Pur,[117] on land he purchased from the Raja of Kahlur.[118] For some time the Guru remained silent and then refused to do as requested. On hearing this, Ram Rai was so annoyed that he announced that

Tegh Bahadur would only live if he showed a miracle. On the orders of the Mughal Emperor Aurangzeb he was murdered.[119]

Guru Gobind Singh, the last living Guru of the Sikh faith, was born at Patna in 1666.[120] When the news of the murder of his father, Guru Tegh Bahadur, reached him, he made an oath to avenge his death. The body of the murdered Guru was burnt, the ashes collected, and a tomb was built in Delhi.[121]

In 1699, Gobind Singh gathered his followers at Anandpur on the day of Baisakhi and established the *Khalsa* (the pure).[122] The Guru introduced the new symbols that are known as the Five Ks, the articles of faith that distinguish Sikhs from the other communities in India. He made it compulsory for Sikhs to have the *kais* (uncut hair), the *kanga* (the comb), the *kara* (the iron bangles), the *karpan* (the sword) and the *kacha* (the undergarment).[123]

The establishment of the casteless *Khalsa* did not suit the Hindu rajas of the Sivalik Hills, who united to remove the Guru from the district. After a few unsuccessful attempts to check the rising force of the Sikhs, the hill rajas asked the Mughal ruler for help. Aurangzeb sent his commanders Dina Beg and Painda Khan, each with 5,000 men, to help the hill rajas crush the rising political tide of the Sikhs. The Mughal powers were joined by the armed forces of the hill rajas, but they failed to defeat the Guru Gobind's forces, and Painda Khan was slaughtered at the First Battle of Anandpur.[124] After continuous fighting, local *jagirdars* united with the Mughal representative Wazir Khan, the Governor of Sirhind (died 1710),[125] who himself asked for the support of the Mughal Emperor Aurangzeb against the *Khalsa*.[126]

After the death of Aurangzeb, the Guru's relation with the next ruler, Bahadur Shah (1707–12), was very good. Wazir Khan felt uneasy about the friendly relations between Guru Gobind Singh and Bahadur Shah, and hired two Pathans, Jamshed Khan and Wasil Beg, to kill the Guru. The two secretly hunted him down and finally assaulted him at Nanded, a city in the Maharashtra state of India.[127] Jamshed Khan attacked the Guru on the left side beneath the heart while he was resting in his chamber after the prayers to God. However, the Guru killed the assailant with his sword, while his guards killed the other assassin.[128] A European medical specialist sent by Bahadur Shah sewed up the Guru's wounds.[129]

Before his death in 1708, Guru Gobind Singh declared that the Sikhs no longer needed a living Guru. He also announced the completion of the Sikh religion and that nobody could become Guru in future. In fact, he declared the *Granth Sahib* to be the living Guru for the Sikhs to follow.[130]

Relationship between Mughal Emperors and Sikh Gurus – Revisited

A series of unfortunate incidents erupted and worsened the situation between the two communities, Sikh and Muslim, who once shared a common faith and had friendly feelings towards each other. The killing of Guru Arjun in 1605 remains the main reason behind the Sikh–Muslim conflict. Before this, the Sikhs had been a peace-loving community, but they turned aggressive and restless after the murder and the whole scenario changed. The Sikhs severely opposed the Muslims and this ill-fated incident proved to be a turning point in the history of the relations between the two. The Sikh community turned to politics and a military build-up. The sixth Guru established a Sikh army in order to avenge his father's death and protect the sanctity of the Sikh religion.[131] They gathered arms for their protection and ended up being known as a warrior community, establishing a powerful Raj (rule) in the Punjab under Maharaja Ranjit Singh. The shocking effects of this unfortunate murder spread over many centuries and are still visible and unforgotten. The relationship between the two religions became increasingly tense because of some very unfortunate incidents, which included the murder of the ninth Guru Tegh Bahadur in Delhi and the battle between the tenth Guru Gobind Singh and the Mughals, which resulted in the murderous attack on Gobind Singh and his sons.[132]

From Babar to Bahadar Shah and from Guru Nanak to Guru Gobind Singh – the last of the physical Gurus of the Sikhs – the relationship between the two communities took many forms and witnessed many stages. Muslim Sufis and the populace largely held cordial and amiable relations with the Sikh Gurus. In endorsing this view, Dilip Singh and Espiritu report that many Muslims, including Sufis and their followers, helped the Sikh Gurus in their mission.[133]

The Muslim musician Bhai Mardana served Guru Nanak until the Guru's death. Guru Nanak also had very friendly relations with Shah Farid and Pir Jalaluddin Qureshi,[134] making long journeys in their company. Hazrat Mian Mir befriended Guru Arjun and stood by him through thick and thin. Moreover, Hazrat Mian Mir's sincere efforts brought about reconciliation between Emperor Jahangir and Guru Hargobind. The bond was further strengthened when Hazrat Mian Mir was invited by the Guru to lay the foundation stone of the holiest place of the Sikhs, the *Darbar Sahib* in Amritsar. Dilip Singh further states that *Guru Granth Sahib*, the holy scripture of the Sikhs, includes a significant number of hymns and spiritual poetry composed by Muslim saints and poets.

In the year 1573, during his visit to the court of Emperor Akbar, Guru Ram Das was given 28 *bighas*[135] and a generous amount of cash. Moreover, followers of the Guru were given exemption from the road tax.[136] The present-day *Darbar Sahib* stands on the land presented to Guru Ram Das by Emperor Akbar.[137]

At the time the Sikh religion took root, the Muslims predominantly ruled the subcontinent, under the Delhi Sultanate and Mughal rule. Hindus had already secured their interests by allying themselves with the Muslim aristocracy and rulers. Being in a minority, Muslim rulers welcomed the Hindus to perpetuate their rule in the subcontinent. This state of affairs was going well: the Muslims were the rulers and the Hindu rajas were their trusted allies, supporting their regime throughout the subcontinent.

Hindu courtiers and aristocracy at times enjoyed better status and privileges than their Muslim counterparts. The emergence of a strong Sikh community and the Sikhs' natural alliance with Muslims because of their common beliefs were clearly a threat to Brahminic vested interests. Even during the time of Guru Arjun Singh, a Sikh delegation from Sri Nagar approached him and complained about the Brahmins. The *pandits* of Kashmir were threatening Sikhs to leave the Sikh religion. As a result, Guru Arjun had to send one of his disciples, Madhu Sodhi, to Sri Nagar to preach the teachings of the Sikh religion.[138] This gives a reasonable understanding of relations between the Hindus and the Sikhs.

The orthodox Muslims, who already felt endangered by the enormous influence of Hindus at the courts of Muslim rulers, were also alarmed at the popularity of Sikhism among the Muslim aristocracy and the masses.

In short, both Hindu nobility and orthodox Muslims felt threatened by the cordial relations between Muslim rulers and Sikhs. Hindus opposed this alliance for fear of being replaced by the Sikh community. Similarly, the Muslim orthodox clergy did not like the alliance for fear of further deterioration in their power and status. These interest groups never let the Sikh–Muslim relationship flourish and strengthen. Subsequently, circumstances and facts were distorted and misrepresented to create stress and differences between the two communities. It is the responsibility of today's historians and researchers to unearth the intellectual and factual distortions in the history of the relationship between Sikhs and Muslims, and to set the historical record straight.

Akbar was an open-minded ruler. He not only respected other religions but also awarded gifts and *jagirs* (rewards of land, estate) to their followers. However, although like his father Jahangir was not an orthodox Muslim ruler, he was significantly under the influence of those *ulemas* (religious scholars) who supported him against his father. Hindus at the court of Jahangir also connived with the *ulemas* to create conditions for the arrest and killing of Guru Arjun. In fact, both the Hindu aristocracy and Muslim theocracy were afraid of the increasing popularity of Sikhism and the corresponding deterioration of their influence in society and at the imperial court.

Available evidence suggests that Akbar's grandfather Babar met Guru Nanak during his invasion of India. Guru Nanak prayed for him and prophesied that Babar and his family would rule India for a very long time. Akbar's father Humayun also met Guru Angad. Akbar himself respected the Sikh Gurus for their peaceful, just teachings.

Although the killing of Guru Arjun is considered the main cause of the Sikh–Muslim conflict, some historians have identified other reasons that encouraged this unfortunate tension between the Sikhs and the Muslims. However, a major role behind this murder and the consequent stress between the two communities is argued to have been played by Emperor Jahangir. In his *Tuzk-e-Jahangiri* he portrayed Guru Arjun in very harsh and provocative words, saying: 'along the River Bias there lives a Hindu named Arjun and many Hindu and stupid Muslims that go around praising him and his teachings'. Jahangir further asserted that it was his duty to halt these views or change them into Islamic beliefs.[139] In fact, Guru Arjun was so popular among the poor that hundreds of thousands of the native people gathered around him.

Guru Arjun's popularity was not the only reason behind his unfortunate assassination. First, Guru Ram Das's eldest son, Parthi Das, wanted to become Guru, but Ram Das had named his younger son, Guru Arjun, to succeed him.[140]

This infuriated Parthi Das. His hatred for his younger brother did not abate even after the death of their father. He continued conspiring against Guru Arjun, falsely complaining to the Mughal Emperor Jahangir about him.[141] Parthi Das and the high Hindu priests used various tactics against Guru Arjun Dev. Parthi Das wanted to take possession of the *Guru Granth* compiled by the Guru. In fact, he was deluded in thinking that this would enable him to claim the Guruship for himself. He and many others played an important role in misleading Jahangir. After the death of Guru Arjun Dev, Parthi Das took possession of *Guru Granth Sahib*, and his descendants continued to protect it and proclaim themselves Guru. Their followers are called *minas*.[142]

Secondly, Chandu Lal, a Hindu courtier in Lahore, also launched a campaign to dislodge Guru Arjun and started complaining to the emperor that Guru Arjun was not as pious a person as he appeared to be. Chandu Lal further complained that Guru Arjun had gathered people who would harm the Mughal Empire,[143] and that he was writing a book against Hindu and Muslim teachings. With the help of these false allegations, Chandu Lal was very cleverly creating hatred in the heart of the emperor and influential Muslim courtiers. Consequently, the emperor decided to take stern action against Guru Arjun once and for all.[144]

Every nation has been blessed with a guide from Allah and thus has been given truth from Allah. The Quran addresses only those Arabs of Mecca as *kafirs* (the people who do not believe in God) who denied the truth preached by Prophet Muhammad (PBUH). The Quran preached a doctrine of co-existence even with those *kafirs* who persecuted Muhammad (PBUH) and his followers. It propounded the doctrine of 'for you is your religion and for me is mine'. However, for various reasons this liberal and open approach of the Quran and Prophet (PBUH) did not always find acceptance with some narrow-minded Muslims and they denounced not only non-Muslims but also those Muslims who did not agree with them on theological matters as *kafirs*. These theological differences are so strong even today that every sect of Islam considers the other sect as having gone astray and being *kafir*. The theologians take religion as a source of power and a matter of sole truth, which creates an attitude of arrogance and superiority.

Besides these conspiracies, there were other interest groups who contributed to Guru Arjun's murder. Sheikh Ahmad Sirhindi[145] and his followers also believed that their version of Islam was the source of sole truth and all those who differed from it had gone astray. Therefore, Sheikh Sirhindi considered it as his mission to revive the true Islam.[146] As he was born on the eve of the second millennium of the Islamic calendar, he was referred to as Mujaddid Alf-e-Sani, that is, renewal of second millennium.[147]

The Mughal court was under the influence of these traditional *ulemas*. It was their strong belief that Islam could only flourish with the help of the state. Khawaja Baki Billah[148] and his follower, Sheikh Ahmed Sirhindi, believed that Sikh and Sufi teachings were against the teachings of Islam, as they were in favour of policies of religious toleration. Akbar's liberalism and tolerance in religious policies were also unacceptable to these *ulemas*, who objected to the open-minded religious views of Akbar and his land offering to Guru Amer Das in Goindwal. They believed this had unnecessarily added to the respect of Guru Amer Das. In fact, they had not felt easy since 1598, when, at the request of Guru Arjun, Akbar remitted the revenue of some *zamindars* (land holders).[149]

However, although the orthodox *ulemas* of Akbar's *darbar* bitterly criticized his religious policies, they were helpless in front of mighty Akbar. They had to live with this open-mindedness of the Mughal emperor until his death, supporting the uprising of his son Jahangir. Consequently, along with Sheikh Farid, minister in the court of Akbar and Jahangir, who was later given the title of Murtaza Khan by Jahangir, they formed a reactionary bloc. Sheikh Ahmed, through Sheikh Farid, influenced Jahangir in the revival of Islam.

Sheikh Ahmed was a strong supporter of conversion to Islam of the *dhimmis* (non-Muslims living in an Islamic state under state protection) and regarded Akbar as the one who stood in the way of spreading Islam. Another staunch supporter of the revivalist movement at the Mughal court was Sheikh Farid, who was a follower of Ahmed Sirhindi.[150] He called Jahangir on his succession the King of Islam.[151] The new Emperor Jahangir was already heavily under their influence. After coming to power, Jahangir readily fell in line with the views and wishes of the orthodox *ulemas*, who continuously pushed him to launch himself as an Islamic leader. Special privileges were given to newly converted Muslims to encourage others to join Islam. On the other hand, these *ulemas* pressed the emperor to enforce *jizya*[152] on non-Muslims for their protection.[153] These orthodox *ulemas* persuaded Jahangir to be the guardian and protector of Islam, to save it from ever-spreading Sikhism and its leader Guru Arjun.[154] So some historians believe that through influencing Jahangir these *ulemas* played a significant role in removing Guru Arjun, and indeed Sheikh Ahmed Sirhindi, rejoicing at the news of the Guru's death, wrote to Sheikh Farid to express his satisfaction.[155] Nevertheless, this does not prove that the murder was carried out under the influence of these orthodox *ulemas* or at their direction.

Some historians have also pointed out that Jahangir was not a secular ruler like his father Akbar, and did not advocate Akbar's *Din-i-Ilahi*,[156] although he did adopt a liberal approach. Unlike Akbar, Jahangir had little love for Sufism. Nevertheless he, too, continued with the practice of *sajda-e-ta'zeem* (the prostration of respect). He once summoned Sheikh Ahmed Sirhindi and expected him to perform the *sajda*. However, the sheikh refused and greeted the emperor in the Islamic way. Jahangir also expressed his anger in his autobiography[157] that Sirhindi had spread a net of falseness and dishonesty and was leading the Muslims into false beliefs. He was angry at his assumed authority to surpass the companions of the Holy Prophet (PBUH), but Sirhindi remained adamant; this further offended Jahangir and he imprisoned him in Gwalior Fort for over two-and-a-half years.[158] However, Sirhindi had a following among a powerful group of courtiers who pressurized Jahangir to set him free, and he was released honourably.[159] Thus, it is not appropriate to say that Jahangir was an orthodox Muslim and that he executed Guru Arjun under the influence of these *ulemas*; he even imprisoned their head when he advised his followers to punish the leader of the Sikh community.

The murder of Guru Arjun was actually a political act rather than a religious one. Those were the days when liberal-minded Khusroo was running from his father Jahangir following an uprising. Khusroo still wanted to wage war against Jahangir, so on reaching Goindwal – the city in which Guru Arjun resided – with his army, he asked the Guru to pray for his victory. The Guru offered him protection and did as requested, which added to Jahangir's hatred for him. Given that the teachings of Guru Arjun were midway between Muslim orthodoxy and Hindu extremism, they helped to gather like-minded secular people around Khusroo, steadily increasing Jahangir's hatred for Guru Arjun.[160] Subsequently many open-minded people joined Khusroo.[161]

Jahangir sent his army to Goindwal to arrest Khusroo, but he had already left for Lahore.[162] However, the army arrested Guru Arjun, seized his land and handed his son into the custody of Murtaza Khan, the Governor of Punjab.[163] Guru Arjun was brought to Lahore and was given to Chandu Lal, his arch-enemy. In order to make things even, Chandu Lal inflicted on him excruciating punishments and eventually ended up killing him.[164] So one can easily understand that the hostility with which Jahangir treated Guru Arjun was not based on religion but was basically a political threat for helping his son. If he had been under the influence of the orthodox Muslim *ulemas* he would never have imprisoned Sheikh Ahmed Sirhindi.

Guru Arjun is the first martyred Guru in Sikh history, seeking to protect his cause and fight for what he believed was right. His death is still largely attributed to the Mughal Emperor Jahangir.[165] The murder was the first serious confrontation between Sikhs and Muslims. Sikhs believed this death to be a sacrifice in the cause of truth and sincerity, and it had far-reaching consequences, transforming the Sikh community into a fighting nation and thus changing the course of the history of the subcontinent, especially the Punjab.

However, there is now a major disagreement among historians as to who was mainly responsible for this incident. At first, Sikh historians believed that Chandu Lal was the one responsible for the murder of Guru Arjun;[166] after publication of *Tuzki-e-Jahangiri*, however, this belief completely changed, because Jahangir and Parthi Das also played an important role in the murder. Jahangir very bluntly wrote that Guru Arjun should be taken to task,[167] and candidly accepted that the reason behind this scandalous act was the Guru's support for Prince Khusroo.[168]

Emperor Jahangir was primarily afraid of the rising popularity of the Guru, but it was also a matter of pride and strategy: a state within the state was not acceptable. Guru Arjun's support for Khusroo further fuelled the situation and Jahangir's apprehensions.[169] Although Jahangir did mean to halt Guru Arjun, religious grounds were not his main motive, as he wanted to avoid direct confrontation with the Sikh community.[170] Instead, he aimed to finish the Guru's reign on political grounds, and the latter's support for Khusroo proved to be his opportunity.[171]

This also presented an excellent opportunity to Guru Arjun's opponents, who played their cards well. Jahangir did not understand the undercurrents of the prevailing situation and went after Guru Arjun and his family, relieving the fears of many who were in one way or another opposed to Guru Arjun and the rise of Sikhism, including Parthi Das, Chandu Lal, other members of the Hindu aristocracy and orthodox *ulemas*.[172]

The murder of Guru Arjun had serious repercussions for the polity of the subcontinent, especially the future of Islam. A number of unpleasant incidents took place between the Muslims and Sikhs, and the two communities were further distanced. This finally led to the arrest and imprisonment of Guru Hargobind. Although he was released at the request of Mian Mir, a friend of Guru Arjun, hostility and distrust further intensified between the two communities.[173]

Sikh historians also criticized Jahangir and Shah Jahan for putting the sixth Guru behind bars and fighting him. They give the reason that Guru Hargobind would not pay the heavy fines imposed on him by Jahangir. These fines had been imposed on the fifth Guru, which after his murder the sixth Guru had to pay. However, this was not the only reason for imprisoning him in Gwalior Fort: the new Guru had started wearing two swords, had his own army and musketeers, started hunting and came into conflict with the Mughal army.[174] As stated earlier, Guru Hargobind also added two new features to Ramdaspur. First, opposite the *Harmandir* he constructed a high platform, which came to be known as the *Akal Takht*, where he conducted his court, and secondly, he constructed a fort called Lohgarh for defensive purposes.[175] These developments, which could not be tolerated by any strong emperor, made him suspicious in the eyes of the administration. Eventually, when the Guru had justified his activities to Jahangir, he was released and was even allowed to pursue them for the rest of Jahangir's reign.[176]

The Mughal Emperor Aurangzeb was mainly held responsible for the murder of Tegh Bahadur. Aurangzeb was an orthodox Muslim ruler,[177] who called Guru Tegh Bahadur to his capital city, Delhi, and asked him to show some miracle or to come to the faith of Islam. The Guru refused to do so and his head was severed from his body.[178] Another reason reported for the murder of Guru Tegh Bahadur was that the Hindus of Kashmir complained to the Guru in Anandpur that Aurangzeb was forcefully converting them to Islam.[179] They pleaded with him to lead them to the 'right way', as they found him to be a very pious and religious person. Hindu priests proved very shrewd at this point, and also used the Guru's 9-year-old son Guru Gobind Singh as a pawn. Gobind Singh pressed his father to offer sacrifice for his piety and goodness and for this noble cause.[180] After listening to the Hindus' plea and his son's innocent sentiments, Tegh Bahadur decided to face the Mughal emperor and sacrifice his life.[181]

M'Gregor gives another reason that Ram Rai, the son of the seventh Guru Har Rai who was at the court of Aurangzeb, had already complained that Guru Tegh Bahadur had stolen his right to be the Guru, and at his request Tegh Bahadur was called to the Mughal *darbar* more than three times. It was not the emperor who insisted that the Guru show a miracle, but Ram Rai. M'Gregor mentions a poem written by the last Guru, Gobind Singh, in which he described the death of his father as a result of the complaint from Ram Rai; the murder took place in the presence of the Mughal emperor.[182]

It is obvious that the Guru had no personal complaints against the Mughal emperor. It was the product of the Hindus' Machiavellian mind that created the sense of urgency and a situation that the Guru could not comprehend when he prepared to take on the Mughal might. Logically, the Hindus of Kashmir should have gone to some Hindu raja or *pruhat* (priest) to confront Aurangzeb; the fact that they chose to involve the Sikh Guru is in itself suspicious. However, just as Aurangzeb was unable to comprehend the undercurrents and motives of the orthodox Muslims, similarly the Guru was unable to see through the Hindu conspiracy, and his innocence proved fatal. Orthodox Muslims and scheming Hindus won the day and the gulf between the Muslims and the Sikhs further widened.

However, Latif reports another reason for the murder of the ninth Guru, Tegh Bahadur. The ninth Guru had started looting the people of the rich agricultural areas of the Punjab, especially wealthy Hindus and Muslims. Many notorious and dangerous people who were against the Mughal Empire escaped the custody of the Mughals and joined hands with the Guru.[183] Aurangzeb sent his army to arrest these people, including the Guru and his allies. As the Guru was being brought to Delhi, he appointed his son Gobind Singh as his successor, the last Guru of the Sikh religion.[184]

Ghulam Muhiyuddin Bute Shah in his *Tarikh-i-Punjab* says that the Guru went on a pilgrimage, and then founded Makhowal. He was summoned to Delhi at the instance of Ram Rai, who poisoned the emperor with the idea that Guru Tegh Bahadur was very proud of his spiritual greatness and that he would not realize his fault unless he was punished. Ram Rai also suggested that Guru Tegh Bahadur be asked to appear before the emperor to show a miracle; if he failed, he could be put to death.[185] The outcome has been described earlier. As a deterrent, the dead body of the Guru was displayed in every street of the city.[186]

This explanation of the murder of the ninth Guru is interesting and rather strange. In Islam, when somebody is captured for looting from innocent people, he is not given the choice to accept Islam as a punishment, nor is he asked to show some miracle to prove his faith and innocence. Moreover, if the accused is a non-Muslim, the matter is decided according to the guidelines of his own religion. Sikhism follows the same pattern. Now we come to the matter of showing a miracle. Why would a plunderer of innocent people not try to save his life? Why would such a worldly person not agree to the emperor's terms? And what were the secrets that were more precious than the Guru's life?

The historian should not limit themselves to narrating events but must also assess their veracity and reliability to set the record straight. Events must be presented in their proper context, with a logical unfolding and explanation. Announcing his son as the tenth Guru also seems quite misplaced in the circumstance of being arrested for something such as looting. It seems that the ninth Guru was already aware of his fate, and that some other important forces and factors contributed to his death. Aurangzeb was a very rigid and strict Islamic ruler under the strong influence of Sheikh Ahmed Sirhindi and his teachings. He had boldly and openly tried to enforce those policies and school of thought, as far as eliminating every non-Muslim and even non-Sunni Muslim throughout the empire.[187]

Another theory to explain the death of Guru Tegh Bahadur only adds to the confusion. This theory holds that Aurungzeb had no hand in the murder of the ninth Guru. It is argued that when the Guru was brought in front of him, the emperor invited him to hear the message of Islam. The Guru, however, refused to accept the emperor's offer and remained silent, adamant in his faith. He was jailed and even under torture remained steadfast. Along with him were three more Sikhs who somehow managed to escape from Mughal captivity. In order not to suffer any further, the Guru asked a fellow Sikh to sever his head from his body. Initially the fellow Sikh refused, but ultimately gave in and killed the Guru.[188] Major Henry Court has endorsed this theory that the death of the Guru was performed by the hand of his servant on his own command.[189]

This theory, too, has its flaws, which are either due to non-reporting or non-availability of a full account of events. How were Guru Tegh Bahadur's companions able to flee the jail, when the Guru could not? Was the command to kill himself worthy of a Guru? Needless to say, every theory to explain the murder of Tegh Bahadur points towards the orthodox Muslims and Hindu *pandits*. While delving deep into each conspiracy theory, one can easily discern that whatever the circumstances of the murder, it was either created or spread by Muslim theocracy and Hindu interest groups. Indeed, it was the request of the Hindu *pandits* that brought the Guru to Delhi to save the sacred cow and the Brahmins.[190] This sad saga concerning the ruin of Sikh–Muslim relations has many more episodes, including the killing of Mati Das, a companion of the ninth Guru, and the throwing of Bhai Dyaal into boiling water; Bhai Mani Singh and Bhai Taru Singh's skins were removed, and others were slaughtered.[191]

As already stated, Guru Gobind Singh was the tenth and the last of the physical Sikh Gurus. He was a warrior, a poet and a philosopher. At the tender age of 9 years, he succeeded his father Guru Tegh Bahadur. He formalized Sikhism and gave a separate identity to the Sikh community, establishing the Sikh *Khalsa* in 1699.[192] At the invitation of Raja Mat Parakash of Sirmaur, he moved to Paonta in April 1685. The Gazetteer of the Sirmaur State reports that the Guru had to leave Anandpur Sahib because of a disagreement with Bhim Chand, the Raja of Bilaspur.[193] Ratan Rai, the son of Raja Ram Rai of Assam, visited Anandpur with his mother and several ministers and presented gifts to the Guru, including an elephant called Prasadi.[194] Some days later, Bhim Chand sent a message to Anandpur, asking the Guru to lend him Prasadi. The Guru suspected that Bhim Chand wanted to gain permanent possession of the elephant, and declined his demand. An atmosphere of confrontation developed between the two on such small issues.[195]

The Mughal Emperor Aurangzeb was very closely and anxiously following these developments and was upset at the outcome. He at once sent off his son to redeem Mughal supremacy and authority in the area.[196] Meanwhile, the Sikh *Khalsa* army, which was against the caste system, could not amass support from the Hindu rajas of the Sivalik Hills, who believed in caste and creed. The Hindu rajas instead united themselves to remove the Guru.[197] However, they failed to intercept the rising power of the *Khalsa* army and finally had to ask the Mughals for aid. Following repeated pleas from the Hindu rajas, Mughal Generals Din Beg and Painda Khan were sent to help them.[198] The Guru was greatly assisted by two Muslim devotees, Maimun Khan and Saiyad Beg. However, the *Khalsa* army was outnumbered and the Guru had to abandon Anandpur.¹⁹⁹ After taking over Anandpur, the Mughal army marched to Sirhind, where the *Khalsa* army caught the Mughal forces in a surprise attack and retrieved the valuables amassed by the army after the fall of Anandpur. Following this success, the Guru returned to Anandpur.

Time passed and Aurangzeb expressed his wish to personally meet the Guru. He ordered the lifting of all restrictions against him, and directed his prime minister to ensure a comfortable journey for him. He also sent Sheikh Muhammad Yar Mansabdar and Muhammad Beg Gurzbardar to convey his respect to the Guru. The Guru passed through what is now called Rajasthan, on his way to Ahmednagar where the emperor was then encamped, but on reaching Baghaur he received the news of Aurangzeb's death in March 1707 and Aurangzeb's son Muazzam ascended the throne as Bahadur Shah. The Guru subsequently decided to return to the Punjab via Shahjahanabad.

During the War of Succession, Bahadur Shah wrote to the Guru for his blessing, not asking for military help, as he knew that the Guru had no army. In fact, the Guru had only three to four hundred Sikh disciples with him at that time, but the *Khalsa* army had been with him earlier because of the threat from the Hindu hill chiefs, and he gave Bahadur Shah not only his blessing but also himself fought for the emperor.²⁰⁰

By invitation, Guru Gobind Singh met Bahadur Shah at Agra on 23 July 1707. The Guru was received with honour and was given the title of *Hind Ka Pir*. He was also presented with a royal robe, a jewelled scarf and Rs.50,000 in cash. Expensive clothes, jewellery and ornaments were sent to Mata Sundari.²⁰¹ The Guru stayed with the emperor in Agra until November 1707. He made Dholpur a centre of his missionary activities and spent many days touring nearby areas before proceeding to the Deccan. The Mughal emperor also appointed him a military commander, and gave him a piece of land on which later his shrine was built.²⁰²

However, meanwhile, a Pathan whose father had been killed by the Guru attacked Guru Gobind Singh.²⁰³ The attackers were killed on the spot, one by the Guru's own hand and the other by his followers. It is also reported that the Guru bought some horses from Gul Khan's father and did not pay him.²⁰⁴ The European surgeon sent by Bahadur Shah stitched the Guru's wound, but it reopened and caused significant bleeding after a few days.²⁰⁵ Reading his fate, the Guru declared the *Granth Sahib* as the next Guru of the Sikhs.²⁰⁶

Dilip Singh, revisiting Sikh history, has aptly tried to dissect, unveil and subsequently refute various 'myths' that have for centuries ruined the sincere and serene relations between Muslims and Sikhs. He logically dismissed the myth that it was Bahadur Shah who actually engaged the Pathan mercenaries to murder the Guru,²⁰⁷ observing that this theory seems to be a highly ambitious concoction of political facts by interest groups. Dilip Singh also laments the thinking of today's students of political science and history, who readily believe in such unreasoned explanations of historical events.

Dilip Singh terms the above account a product of 'Brahminic blend' and ambition. He allocates a significant portion of his book *Life of Sri Gobind Singh Ji* to dispelling and arguing against this theory that sowed the seeds of further disharmony between Muslims and Sikhs. He breaks down all the events spanning eighty days before the attack on Guru Gobind Singh and analyses them to prove that the story was nothing but a mere farce. He elaborately highlights that a relation of respect and trust existed between the Mughal Emperor Bahadar Shah and Guru Gobind Singh. He also proves that close bonds existed between the two, long before Bahadur Shah ascended the throne.[208]

The emperor was a sympathizer of the Guru and bestowed upon him the robe of honour symbolizing brotherhood and respect. Bahadur Shah even enabled the Guru to freely undertake his missionary activities across the Mughal Empire. Furthermore, he assigned an orderly to ensure the wellbeing of the Guru and his disciples during his lifetime. These acts of benevolence prove that the shrewdness and malaise of Wazir Khan of Sirhind was in fact behind the Guru's homicide. Threatened by the closeness between the Guru and the emperor, Wazir Khan planned to murder the Guru and settle the score.[209] Indeed, Wazir Khan was involved in the murder of the Guru's sons, another reason for fearing the Guru's closeness to the Emperor.

Dilip Singh further reports that the Pathans and his mercenaries admitted, before being killed, that Wazir Khan had hired them to kill Guru Gobind Singh. Bahadar Shah was then in Maharashtra, and on hearing about the attack on the life of the Guru, at once sent his own medical specialist, Mr Cole, to treat him. He also ordered the arrest of 700 Pathans residing in the region where the incident took place. However, Guru Gobind Singh requested the emperor not to arrest innocent Pathans, to avoid unrest in the region.[210]

Dilip Singh's work has uncovered some of the veiled complexities of relations between Sikhs and Muslims. Such a sincere effort to bring about rapprochement between the two communities is praiseworthy and mutually beneficial to both. His work has, indeed, instilled the need to revisit the history of this relationship from a different perspective.

Sikh–Muslim Relations – Later Developments (1708–99)

After the death of Guru Gobind Singh, relations between the two groups deteriorated even further. The physical Guruship ended with the demise of Guru Gobind Singh, who announced the *Adi Granth* as the last Guru for the Sikhs. During his stay in the Deccan, Guru Gobind met a man named Banda Singh Bairagi, who had been born in Kashmir in 1670 and whose real name was Lachman Dev. Although initially sceptical, Banda Singh Bairagi became a supporter of the Guru after meeting him, winning his trust, and very soon Gobind Singh pronounced him guardian of the Sikhs.[211] He was also given authority to control the Sikh forces against the Mughal army in reprisal for Guru Gobind's sons, who were mercilessly murdered by the Governor of Sirhind, Wazir Khan.[212] He assembled a strong, armed force of Sikhs in the Punjab and began battle. The principal battle was fought in 1709 at Sonipat,[213] where the Sikhs got the better of the Mughal army.²¹⁴ In the same year, Banda Singh crushed the Mughal army at the Battle of Samana,²¹⁵ captured the city and executed more than ten thousand Muslims. This triumph gave the Sikhs a major financial advantage, as Samana was well known for minting coins.²¹⁶

The Sikhs captured Sirhind in 1710 and slaughtered the governor, Wazir Khan, alongside Diwan Suchanand (who was in charge of the two youngest children of Guru Gobind Singh).²¹⁷ Banda Singh's rule over the whole of the Punjab east of Lahore prevented correspondence between Delhi and Lahore, the capital of the Punjab, and this encouraged Bahadur Shah to march against the Punjab.²¹⁸ The whole imperial power was assembled to annihilate and execute Banda Singh,²¹⁹ and every officer was ordered to join the emperor's armed force. The Mughal army under the command of Munim Khan reached Sirhind before the arrival of Banda Singh and took it and the regions around it. The Sikhs moved to Lohgarh for their last fight, to crush the Mughal army; reinforcements were called up and they attacked the fort with 60,000 troops.²²⁰

Emperor Bahadur Shah was shocked by the failure of his army to kill or catch Banda Singh.²²¹ His successor, Farrukh Siyar, appointed Abdus Samad Khan as the Governor of Lahore.²²² During this time the Sikhs were being hunted down, particularly by Pathans in the Gurdaspur area. Farrukh Siyar (emperor 1713–19) requested the Mughal and Hindu authorities to continue with their troops to Lahore to strengthen his army.²²³

In March 1715, Banda Singh was in the town of Gurdaspur when the armed force under the leadership of Samad Khan, the Mughal Governor of Delhi, attacked the Sikh army.²²⁴ Banda Singh was arrested and put in an iron cage. The remaining Sikhs were imprisoned²²⁵ and sent to Delhi.²²⁶ After some months of imprisonment, in 1716 Banda Singh was killed.²²⁷ This was the end of the man who was responsible for slaughtering thousands of Muslims wherever he found them in Sirhind as well as in Ghuram, Thaska, Kunjpura, Shahabad, Ambala and Banur.²²⁸ His rule left a very bad impression on Sikh–Muslim relations for the rest of time, and the later Mughal period was demonstrably hard for the Sikhs. Mir Mannu, Governor of the Punjab (1748–53), took exceptionally severe action against the Sikhs, who continued to do battle with the Muslims. There is a popular Sikh rhyme about Mir Mannu's merciless actions against them:

Mannu asadi datri, asi Mannu day soey
*Jiyon Jiyon Mannu vadhda asi doon sawaey hoey.*²²⁹

The terrible administration of the Mughals brought about the formation of the Sikh *misls* and their brutal assaults on the Muslims. The Sikhs had solid cooperation in defence against the attacks started by Ahmad Shah Abdali and his Durrani Empire. Ahmad Shah Abdali's assaults on the Punjab forced the Sikhs to conceal themselves in the forests, but after his return to Afghanistan they emerged and executed Muslims.

In 1762 Ahmad Shah Abdali mercilessly executed the Sikhs in Melerkotla. Almost 25,000 Sikhs were killed in a solitary day's fighting, known in Sikh history as *Vadda Ghallughara*.²³⁰ Ahmad Shah was sure that the Sikhs would not have the capacity to face him again for at least fifty years.²³¹ In April he destroyed the *Harmandir Sahib*, and as a demonstration against expected retaliation, the pool around it was filled with the remains of cattle.²³² However, even this act could not crush the Sikhs.²³³ Four months later they observed Divali in the *Harmandir Sahib* and fought Ahmad Shah Abdali in a pitched battle, forcing him to withdraw from Amritsar. Ahmad Shah left Lahore for Afghanistan on 12 December 1762,²³⁴ only to attack India for the eighth time in 1766. The Sikhs were irritated by his repeated attacks, and this time wanted to weaken his position to such an extent that he would never return to the Punjab. They left Lahore and took up positions in different parts of the Punjab. This time when Ahmad Shah came to Lahore, he immediately decided to negotiate with the Sikhs, as he had suffered in his previous invasions. However, the Sikhs were not ready to compromise with him. They knew his situation extremely well, and internal problems forced him to retreat to his own country.²³⁵

The Sikh victory prevented any other power from ruling the Punjab, and Ahmad Shah Abdali and his successors were no longer considered a threat. Thus the Sikhs surrendered to none, crushed the Mughals and Durranis, and became leaders of the Punjab.

Conclusion

Sikhism grew at a time when both Islam and Hinduism were caught in the vicious circle of fundamentalism and the caste system. Religions were more a source and sign of superiority for the nobility and the orthodox than salvation for the common man. Muslims were divided into faiths and factions and Hindus were immersed in the caste and creed system. The gulf between the common man and the theocracy was widening fast, the former poor and unaware of the blessings of religion and faith. Myopic and self-centred interpretation of religion and its teachings was further squeezing the poorer segments of society. Under these circumstances, Sikhism was seen as a redeemer and saviour.

The subcontinent, being a heterogeneous polity, needed an open-minded and tolerant system of administration and justice for the smooth functioning of the empire. Early Mughal emperors understood this and hence adopted very liberal and fair policies in their dispensation of state functions. Therefore, from Babar to Akbar the relations between the two communities were based on harmony, tolerance and understanding. However, Akbar's liberalism was not acceptable to orthodox Muslim notables including *ulemas*, and a movement was started by the Naqshbandi *ulemas* for the revival of Islam. This movement was, indeed, against Akbar's policy of *sulh-i-kul* (absolute peace, conciliation with all).²³⁶

Unlike Hinduism, both Islam and Sikhism teach tolerance, equality, love for mankind and belief in one God. Both religions forbid worshipping anything but the one God, and the tenth Guru Gobind Singh called himself an 'image breaker'. There is no difference between a prince and a peasant in both religions. Both religions strongly support intermarriage and inter-dining. The charitable giving of *zakat* in Islam and *daswant* in Sikhism is used to help needy people.[237] These similarities brought the two communities closer together. This closeness left little space for the Hindu nobility, who would lose all the benefits and benevolence of the Mughal Empire. The astute Hindu mind instantly sensed this threat and therefore the Hindus put all their energies into keeping the two communities apart in one way or another. At the same time, a group of orthodox Muslims faced the same dilemma. Both their religious authority and their position at court were challenged; thus Hindu cleverness was aided by Muslim fundamentalism to set the stage for tearing apart the brotherhood and harmony between Sikhs and Muslims.

This illicit bond between Hindu aristocracy and Muslim orthodox theocracy resulted in many unfortunate incidents, which first created and then deepened the enmity between the two communities. One can easily see the deadly consequences of this cohort, first in the form of the murder of Guru Arjun by Emperor Jahangir on political grounds and later in the shape of the murder of the ninth Guru by Aurangzeb for not accepting Islam. The death of the tenth Guru was also the end product of complex conspiracies hatched by this alleged alliance. It was all done in the name of that religion which ordains no coercion or duress in accepting Islam, a religion that preaches peace and respect for mankind and others' religions.

The annals of history offer adequate evidence and material to highlight how Hindu shrewdness and Muslim orthodoxy manoeuvred the Gurus' fall. Muslim rulers always played into the hands of Hindu *pandits* and willingly helped their designs come true. However, history must not forget that even under the worst circumstances, the common Muslims always helped the Gurus. They stood by them, fought for them, and many died for them. Many Muslim saints also remained associated with Gurus. Unfortunately, some of the most loyal Muslims were treated very harshly during later days, including Syed Badar-ud-Din, commonly known as Bhudhu Shah, a close friend of Guru Gobind; this noble Muslim lost his sons while protecting Gobind Singh from the armed attacks of the Hindu mountain chieftains. Later Bhudhu Shah lost his family and fortune to the brutalities of Banda Singh.[238] Syed Bhikha Shah was another devotee who sacrificed his life for the Guru. In fact, he prophesied the spiritual elevation of Guru Gobind Singh. Moreover, Nabi Khan, Ghani Khan and Syed Muhammad Nurpuri risked their lives while saving Guru Gobind Singh from Wazir Khan, the Governor of Sirhind. The murders of Guru Arjun, Guru Tegh Bahadur and finally Guru Gobind Singh still remain obscure and disputed under the intricate layers of the subcontinent's history. However, one thing becomes clearer after each discourse: it was not religion or faith but the political ambitions and designs of Hindus and Muslims, and later those of Sikhs themselves, that were mainly responsible for the unfortunate events.[239]

On the other hand, these developments left indelible imprints on Sikhism. After the death of Guru Arjun, and even during his lifetime, Sikh Gurus deliberately entered into politics and the formalization of their religion. These ambitions to gain political as well as economic power further alarmed both foes and friends. Mughal emperors as well as Hindu rajas also became sceptical of the political designs of the Sikh Gurus and Sikhism. These ambitions, indeed, brought the

Sikhs face to face with the Mughal emperors. While this was a matter of concern for the rivals of Sikhism, it was also an opportunity for them to strike at Sikhism. These designs actually gave its enemies a chance to provoke the Mughal emperors against Sikhism. The rising power and popularity of Sikhism were taken as a threat to the existence of the Mughal Empire. These apprehensions, uncertainties and confusion worsened the relation between the two communities. The mischief-mongers further fuelled the situation that claimed the lives of the ninth and tenth Gurus, and many more.

An unintended consequence of the pressure on Sikhism from both Hindus and Muslims came about in the form of consolidation of Sikhism as a formal religion. In order to protect their minority status, the Sikh population united and took on the shape of a distinct community with an independent identity, despite many cross-cultural and religious similarities with Islam and Hinduism. Sikhism not only consolidated its spiritual gains but also its military might. From providing help to Khusroo to fight for Bahadur Shah, it gained in confidence. Following an inverse relationship, while Sikh military power continued to increase, the Mughals became weaker. During all those years while the Mughals were fighting their own blood relations, the Sikhs were expanding their political power and military strength, which best manifested itself during the reign of Maharaja Ranjit Singh.

In light of the above facts and analyses, it is imperative to revisit the history of Sikh–Muslim relations. Dilip Singh concludes that the Hindu intelligentsia deliberately marred the relationship between the two communities. Another point that needs to be stressed is the fact that the Sikh Gurus were never in direct opposition to Islam, only to the biased policies and treatment of the Mughal nobility and the *darbar* that heaped many injustices on them.

In short, the above-mentioned facts clearly show that although the relationship between Muslim and Sikh gradually began to sink from friendship to estrangement, originally this change was between the rulers and the Gurus and not between common Muslims and common Sikhs.

Nevertheless, the sufferings and oppression later meted out by Banda Singh and Muslim rulers against the common Sikhs and Muslims respectively actually remain responsible for the parting of the ways between the two communities. This situation became worse when Banda Singh started plundering the Muslim-majority areas to avenge Guru Gobind Singh. On the other hand, after the execution of Banda Singh, the Sikhs suffered at the hands of the Mughal governors. In the 1750s the Sikhs reorganized themselves, but again suffered at the hands of Ahmed Shah Abdali, who several times attacked the Punjab. He not only razed the sacred place of the Sikhs, the *Harmandir Sahib*, but also in 1762 killed almost 10,000 Sikhs in one day. During this period the Sikhs, too, killed many civilians who were supporters of Ahmed Shah Abdali, and also destroyed places of Muslim worship. Against this background, Maharaja Ranjit Singh showed an extraordinary degree of lenience and kindness towards his Muslim subjects.

Chapter 2

CONQUESTS OF MAHARAJA RANJIT SINGH: TREATMENT OF THE FALLEN MUSLIM RULERS AND POPULATION

Ranjit Singh emerged on the stage of the subcontinent when the whole of the Punjab was politically, socially and even economically at its lowest ebb because of the process of decadence of the Mughal Empire, the invasions of Nadir Shah and Ahmad Shah Abdali, and the War of Succession among the Sikh groups called *misls*. Consequently, the state machinery had collapsed and nobody was interested or ready to protect the people from looting and plunder. Rulers were busy accumulating wealth or feuding with each other over petty matters. Afghan power was decaying and the British were not yet powerful enough to take over the whole of the subcontinent. A huge governance and power vacuum emerged in the subcontinent, especially in the Punjab. The result was ever-increasing sociopolitical unrest and uncertainty, a weakening state and polity, poor social services, and an acute sense of insecurity. Under these circumstances, someone was needed to remove the painful rule of greedy and callous rulers.

Ranjit Singh came and conquered the entire province of the Punjab and also brought a ray of hope for peace and prosperity in the land. Frustrated by the existing rulers, people not only welcomed him, but they supported him against their own rulers and rajas. Starting from Gujranwala, he was successful in capturing and subjugating great and small states in and outside the Punjab. This remarkable achievement, coupled with his policies as a ruler, earned him the name 'Lion of the Punjab'. Therefore, it is of immense importance to investigate how he emerged as the most powerful ruler of the Punjab. This chapter attempts to reveal how he captured and subdued the different parts of the Punjab and how he treated the fallen rulers and populace, including Muslims, while subjugating or capturing their states.

Early Life

Ranjit Singh was born on 13 November 1780 to Maha Singh and Raj Kaur in Gujranwala, Punjab.[1] At first, he was named Budh Singh, but when Maha Singh received the news of his son's birth on his return from a victorious battle against the Chattha chief, Pir Muhammad, he renamed him Ranjit (Victor in War).[2] Ranjit Singh lost his left eye in childhood from an attack of smallpox. He had no formal education and spent most of his time in hunting and riding, having a great love for horses from an early age. He fought his first battle alongside his father Maha Singh against the Bhangi chiefs, but lost his father in his childhood. Ranjit Singh's grandfather, Charaht Singh was one of the foremost leaders of the *Khalsa* in their struggle for power; he had occupied large areas in three *doabs*, and was the founder of the Sukarchakia *misl*.[3]

Maha Singh added to his own father's territories, and Ranjit Singh inherited a large and well-administered land along with a well-trained army of 5,000 men.[4] He strengthened his position by his two marriages, one in the family of Jai Singh Kanaya and the other in the family of Kamar Singh Nakai, south of Lahore.[5] He married his first wife, Mahtab Kaur, daughter of his mentor Sada Kaur, the head of the Kanaya *misl*, in 1796. Sada Kaur gave him active support and courage during the early part of his conquests, and was as passionate as was Ranjit Singh himself.[6] At that time, the Sikhs ruled most of the Punjab under a joint *Sarbat Khalsa*[7] system, dividing the territory among groups known as *misls*.[8]

An astute military campaigner, Ranjit Singh learned the art of war at a tender age. Although childhood smallpox had blemished his appearance, he had a convincing personality with endless curiosity and extraordinary energy. Hunting and riding were his childhood passions. He was not destined to be a man of letters, but an outstanding military tactician. With his gifted leadership as a commander and military genius, he turned a crowd of *Khalsa* soldiers into a formidable army that, out of nowhere, carved out a huge kingdom for themselves.[9] This author takes the position that while annexing territory into his kingdom, Ranjit Singh did not view any state or ruler from the perspective of a Sikh leader; rather, like any expansionist of his time, he had the ambition to subjugate the entire Punjab, northwestern areas, Sindh and even all India. He adopted tactics such as creating rifts between the rulers and their opponents, developing a spy system and creating his image as a *messiah* (redeemer), to facilitate his conquests.

Maharaja Ranjit Singh's political and military shrewdness helped him rule over the Punjab for forty years from 1799 to 1839. He fought many battles and won all of them. While he defeated most of the Muslim, Sikh and Hindu rulers in the Punjab, he also halted Afghan and British armies. It was only after his death that the British entered the Punjab. The Lion of the Punjab was admired for his remarkable achievements as the conqueror who brought the Punjab under one central government, popularly known as the *Khalsa Sarkar*. He proved himself an intelligent and resourceful ruler with a highly ambitious political agenda. He came to fame in the Punjab by winning battles against the Afghan king. Zaman Shah, the king of Kabul and the grandson of Ahmad Shah Abdali, tried to re-establish the Durrani Empire in the Punjab, but 17-year-old Ranjit Singh intercepted him and defeated him at the battles of Amritsar (1797 and 1798) and Gujrat (1797).[10] After these battles, Ranjit Singh emerged as hero of the Sikhs and this encouraged him to aim to become ruler at the Punjab level. These victories against the Abdali rulers of Afghanistan paved the way for his unending campaigns to subjugate the Punjab, northwestern areas and Sindh.

Conquests of Maharaja Ranjit Singh

After the departure of the Afghans from the Punjab, their deputies and governors failed to keep tight authority; consequently, numerous large and small independent territories mushroomed, some of whom still held allegiance to the Afghan rulers. Ranjit Singh, knowing their weak position, sent letters asking them to accept him as their ruler and show their allegiance to the Maharaja of the Punjab. The Muslim *sardars* refused to accept his authority, especially the chief of Jhang under Ahmad Khan, Kasur under Nizam-ud-Din Khan and Multan under Nawab Muzaffar Khan.[11]

Dera Ismail Khan was being governed by Abdul Samad Khan; Mankera, Bannu and the neighbouring territories were respectively under the control of Muhammad Shah Nawaz Khan, Moeenud Doula and Swar Khan Katti Khel. Dera Ghazi Khan and Bahawalpur, along with a vast tract adjoining Multan, were ruled by Daud Potra and Bahawal Khan respectively. Sials ruled Jhang, and Fateh Khan Barakzai ruled Peshawar. Attock Fort was in the possession of Wazir Khan and Jahandad Khan. The Kangra Hills were under Sansar Chand, while independent Sikh *sardars* governed areas from Hoshiarpur to Kapurthala.[12] Ranjit Singh's forces invaded and subdued all of them.

The British were another powerful player in the subcontinent. While Ranjit Singh knew the weaknesses and vulnerabilities of indigenous Muslim, Hindu and Sikh rulers, he also understood the power and might of the British East India Company army. Therefore, despite all his ambitions and preparation, he did not venture into their territories. Instead, he focused on frail fiefdoms in the Punjab who were fighting with one another for more power internally.[13] With the fall of every ruler, Ranjit Singh became stronger and stronger and his ambition soared higher and higher. He continued to consolidate his military strength and skills, soon after the occupation of Lahore starting a long campaign against the neighbouring Muslim, Hindu and Sikh rulers to bring them under his control.

Conquest of Muslim States: Lahore

The occupation of Lahore by Ranjit Singh in the summer of 1799 marked a watershed in his career and in the history of Sikh rule in the Punjab. His political achievement as the ruler of Lahore has so completely overshadowed his late eighteenth-century predecessors that the year 1799 appears to many historians to mark the beginning of sovereign Sikh rule in the Punjab.

Ranjit Singh attacked and captured Lahore without much effort from the Bhangi *misl* who had won it from the Afghans in 1765. He was actually invited by some Muslim and Hindu *sardars* who wanted to see the end of the Bhangi *sardars* and their cruelties.[14] S. M. Latif gives the names of some important persons who signed the letter inviting Ranjit Singh to attack the fort at Lahore: Hakam Hakim Rai, Bhai Gurbukhsh Singh, Mian Ashok Muhammed, Mufti Muhammed Mokarram and Mir Shadi, all from very well-known and noble families.[15]

Nawab Nizam-ud-Din, ruler of Kasur, was also ambitious to seize Lahore, trying to convince the *chaudharis* (elites of an area) of Lahore to help him capture it from the Bhangi *sardars*,[16] but the notables mentioned above preferred to invite Ranjit Singh rather than the Muslim rulers of Kasur or Multan. In fact, they believed Ranjit Singh to be a more benevolent, fairer and secular monarch than the Muslim rulers. They opened the gates of Lahore for Ranjit Singh and allowed an effortless entry into the city. Available evidence reports hardly any significant bloodshed during this 'conquest'.[17]

Kasur

Pathans, loyal to Kabul, ruled Kasur. During the Abdali attacks, the ruler took the side of the Afghan, Tamur Shah, and plundered Sikh territory. When Tamur Shah attacked Lahore and Amritsar in 1797, the Kasur ruler, Nizam-ud-Din Khan, promised to help him. The people of Lahore, especially the Muslims, suffered considerably at the hands of Nizam-ud-Din and the Abdalis, whose retreating forces looted the surrounding towns.

The Bhangi *sardars* joined forces with the Nawab of Kasur to recapture Lahore. Sahib Singh Bhangi of Gujarat, Gulab Singh Bhangi of Amritsar, Jassa Singh Ram Garhia, Jodh Singh of Wazirabad and the Nawab of Kasur forged an alliance. All of them were afraid of Ranjit Singh's growing power and influence in the area. The combined forces of the Bhangi *sardars* and Pathans attacked Lahore, but after a lapse of two months both sides still stood firm. However, to Ranjit Singh's luck, one of the important allies of the opposing forces, Gulab Singh, died of excessive drinking during the fight. While this ill-timed death brought relief to Ranjit Singh, it shattered the confidence and determination of the Bhangi forces, who could not keep the ground and fled the field. Ranjit Singh emerged victorious and the undisputed Maharaja of the Punjab, and the *Khalsa* army grew stronger and more experienced.[18] In order to teach Nizam-ud-Din of Kasur a lesson, Ranjit Singh fell on Kasur in 1801.[19]

The ruler of Kasur had forged the alliance with the Bhangi *sardars* because he feared that Ranjit Singh's rising power and influence in the area might endanger his own throne.[20] Ranjit Singh no doubt wanted to expand his territory, but realizing that the Nawab of Kasur had conceived the alliance against his kingdom, he decided to subdue Kasur after defeating the allied forces. He invaded Kasur first in 1801 and again in 1802,[21] finally annexing it in 1807.[22] Great celebrations were held in Lahore and Amritsar to commemorate the victory of Kasur.[23]

In analysing the annexation of Kasur, several startling facts emerge. Many factors were responsible for the unfortunate fate of Kasur at the hands of the Sikhs. Nizam-ud-Din, despite his weak military strength and compromised position, was bent upon taking over Lahore. In spite of losing to Ranjit Singh many times, Nizam-ud-Din kept conspiring against him and defying the agreed terms and conditions of defeat. Ranjit Singh invaded Kasur five times and every time returned the *nizamat* to the Muslim ruler. He was a natural and strategic ally of Kasur itself. Nonetheless, the Afghan rulers again and again broke the treaties and connived with enemies of Ranjit Singh, thus provoking a powerful foe. Even Nizam-ud-Din's brother-in-law, Qutab-ud-Din, who replaced him, did not sit by idly, and very soon started making alliances with the enemies of Ranjit Singh.[24] Qutab-ud-Din also looted some areas of Lahore and thus further annoyed the Sikh ruler. Before attacking Kasur, Ranjit Singh had sent his trusted minister Fakir Azizuddin to convince the Pathan ruler to abide by the agreed terms of surrender. However, Fakir Azizuddin was instead humiliated by the Pathan ruler and condemned for rendering service to Ranjit Singh.[25]

Ranjit Singh very generously ignored Nizam-ud-Din's blunders and continued to return the *nizamat* to the Pathan rulers. This happened not once but five times, but the Pathan rulers continued to violate the terms of peace.[26] In fact, they failed to see the strategic significance and power of the Sikhs and failed to maintain cordial relations with Ranjit Singh. They neither tried to befriend him nor to neutralize his strength with treaties, pacts or networking. Instead, they kept on challenging him without considering their capacity or the results. On the other hand, Ranjit Singh understood his strengths and had clear thinking about his relations with the Muslim rulers. He was not interested in the annexation of Kasur but only in its revenue. Nevertheless, the Pathan ruler forced him to strike a final blow and take over Kasur. The Sikh army captured Qutab-ud-Din while he was fleeing from the fort. When Ranjit Singh asked him about the violation of the treaty, the Pathan ruler had no answer but made a plea for pardon. Ranjit Singh pardoned him and also granted him the estate of Mamdot, which brought an income of Rs.190,000 annually.[27] Although the Maharaja gave these Afghans *jagirs*, they continued to pose problems for him.[28] However, he did not stop here. He also granted an estate in Maruf to the son of Nizam-ud-Din, the former ruler of Kasur who had been killed by his own family members.[29]

Multan

The province of Multan was known as *Dar-ul-Aman* (abode of peace) during the time of Akbar the Great. While Multan bordered British territories on one side, it had Bahawalpur to the north, and touched the districts of Shikarpur and Jacobabad in Sindh and the districts of Sibi and Mari in Baluchistan.[30]

After the decline of the Mughals in the Punjab, Nadir Shah Durrani captured the Punjab and appointed a Pathan (Pakhtun) as Nawab of Multan, in 1739. Similarly, Ahmad Shah Abdali appointed an independent governor for the newly secured areas of the Punjab with enlarged territory. The Bhangi *sardar*, Hari Singh, attacked these areas in 1799 but was repelled by Tamur, the son of Ahmad Shah Abdali. Later, Tamur handed over this part of the Punjab to his relative Muzaffar Khan Saddozai, who was theoretically under the Afghan ruler but in practice had become independent.[31]

Numerous factors enticed Ranjit Singh to subjugate Multan. Enjoying a rich Muslim civilization, Multan was a fertile, productive and cultured province – qualities which made it a great attraction to an invader. Multan was also important to Ranjit Singh for its strategic location and economic potential, as it was on a major trade route with states to and beyond the Bolan Pass. It collected revenue from all the states, totalling Rs.680,975 a year, which provided a constant source of income for the province.[32] The other reason for Ranjit Singh to capture Multan was to prevent the union of the Muslim forces of Bahawalpur and Sindh.[33] He built his case on the plea that Multan belonged to Abdali and as successor or deputy of the Abdalis in the Punjab, he had every right to inherit the province of Multan as well.

Ranjit Singh could not resist these attractions and attacked Multan in 1802. Initially, he demanded that the Nawab surrender the city to the *Khalsa* army, arguing that he was the rightful heir of the king of Kabul.[34] On the Nawab's refusal, Ranjit Singh's army marched towards Multan.[35] It attacked Multan a number of times but did not take over until 1818. The question arises as to why he delayed its annexation. Some historians attribute this delay to the Maharaja's generosity in allowing his opponents to prove their loyalty and submission to him. Others suggest that he was more interested in the treasury of Multan than occupying the city. Another explanation is that he did not think the *Khalsa* army strong enough to annex Multan before 1818, which is why he abandoned it as many as six times.[36] Every time the Maharaja attacked Multan, he just took the *nazrana* (tribute) and returned to Lahore. However, in 1818 he had become strong enough to conquer Multan.[37] Historians, including S. M. Latif, Lepel Griffin and Diwan Amar Nath, appreciate the political wisdom of Ranjit Singh because Multan had been subjugated without bloodshed, looting or plunder.[38] However, Kanhaiya Lal presents another side of the picture about the Multan expedition. He writes that the conquest of Kasur had left the *Khalsa* army worn out, and Ranjit Singh had to struggle to persuade his forces to march towards Multan and subsequently had to rethink his war strategy.[39]

Multan was invaded so many times by the Sikh army that even Nawab Muzaffar Khan in 1810 requested the British for help against the Sikh ruler, as he was tired of paying the annual *nazrana*. The British, however, refused to help him, arguing that they already had a treaty with the Sikh ruler of the Punjab.[40] Also, before this invasion, Ranjit Singh had met Shah Shuja, the king of Kabul, who had been thrown out of Afghanistan. Shah Shuja appealed to Ranjit Singh to hand over Multan after its conquest. Earlier, in 1803, Muzaffer Khan had defeated Shah Shuja and offered to let him to stay in Multan. However, Shah Shuja refused. Ranjit Singh wanted money from Shah Shuja so he promised to hand over Multan to him. However, when Shah Shuja failed to pay him the promised riches, Ranjit Singh decided to invade Multan for himself.[41]

After getting hold of most of the Punjab, in 1818 Ranjit Singh finally decided to annex Multan. On 2 June 1818, a Sikh called Sadhu Singh attacked the fort and made inroads into the wall. Encouraged by his bravery, the Sikh army joined him and reached the *Khizri Darwaza* (one of the gates) of the fort.[42] The old Nawab, with some faithful soldiers and his eight sons, continued to fight fearlessly, until he and five of his sons were killed.[43] One of the remaining sons received a serious facial injury and the other two were taken prisoner. Following the conquest of Multan, the Nawab and his sons were buried with honour near the shrine of Sultan Bahauddin (RA).[44]

News of the conquest of Multan reached Lahore three days later. In celebration, the Maharaja gave a pair of bracelets to the messenger, and Diwan Chand was awarded the title of Zafar Jang Bahadar.[45] Sarfraz Khan, the son of Muzaffar Khan, was brought to Lahore, where the Maharaja treated him with honour and placed his seat near him. Initially he was under strict scrutiny, but when matters had been settled in Multan, he had full freedom to move around and was always treated with respect.[46] Maharaja Ranjit Singh also granted him a state in Sharkpur and Naulakha.[47] However, after the fall of the Punjab, the British took this *jagir* from his family on his death.[48] Nawab Muzaffar Khan's second son was in the custody of Diwan Chand, who brought him to Lahore some days later. Maharaja Ranjit Singh also honoured him and granted him a proper place in his *darbar* and a respectable state with a pension.

One of the aspects of Ranjit Singh's character was his kindness. He always treated fallen rulers with reverence and benevolence. When Bhai Govind Ram told the Maharaja in 1839 that Nawab Sarfraz Khan of Multan was short of funds, he willingly awarded him Rs.2,000 and a pashmina, worth Rs.6,000.[49]

The fall of Multan proved to be strategically and economically a great conquest. It ended Afghan rule in the southern Punjab and also opened up the riches and fertile land of the south for revenue of nearly Rs.700,000 a year.[50] It influenced and left a strong impression on all the other rulers of the Muslim states of Dera Ghazi Khan, Bahawalpur and Dera Ismail Khan.

Multan was an important city for the ruler of Lahore, not only economically but also geographically. Some historians[51] criticized Ranjit Singh for his invasion of Multan. They also portrayed these invasions as a Sikh–Muslim religious conflict, but a true historian can easily see that Ranjit Singh was expanding his territory and Multan was the most important region with a large amount of revenue. If he invaded Multan again and again, there was some reason behind it. During the first invasion the Nawab accepted his rule and promised to pay him a yearly tribute. The other invasions happened because the Nawab broke his promise and joined hands with the enemies of Ranjit Singh. It was not at all a religious war on either side. Before his invasion, the ruler of the Afghan family, Shah Shuja, had asked Ranjit Singh to help him in conquering Multan. It is also interesting that Nawab Muzaffar Khan also requested the British East India Company to help him against Ranjit Singh.

Jhang

The Muslim *sardar* Ahmed Khan controlled the territory of Jhang. He ruled peacefully and the people were happy with his style of government. He had good relations with the neighbouring states and was known to be a brave ruler. Ranjit

Singh knew that the fall of Jhang would add to his own prestige and power.[52] He sent his agents there to collect tribute from the Muslim ruler, but the agents remained in Jhang for a month without any result.

Enraged, Ranjit Singh finally started preparations to invade Jhang in 1803.[53] Ahmad Khan gathered around him a large army consisting of different Muslim tribes such as the Kharals, Sials and Bharwanas. The Sikh army, with the help of cannons, destroyed a large part of the Muslim army.[54] Ahmad Khan fought bravely with his sword.

Ranjit Singh besieged the city and cut off all supplies from every side. After three days, the Hindu subjects of Jhang tried to open the gates of the fort in return for a promise of amnesty by the *Khalsa* army. The news reached Ahmad Khan, who posted guards outside the doors of the Hindu *chaudharis* to prevent them from opening the gates. However, two days later, when Ahmad Khan's army heard the arrival of the Sikh army at the city's outskirts, they left the Hindus' *havelis* (villas) to save their own families. Even Ahmad Khan decided to save his family and fled to Multan,[55] and the *chaudharis* gave Ranjit Singh the news of his departure.[56] The battle of Jhang caused heavy casualties on both sides.[57] Muzaffar Khan angered the Maharaja by offering protection to Ahmad Khan and his family.[58]

Eventually, talks between the Maharaja and Ahmad Khan regarding the future of Jhang state resulted in an agreement whereby Ahmad Khan accepted to pay a tribute of Rs.60,000 annually to the Sikh ruler if the throne of Jhang was returned to him. Nevertheless, in 1816, owing to non-payment of the *nazrana*, Ranjit Singh's forces again attacked Jhang and forced Ahmad Khan to pay a heavy tribute. This time Ahmad Khan did not have sufficient money and was brought to Lahore, and Jhang was annexed. The Maharaja treated the former ruler of Jhang kindly and granted him the state of Mirowal in Amritsar District, worth Rs.12,000 annually.[59] In 1818, his son also received a state worth Rs.3,000; on his father's death he succeeded to his state, and in 1830 was granted another state in Mianwali district.[60]

In 1803, the forts of Sahiwal and Garh Maharaja were also forced to pay tribute to the Maharaja. The *sardars* accepted the Sikh terms for fear of attack and complete annexation. Fateh Khan, the chief of Sahiwal, agreed to pay a tribute of twenty-five horses and twenty-five camels a year, but was unable to pay the annual tribute of Rs.150,000; consequently, the Sikh army attacked Sahiwal.[61]

In 1810, Ranjit Singh called Fateh Khan to his court, but he sent his son Lal Khan on his behalf. Ranjit Singh in the meantime attacked Khushab and expelled its chief, Zafar Khan. On his way back, he also captured Sahiwal and imprisoned Fateh Khan and his family. Fateh Khan was freed in 1811 and a state worth Rs.14,400 was granted to him; in return, he was required to supply fifty horsemen every year. In 1812, Fateh Khan returned to Lahore and was forced to stay in the *darbar* for three years. He escaped and claimed shelter under the Baloch governor of Mankera, before going on to Multan. He finally retired to Bahawalpur, where he stayed until his death in 1820.[62]

Ranjit Singh's design to capture Bahawalpur and Sindh could not be realized, largely because of the East India Company. In 1807, he tried for the first time to attack Bahawalpur but returned after being awarded some money. He continued to receive money from Bahawal Khan until the Nawab's death. When he demanded tribute from Nawab Sadiq Muhammed and the Nawab refused to pay, Ranjit Singh attacked Bahawalpur. He kept on attacking until 1831, when Bahawalpur state and the East India Company entered into an alliance. Bahawalpur became an independent state and just escaped from the hands of Maharaja Ranjit Singh.[63] Ranjit Singh tried to attack Sindh as well, but because of the East India Company, he did not succeed. Therefore, the Sikh chiefs had little control over the western part of Sindh including Sagar *doab*, the areas of Fatehjang, Pindigheb and Bhakhar.[64]

Peshawar, Attock, Hazara, Dera Ghazi Khan, Dera Ismail Khan, Mankera and other areas

Peshawar, now a large city and capital of the province of Khyber Pakhtunkhwa (KPK), Pakistan, was then part of the Afghan kingdom. High mountains to the north, lower hills to the south, the river Indus to the east and the famous Khyber Pass to the west surround it.[65] It is a fertile land with an abundance of fruit, and was called a *shehr-e-sabz* (green city) in the time of Ranjit Singh.[66]

The greatest legacy of Ranjit Singh is his conquest of Hazara and Peshawar and the consolidation of the northwestern frontier. Indeed, if this consolidation had not happened, all these regions, along with the entire trans-Indus territories, would have been part of Afghan territory, and would not have become part of the British Empire.[67] Pakistan would not have inherited them, as they would still have been in Afghanistan. Hence, Ranjit Singh's achievement in this context is of transnational importance.

All these trans-Indus areas were included in the province of Kabul, which had the same standing and significance as that of Lahore and Multan. Although these areas were under the control of Mughals they were never subdued. The Attock District Gazetteer states that 'the Mughal control was always more nominal than real. They appear to have been content to levy revenue and there is nothing to show that any serious administration was attempted. The whole district paid only about half a *lakh* of rupees and the head of each tribe remained practically independent.'[68]

This nominal influence of the Mughals was further eroded after Nadir Shah's invasion. Ahmad Shah Abdali, the founder of modern Afghanistan and successor of Nadir Shah, brought all the trans-Indus areas and some parts of West Punjab under the control of Kabul. However, repeated invasions by Ahmad Shah Abdali could not crush the Sikhs, but had the opposite effect and greatly helped the Sikhs' rise to political power.[69] The Sikhs gained almost all the Punjab from the successors of Ahmad Shah Abdali, from Sirhind to Lahore, Multan and Derajat; the whole area was divided among Sikh *sardars*.

It seems appropriate to discuss the condition of Peshawar before the advent of Ranjit Singh. Shah Mahmood, the grandson of Ahmad Shah Abdali, was the ruler of Kabul with Fateh Khan Barakzai as his minister. All the territories across the Khyber Pass were given to Sardar Yar Muhammad, Sultan Muhammad Khan and

Dost Muhammad Khan, the brothers of Fateh Khan. Shah Mahmood did not like the increasing power of Fateh Khan, so his son killed him. Azim Khan, the ruler of Kashmir, who was also a brother of Fateh Khan, avenged his brother's murder by imprisoning Shah Mahmood and his son with the help of Shah Mahmood's cousin Ayub, who became the ruler of Kabul.[70]

Under these circumstances, Ranjit Singh decided to attack Peshawar in 1818. Both the Muslim rulers left the city and fled to Yousafzai tribes. When Ranjit Singh had captured the city, he decided not to annex Peshawar. He took Rs.25,000 in tribute and handed over the territory to his old friend Jahandad Khan, the governor of Attock.[71]

Yar Muhammad Khan, the former ruler of Peshawar, again attacked and regained his territory. Ranjit Singh sent his forces to recapture the city, and Yar Muhammad Khan strategically offered him an annual tribute of Rs.1 *lakh*.[72]

Azim Khan did not like the way his brother was ruling Peshawar. He appealed for a *jihad* (holy war) against the Sikhs, and a large army was gathered in the name of Islam. Ranjit Singh also sent a large army under the command of Prince Sher Singh. French officers, including Generals Ventura and Allard, had trained the Sikh soldiers, and many famous and brave Sikh generals were leading them, including Hari Singh Nalwa, Attar Singh Sindhianwala, Dhinna Singh Malwai and Diwan Kirpa Ram, son of Diwan Mohkam Chand; Misr Diwan Chand and Ranjit Singh also joined them subsequently.[73]

Initially the Afghans won the battle and the famous Sikh *Akali* leader Phula Singh was killed during the fight, but the Sikh army fought very bravely against the Afghan forces and eventually won.[74] In the battle at Naushehra, 4,000 Pathans and 2,000 Sikhs were killed.[75] Azim Khan became disheartened and died of a heart attack.[76]

Ranjit Singh won a decisive victory and the Pathans were dispersed forever in 1823. In March 1824, he again entered the city and was welcomed overwhelmingly by the people of Peshawar. Yar Muhammad Khan, who had earlier fled, returned and was appointed governor again on condition of paying Rs.110,000 annual tribute.[77]

This was a significant trial for the Pathan tribes who had gathered for religion under Azim Khan Barakzai. However, they lost the battle and the whole territory again fell into the hands of the Sikh ruler. Although Ranjit Singh won the battle against the Afghans, he trusted Yar Muhammad Khan one more time and made him governor of Peshawar, after which he returned to Lahore. On his return, songs of celebrations were sung, and all the communities also celebrated the Muslim festival Shab-e-Barat. At night oil lamps were lit and rockets fired, and the Maharaja himself threw silver and gold coins into the crowds.[78] Peshawar remained as an attached territory of the Lahore *Darbar*, however; the weakening situation in Afghanistan further helped the Sikhs to annex Peshawar.[79]

Tehrik-e-Mujahidin

Tehrik-e-Mujahidin was an armed movement started by Syed Ahmad against the Sikhs in the northwestern areas during the Sikh rule to establish a Muslim state.

Syed Ahmad was a dominating personality in the early nineteenth century. His name is associated with the religious, social and political revival of the Muslims in India. He was born in 1786 into a Syed family. In his early life, he was strongly influenced by Shah Abdul Aziz, a renowned religious personality of the time. He was a learned person and well known for his understanding of Muslim theology. He was a strong man and had an association with the Amir Khan of Tank, where he learned many military skills.[80] In the declining days of the Mughals, the Marhathas, British, Rajputs, Jats and Sikhs were gaining power. He was especially concerned about the ever-deteriorating condition of the Muslims and the rising power of the Sikhs in the Punjab. Therefore, he turned his attention to the northwestern areas, gathered Muslim combatants and started *Tehrik-e-Mujahidin*.

On 30 July 1821, Syed Ahmad started his *hajj* (pilgrimage) with 400 followers. According to Mian Muhammad Saeed, he went on *hajj* to secure the help of Muslim countries.[81] After returning from Mecca, he began his two-year preparations for *jihad*. He asked the Muslims to join him against the infidel Sikhs who had committed numerous crimes against the followers of the Holy Prophet. During *hajj*, he also tried to make a Muslim alliance against the British; however, it seems very strange that he hardly ever made any statements or alliances in the subcontinent itself against the British.[82]

Mirza Hairat Dehlvi tells in the *Itayat-e-Taiba* that after discussion with Shah Ismail, Syed Ahmad conveyed to the lieutenant governor of the northern areas of the British, through Sheikh Ghulam Ali, chief of Allahabad, that he was forging an alliance for *jihad* against the Sikhs and expected no objections from the British government. The lieutenant governor wrote back that as long as the harmony of their lands was ensured, they had no opposition to such arrangements.[83] There are some reports that Syed Ahmad was provided with money and men by the British East India Company government in Calcutta.[84] Although the British were also infidels in his eyes, he made it clear that the war was against the Sikhs and not against the British.

Syed Ahmad left Delhi with 500 followers. The Nawab of Tank also aided him. From Tank, he reached Sindh, where he was well received by the Mirs of Sindh. They showed great respect and hosted the whole gathering. The Nawab of Bahawalpur also provided help to Syed Ahmad. Subsequently he declared *jihad* against the Sikhs, and his followers declared him *Imam* (leader of prayers) or *Amir-ul-Momneen* (leader of the Muslims). Even Peshawar accepted him as ruler. *Shariah* ordinance was issued and Islamic laws were enforced in Peshawar; for example, prostitution was stopped and wine shops were closed.[85]

Hari Singh Nalwa defeated Syed Ahmad at the first encounter at Akora,[86] although the latter gathered his followers and returned, this time killing the Afghan *sardar*, Yar Muhammed Khan and capturing Peshawar.[87] Ranjit Singh sent Prince Sher Singh along with General Ventura to retrieve the city and Syed Ahmad again fled. After settling affairs, the Sikh army returned to Lahore. Sultan Muhammad Khan was appointed the new ruler of Peshawar. Meanwhile, Syed Ahmad reached the valley of Kashmir and preached among the Kashmiris.[88] However, he reemerged, gathered his followers and again fell upon Peshawar, unseating the governor and seizing the city. The affairs of the state were sustained for some time but very soon even the Muslims turned against him. At the same time, Ranjit Singh came out to teach a lesson to Syed Ahmad, who escaped to the hills before the Sikhs had reached Peshawar. Syed Ahmad by force took the *nazrana* from the governor of Peshawar, who promised to pay him Rs.3,000 a month on condition that two *molvies* (Muslim religious persons) would manage the affairs of the city according to the *shariah*.[89]

The Pathans resisted the introduction of some religious innovations by Syed Ahmad, such as the collection of a tenth share of land income for religious and state purposes. They were also becoming restless at the incursion of people on their land, as Muslims from the whole subcontinent were coming to join the *jihad* movement. The demands they were making for food and especially for women were not acceptable. It is said that Syed Ahmad was marrying young Pathan girls to young men from India, with a view to bringing the Pathans into the mainstream of the subcontinent. These forced marriages were a humiliation to the Pathan tribesmen, who took pride in the traditions of bravery that had always been shown by their ancestors.[90]

Syed Ahmad was strongly influenced by the teachings of the *Wahabi ulemas* of Najd,[91] publicly rejecting the bow of respect before the shrines of saints or paying for blessings at the tombs. He denounced offering alms and food for the absolution of the souls of the dead, believing that these rituals could not benefit them. He also did not believe in the miracles of the saints. However, these beliefs were not acceptable to the Muslims of that area.[92] Given his extreme views and staunch beliefs, the Yousafzai tribes themselves turned against him. Even *qazis* and *mullahs* became disillusioned, and a wave of hostility broke against Syed Ahmad. The tribesmen murdered his followers from other parts of the subcontinent and he himself was forced to step down from Peshawar. He went to Muzaffarabad, but was chased and killed by Prince Sher Singh in the hills of Balakot.[93] Sher Singh arranged a respectable burial with precious shawls as a sign of respect for a brave opponent, and Ranjit Singh was pleased to hear about the prince's conduct towards the defeated leader.[94] As described above, Ranjit Singh still did not choose to rule Peshawar directly and instead appointed Sultan Muhammad Khan, a brother of Yar Muhammad Khan, as ruler.[95]

Tehrik-e-Mujahidin, the movement started by Syed Ahmed, left some significant lessons and patterns that can help understand the polity of Peshawar and the rule of Ranjit Singh. The Pathans did not tolerate the religious restrictions and innovations introduced by Syed Ahmad and they came out very strongly against him. How could such a race and society tolerate a ban on *aazan*[96] or other restrictions on their religion during the Sikh regime? Ranjit Singh had learned not to restrict the Muslims from undertaking their religious duties, especially in the Muslim-majority areas. From his first conquest of Peshawar he had not ruled Peshawar directly, only receiving tribute from the Pathan *sardars* and not interfering in internal matters. Even after the fall of Syed Ahmad, he did not try to annex Peshawar, to avoid future trouble from the Muslims. We as historians and analysts of human narratives and historical patterns need to understand and dissect the reported facts with logic and caution. Fiction needs to be separated from fact.

Tired of all this melodrama and continuous pricking by Afghans in the northwestern areas, Ranjit Singh eventually decided to annex Peshawar and appoint his own governor. While the Afghans were busy fighting and weakening each other, he dispatched Prince Nau Nihal to Peshawar along with Sardar Hari Singh Nalwa and General Ventura.[97] The tribal leaders of Peshawar had already sent their families out of the city. Apparently the expedition was meant to recover and increase the amount of tribute; however, the Sikh army had its own designs on annexing Peshawar. Hari Singh Nalwa sent a message to Sultan Muhammad that Nau Nihal wanted to visit the city; therefore, it would be better for Sultan Muhammad Khan to leave the city, which he promptly did. Subsequently the Sikh army formally occupied Peshawar on 6 May 1834.[98]

The annexation of Peshawar annoyed Dost Mohammad Khan. He declared *jihad* against Ranjit Singh, and again many different tribes joined forces with him. In order to stop Dost Muhammad Khan and his allies, Ranjit Singh sent his trusted minister, Fakir Azizuddin. A brief account of the discourse that took place between Dost Muhammad Khan and Fakir Azizuddin follows:

> The rulers of Afghanistan were never reconciled with the fact that Peshawar had slipped out of their hands and went to Ranjit Singh. When Dost Mohammed Khan attacked Peshawar in 1834 to regain it, Ranjit Singh sent Faqir Azizuddin his prime minister for negotiations. When the Fakir reached his camp and talks started, the courtiers gave it a religious bent and he was taunted severely for his allegiance to a non-Muslim. Shrewd as the Fakir was, he asked all present that being a good Muslim, wasn't it his moral duty to loyally serve his king? The aggressors, who were in no mood to let go, cleverly started alluding to the massive bloodshed of Muslims on both sides if the war ensued. The Faqir paused and then asked Dost Khan if he convinced Ranjit Singh to give Peshawar back to him, would he return peacefully? The answer was a resounding 'yes'. And then the Fakir retorted: 'don't brand your campaign Islamic, it is a fight for a piece of land.[99]

Ranjit Singh himself led the army to Kashmir to face Dost Muhammad Khan, but the latter left without a fight on hearing that it was Ranjit Singh himself leading the army. Sultan Muhammad Khan and his brother Pir Muhammad Khan were given the *jagir* of Kohat and Hashat Nagar, which was worth of about Rs.300,000 a year. They were also given territory in *doabs*, which grossed Rs.25,000 a year.[100] In 1837, Dost Muhammad Khan again attacked Peshawar. Hari Singh Nalwa lost his life in the famous battle of Jamrud, but Dhian Singh reached Peshawar with reinforcements, at which point the Afghans withdrew.[101]

In 1838, the Sikhs, the British and the former ruler of Afghanistan, Shah Shuja joined forces to win the throne of Kabul for Shah Shuja. However, despite the alliance with the British, Ranjit Singh did not allow them to pass through the Punjab.[102]

In a detailed account of the proceedings of the court of the Maharaja on 25 August 1825, Sinha reports that 'the Qazis, Syeds, Ulemas and Faqirs of Peshawar were given great *khilats* (dresses) and each was given a jagir for his upkeep when the Maharaja annexed Peshawar'.[103]

When the Maharaja's victory procession passed through the avenues of Peshawar, Ranjit Singh issued strict directions to his *sardars* and men not to harm any mosque, not to disrespect any lady and not to devastate any crops. The Muslim clerics were pleased to the point that they welcomed the victory. Moreover, the Muslim generals of the *Khalsa* army led the convoy. Available records of his *darbar* journals and proceedings amply highlight that, following the conquest of Peshawar, Ranjit Singh paid tribute and charity to the shrines and the *fakirs*, the educated individuals and the *Syeds* as well.[104] His secular approach earned him many prayers and blessings from the Muslim population when he fell sick in 1826.

The whole saga of deadly battles, convoluted intrigues and religious revivals lead to one major inference – that Ranjit Singh was interested only in the revenue from Peshawar and nothing else. He showed little ambition for extending the boundaries of the Sikh Empire or spreading the Sikh religion across the northwestern areas of the subcontinent, but only for accumulating more and more wealth. The *sardars* of these tribes remained independent after paying the agreed annual taxes and tribute to the Maharaja, who rarely interfered in their administrative affairs.

Situated on the bank of the river Indus,[105] the fort of Attock had great strategic importance for monitoring the movements of enemies coming from the north. For this reason it was called the northern gate of the subcontinent. Although enthusiastic about taking the fort, Ranjit Singh dropped the idea because of the expected hardships. Jahandar was the ruler of Attock at that time, and the Afghan and Sikh armies had already defeated his brother, Ata Muhammad Khan, the ruler of Kashmir. After the death of Atta Muhammad Khan, Jahandar knew his fate and expected invasion by the Afghans and Sikhs, well exposed to the ambitions of both. He therefore decided to win the trust and friendship of Ranjit Singh, who reciprocated wholeheartedly. Many letters were exchanged between the two rulers. During these talks, Fakir Azizuddin represented the Maharaja. Finally, the ruler of Attock agreed to hand over the fort in return for a safe haven and a suitable area to rule; he was subsequently granted the area of Waziristan.[106]

Ranjit Singh sent an experienced special convoy to Attock to control the fort. However, they were informed that the Afghan forces had to be paid before giving up the fort. In fact, the soldiers had not been paid for months. Ranjit Singh agreed to pay their salaries first and then take over the fort.[107] All this was done so secretly that the Afghan government had no idea until the end. On learning of the handing over of Attock Fort, the prime minister, Fateh Khan, tried every means to get it back, unsuccessfully. He prepared his army and reached Peshawar by the unfamiliar route of Pakhli and Dhamthor.[108] On reaching Peshawar, he sent a message to the Sikhs to leave the fort. The Maharaja, however, refused to do so, keeping Fateh Khan engaged in futile talks to buy time to strengthen his position in Attock. Fateh Khan did not see this and continued to waste time in unfruitful talks and letters. In the meantime, Ranjit Singh cleverly and steadily continued to strengthen his hold on Attock. When Fateh Khan reached Attock, the Maharaja blankly refused to leave the fort. While Fateh Khan besieged it, reinforcements and ammunition under the command of Diwan Mohkam Chand arrived. Both armies stood against each other for some three months. Finally on 13 July 1813, the two armies fought on the plains of Khizru and the Sikhs emerged victorious.

This battle was significant in the history of the Punjab for several reasons. It infused a sense of superiority in the Sikhs, which added to their confidence and valour. They fought fearlessly and won many battles for Ranjit Singh. In a short span of time they not only took Peshawar from the Afghans but also attacked Kabul. Fully recognizing the importance of the fort of Attock, Ranjit Singh did all he could to keep it in his hands.[109]

After the victories of Kashmir and Peshawar, the Hazara tribes were worried that they would be the next to be attacked by the Sikh forces. They therefore decided to rise against Lahore. On learning this, Ranjit Singh dispatched an army under the command of Sher Singh, who was victorious in every fight. In their final encounter, the Hazaras ran from the battlefield. Ram Deyal chased them, but they turned back and again attacked the Sikhs, killing many soldiers including the Sikh General Ram Deyal, which was a severe blow to the Sikh forces. However, the Sikh army eventually won the battle, completing the conquest of the entire area of Hazara.[110]

Hazara is located with Kashmir to the west, Peshawar to the east and Attock on its northwest borders. It was conquered and subsequently attached to the Sikh kingdom in 1820, and Ranjit Singh appointed Amar Singh Majithia, also known as Amar Singh Kalan, as its first *nazim* (governor). He remained *nazim* for two years, successfully handling the defiance of Tarin and routing Dhund, Tanol and Kharal tribes, although this ended at his death.[111] Hari Singh Nalwa was then appointed *nazim* of Hazara.[112] Nevertheless, the Hazara tribes remained uncontrollable until formal military posts were created and manned by regular soldiers. Hari Singh Nalwa successfully fortified the Sikh position by garrisoning the wilderness of Hazara.[113]

Dera Ghazi Khan was conquered in 1819. It was first given to Sadiq Muhammad Khan, the Nawab of Bahawalpur, for Rs.4 *lakh* a year, but later given to General Ventura, who held the charge for two years and left it with a good reputation. Then in 1832, Diwan Swan Mal took charge, and during his time agriculture and commerce were promoted more than ever before.[114]

Meanwhile, Ranjit Singh, with the help of his French officers, conquered Darband, Mankera and Dera Ismail Khan. Nawab Hafiz Ahmad Khan, who was an independent ruler of these areas, was paying tribute to the Afghan ruler for his protection.[115] These areas were especially important to Ranjit Singh, as the caravan route from Persia and Baluchistan passed through them to India. These areas were not as fertile, but Mankera was important in terms of income generation and political power.[116] The Nawab of Mankera accepted the offer of a *jagir* with safe residence in Dera Ismail Khan, and handed over the fort to the Sikh ruler.[117] Ranjit Singh never annexed the area of Bannu, which remained under the control of the Muslims, although these tribes paid an annual tribute.[118]

Kashmir

After the fall of Atta Muhammad Khan, Fateh Khan appointed his other brother Muhammad Azim Khan as the governor of Kashmir.[119] He was courageous and intelligent and kept a strong hold on Kashmir. This worried Ranjit Singh, who decided to take over Kashmir as soon as possible. In fact, the fort of Attock was under threat because of the grip of the Afghans on Kashmir. The Maharaja planned to attack Kashmir immediately after the battle of Khizru and set off in October 1813.[120] He ordered all *sardars* to come together in Sialkot, but a heavy snowfall forced him to return to Lahore. In 1814, he again decided to attack Kashmir. He divided the Sikh force into two parts, one supervised by himself and the other under the command of Diwan Ram Deyal, the grandson of Diwan Mohkam Chand. Diwan Ram Deyal reached Behram Gullah on 18 June 1814.[121] During this time, many problems arose between the Sikhs and the Afghans, which the Sikhs successfully overcame. On 24 June, the Sikh forces faced the Afghans and won the battle, but in the next fight the Afghans defeated the Sikh army. Ranjit Singh could not reach Ram Deyal because of excessive rain and, despite his best efforts to reach Kashmir, had to return to Lahore. Attacks by Azim Khan forced Ram Deyal and his army to stay outside Kashmir. Due to this failure, the areas around Kashmir remained out of Lahore's direct control.[122] However, Ranjit Singh's conquests of Rajodi and Bhambhar re-established his control over these areas.[123] Despite the setbacks, Ranjit Singh never lost his desire to capture Kashmir, and he got his chance in 1819.

After Azim Khan also left for Kabul with the major part of his army, the strength and hold of the Afghan forces were reduced, and Ranjit Singh took full advantage of the situation to attack Kashmir. The leading half of his army was under the command of Prince Kharak Singh, and Ranjit Singh led the second half. He deputed a number of soldiers for speedy delivery of messages across the whole rank-and-file of the army.[124] The Sikh army became stronger when the forces of Sultan Khan, ruler of Bhimbhar, joined the Maharaja. Obtaining help from Bhimbhar was a strategic and bold decision, which earned Ranjit Singh a great victory.[125] The Sikh forces won a battle at Rajori, and then set off for the next destination under the command of Prince Kharak Singh, accompanied by Misr Diwan Chand. After passing through rough, tough terrain, the army finally reached and captured Poonch. This put the Sikh forces directly in front of the Afghans on the field of Panj Pir.[126] The Afghans lost this battle and the Sikhs reached Aliabad, where they now faced the army of Jabbar Khan, the brother of Azim Khan. Both forces fought fearlessly, but the Sikh army emerged victorious, largely due to the military skills of Phula Singh, one of Ranjit Singh's able generals. The Afghan forces ran away and the Sikhs collected much loot. Jabbar Khan retreated first to Sri Nagar and from there through Bara Mullah to Peshawar. On 4 July 1819, the Sikh forces entered Sri Nagar, under strict orders, enforced by Misr Diwan Chand,[127] not to harm the citizens in any way. When it was announced that the people were to be given an amnesty, the population was overjoyed and happily accepted the Sikh rule.[128] Misr Diwan Chand was given the title of Zafar-e-Jang and was nominated governor of Kashmir. Fakir Azizuddin and Reza Ansari were sent to study the climate of the valley, along with Diwan Devi Das to organize the system of revenue.[129] The conquest of Kashmir naturally was an extraordinary addition to the kingdom of Maharaja Ranjit Singh, leading to increased revenue. In fact, he told C. M. Wade of the British political department that Kashmir was the most productive of all his provinces, with annual revenue of Rs.25 *lakh*.[130]

Sikh rule in Kashmir lasted for some twenty-seven years. During this period ten governors were appointed to administer the valley. Two were Muslims, three Sikhs and five Hindus: Misr Diwan Chand, Diwan Moti Ram, Sardar Hari Singh Nalwa, Diwan Chunni Lal, Diwan Kirpa Ram, Bhīma Singh Ardali, Prince Sher Singh, Colonel Mahan Singh, Sheikh Ghulam Muhaiy-ud-Din and Sheikh Imamuddin. However, because of their corruption, Ranjit Singh was not happy with the performance of any of his governors. He once commented that all the people he had sent to the beautiful valley of Kashmir proved to be *haramzadaz* (bastards), adding that he should have sent one of his sons or himself for the administration. This was the very reason that he kept on changing the governors on the reports from Kashmir.[131]

Conquest of Sikh States

In order to unite the Punjab into one kingdom, Ranjit Singh waged a series of wars against his rivals throughout his regime. Whosoever came across his path, he removed them all. Not only were the Hindu and Muslim rulers subdued, but the Sikh *sardars* were among the first to be taken to task.[132]

People complained about unjust treatment from the ruling class of Bhangi *misl*. Inflation, black marketing, skewed distribution of resources, lack of economic opportunities and greed were indicative of the rule of Bhangi *misl*. The Bhangi *sardars*, rulers of Lahore, were totally insensitive to the needs of the citizens and the city itself. Under these circumstances, local Muslims, *chaudhari* and *khatri* traders welcomed Ranjit Singh and Sada Kaur. On 7 July 1799, Ranjit Singh arrived with 5,000 troops near the Shalimar Gardens. The Bhangi *sardars* left the town hurriedly and Ranjit Singh took over Lahore and laid the foundation of a great Sikh kingdom.[133]

Gulab Singh died in 1800 and was succeeded by his son, Gurdit Singh, who was then aged 10. He managed the affairs of the *misl* through his mother, Mai Sukkhan. After taking over Lahore, Ranjit Singh was now looking at Amritsar where the Bhangis still held sway. The *Zamzama* cannon was both a constraint and an attraction for Ranjit Singh. In 1802, he fell on Amritsar and Gurdit Singh and his mother left the city without any resistance, leaving it open to Ranjit Singh. He steadily subdued all the Bhangi *sardars* including the last, Sahib Singh of Gujrat.[134] By 1810, all the Bhangi areas including Lahore, Amritsar, Sialkot, Chiniot and Gujrat were integrated under Ranjit Singh.[135] He had granted a few villages to Sahib Singh to live a respectable life, but on his death he seized them back.[136]

Tara Singh Ghaiba, the Sardar of Dallevala *misl*, was intelligent and aware of the strength and designs of Ranjit Singh. He got closer to the Maharaja and became a trusted subordinate, accompanying him in his operations against Malva. After Tara Singh's death in 1807 at the age of 90, Ranjit Singh seized all the areas under the control of the Dallevala *misl*.[137] Taking over the Dallevala territory shows that expansion in his kingdom was more important to him than was Sikhism. Consolidation of the Punjab and the greatness of his kingdom were paramount. His behaviour and treatment was the same for all the rulers, whether Muslim, Hindu or Sikh.

The leader of the Nakai *misl*, Ran Singh, died in 1781 and his eldest son, Bhagvan Singh, succeeded him. Raj Kaur, the daughter of Ran Singh, was the wife of Ranjit Singh. After the death of Bhagvan Singh, his younger brother, Gian Singh, became leader of the *misl*. When Gian Singh died in 1807, he left a son, Kahn Singh. Subsequently Ranjit Singh took over all the family's possessions in the Nakai *misl* and granted Kahn Singh a *jagir* with an annual income worth Rs.15,000.[138]

Ranjit Singh also captured all the areas under the control of the Ramgarhia *misl*. He defeated Divan Singh and Jodh Singh and took over the fort of Ramgarh. Both Diwan Singh and Jodh Singh were given grants adequate to live a respectable life.[139]

Sada Kaur, a member of the Kanaya *misl* and mother-in-law of Ranjit Singh, led armies side by side with him. She was ambitious for the future of her son-in-law. Although the marriage between her daughter Mahtab and Ranjit Singh was not a happy one, she still did all that she could in winning Lahore and other areas. Initially, Ranjit Singh and Sada Kaur understood each other very well, although the union did not last long.[140] Ranjit Singh's second marriage and his affection for the second wife offended Mahtab Kaur, who returned to her mother's home, only occasionally visiting Ranjit Singh.[141] Mahtab Kaur was infuriated further when Ranjit Singh did not designate her son as crown prince, nor did she attend the marriage ceremony of Prince Kharak Singh.[142] On the death of Mahtab Kaur, Ranjit Singh was unwilling to attend the last rituals, participating only through the intervention of his influential courtiers.[143]

The differences increased as Sada Kaur started conniving with the British through Sir Charles Metcalfe and Sir David Ochterloney. Ranjit Singh did not like this; he hounded the Kanaya family, and seized their territory and all possessions. Batala was granted to Prince Sher Singh as a *jagir*. The remaining land belonging to Sada Kaur was put under the authority of Desa Singh Majithia.[144]

Haqiqat Singh was another important leader of the Kanaya *misl*. He was the son of Baghel Singh, a Siddhu Jat from the town of Julka. He remained associated with Jai Singh and fought for him. Haqiqat Singh did not like Ranjit Singh. He had consolidated his lands including Kalanaur (Kahngarh), Adalatgarh and Pathan Kot, and in 1760 he established another town, Sangatpura. He had also built a fort at Fatehgarh. Haqiqat Singh died in 1782 and his only son Jaimal Singh, then a minor, succeeded him. Haqiqat Singh's granddaughter Chand Kaur was the wife of Prince Kharak Singh, the eldest son of Ranjit Singh. Jaimal Singh passed away in 1812 leaving no child. Ranjit Singh readily grabbed his wealth, stored in the fort of Fatehgarh. However, he allowed Jaimal Singh's widow to receive the income of the region as a subsistence allowance. All the remaining lands of the Kanhaiya *misl* were gifted to Prince Kharak Singh.[145]

Conquests of Hindu States

Given that Ranjit Singh wished to become ruler of the whole Punjab, he waged wars irrespective of religious distinction and subdued not only all the Muslims and Sikhs but also the Hindus. Sansar Chand was the ruler of Kangra. He gradually took over most of the neighbouring territories, for some twenty years ruling over most of today's Himachal Pradesh. However, in pursuit of his expansionist policy, he directly ran into the Gurkhas of Nepal. The Gurkhas and chieftains of the hill states together fell on Kangra in 1806. Sansar Chand lost and was confined to the outskirts of Kangra. However, the Gurkhas failed to take the fort of Kangra, which Ranjit Singh captured in 1811.[146] William Moorcroft, who visited Kangra in 1823, called on Raja Sansar Chand and his son Anirudh, who were then living as dependants of Maharaja Ranjit Singh. He reports that indeed, their hardship was largely the result of their own wrongdoing.[147] In 1828 when Anirudh visited the court of Lahore, Ranjit Singh asked for his sister's hand for Prince Hira Singh. Anirudh agreed reluctantly, but moved with all his family to the other side of the Sutlej under the shelter of the British.[148] He died the same year and Ranjit Singh annexed all his territories; a *jagir* was given to the younger brother of Anirudh. Ranjit Singh married two of the daughters of the Sansar Chand and one of them committed *suttee* on his death.[149]

Dessa Singh Majithia took over Haripur from Raja Bhop Singh in 1813. Ranjit Singh pushed the Rajas of Noorpur and Jaswan out of Sialkot in 1815 for not complying with his orders. The Raja of Datapur himself offered his territory to Ranjit Singh in 1818, being given a *jagir* in Lahore in return. Siba also submitted to Ranjit Singh and later became a close aide to the Maharaja. Ranjit Singh acquired Kotlher in 1825; the raja was granted a *jagir* worth Rs.10,000 annually. Several other chiefs surrendered themselves and received *jagirs* in return: Chamba, Noorpur, Kotla, Shahpur, Jasrota, Basoli, Mankot, Jaswan, Mandi, Suket and Kulu.[150]

Story of the Famous Koh-e-Noor Diamond

One charge against Ranjit Singh is that he took the Koh-e-Noor diamond from a Muslim ruler of Kabul and treated him inhumanely; therefore, it would be helpful to have an unbiased review of the whole story.

The Koh-e-Noor diamond was found in Golkanda (India) and presented to the Mughal Emperor Shah Jahan by a local merchant.[151] It was embedded in the famous Peacock Throne of Shah Jahan.[152] When Nadir Shah Durrani invaded Delhi, he did not find the diamond until a woman disclosed that the Emperor Ahmed Shah Rangila had it in his turban.[153] After the murder of Nadir Shah, the diamond went to Ahmad Shah Abdali, then to his son Tamur and to Tamur's son

Shah Zaman.[154] One of Shah Zaman's brothers, Mahmood, blinded and deposed him, but was unable to get the diamond. Subsequently it fell into the hands of another brother of Shah Zaman, Shah Shuja, the ruler of Afghanistan, who was exiled by his brother Mahmood. Shah Shuja's family was at that time living under the protection of Ranjit Singh.[155]

The story briefly goes that Afghan envoys approached Ranjit Singh to join the Kabul government in invading Kashmir. Shah Shuja himself was in the custody of the ruler of Kashmir. The Afghan agents offered Ranjit Singh an equal division of the loot, and in addition Rs.9 *lakh* a year.[156] The first wife of Shah Shuja and her sons heard that Ranjit Singh was planning to attack Kashmir, and they knew that if the Afghans captured it they would kill the former ruler of Afghanistan, Shah Shuja. The refugee family therefore made the counter-offer of handing over the precious diamond to Ranjit Singh for the safe return of Shah Shuja.[157]

Sohan Lal Suri agrees that the wife of Shah Shuja was so terrified by the invasion of the Barakzais that she offered Ranjit Singh the invaluable diamond in return for her husband's life.[158] Diwan Mohkam Chand, who was leading the Sikh forces, reached the fort of Sher Garh before the Afghans. While the Afghans were busy looting the treasury, the Sikh soldiers found Shah Shuja and brought him to Diwan Mohkam Chand. When Fateh Khan of Kabul heard the news of the capture of Shah Shuja, he demanded his custody, which was refused by Diwan Mohkam Chand. Later the Afghans tried to get him back by force but failed. Fateh Khan accused Mohkam Chand of breaking his promise and refused to share the loot with the Sikh forces.[159] Shah Shuja was safely delivered to his wife, Wafa Begum, and now it was her turn to fulfill her promise.

The very next day the Maharaja sent a note to Shah Shuja and his family asking for delivery of the Koh-e-Noor. Neither Shah Shuja nor his wife bothered to answer the note. Although the diamond was so valuable, yet Ranjit Singh had paid too much for the release of Shah Shuja, sacrificing over a thousand lives, the treasury and his share in the loot along with the Rs.9 *lakh* per year as tribute, which Fateh Khan refused to pay.[160] Even the living expenses of the royal family of Shah Shuja were high; for example, it is written in diaries in the Fakir Khana Library that Wafa Begum used to give alms every day of not less than Rs.5,000.[161]

On the following day, Bhaia Ram Singh went to Shah Shuja's residence, Mubarak Haveli, to receive the Koh-e-Noor diamond. He was told that the diamond was in the custody of a jeweller as a mortgage in Afghanistan. Ranjit Singh did not believe this story and again demanded delivery of the diamond,[162] offering Rs.3 *lakh* along with a *jagir*. The exiled ruler accepted this offer but requested time. Ranjit Singh again sent his messenger but all in vain, breaking the limits of patience of the Maharaja, who now posted guards around Shah Shuja's residence.[163]

According to Colonel D. Ochterloney, a British agent at Ludhiana, the soldiers of the Maharaja daily insulted Shah Shuja.[164] After fifteen days, Fakir Azizuddin, Jamadar Khushal Singh and Bhai Gurbukhsh Singh were sent to ask Shah Shuja to hand over the diamond. He replied yes, but said that the Maharaja himself should come to receive so precious an object. Ranjit Singh with some of his ministers came to Mubarak Haveli to receive it. The two sat silently in front of each other for some time, then Shah Shuja ordered his servant to bring him the diamond, and he untied the bundle and presented the diamond to the Maharaja.[165] Shah Shuja himself admitted that Ranjit Singh offered him a *jagir* worth Rs.50,000 and the recovery of his territory.[166]

On many occasions it has been shown that Ranjit Singh was very fond of jewellery and horses, trying his best to acquire them wherever he found them, from Muslims, Hindus or Sikhs. The manner in which Muslim rulers looted their own Muslim subjects is well documented; one of many examples is the attack of Nadir Shah Durrani on Delhi and the way he plundered the city and murdered Muslims. It was none other than Nadir Shah Durrani who took the Koh-e-Noor diamond from the Mughal king, Ahmad Shah Rangila. To suggest that Ranjit Singh was treating Shah Shuja in this manner just because he was a Muslim therefore seems quite arbitrary.

Conclusion

Maharaja Ranjit Singh with his military genius and political insight achieved great success and splendour. During his lifetime he fought many battles and subjugated many rulers, but he treated them all with openness and tolerance. Like any great ruler, he showed much benevolence and generosity to his conquered enemies. He never killed any defeated rulers or their families, but took good care of them and granted them sufficient lands and funds for a decent living.

Even those historians, especially British and Muslim, who openly criticized Ranjit Singh acknowledged that he granted *jagirs* to many fallen Muslim and Hindu rulers, and treated them benevolently. He respected the rituals and rites of his Muslim subjects and did not prohibit their customs and traditions. He often sent gifts to the *ulemas* and nobles on holy occasions such as Eid. In this regard, Sir Henry Lawrence observes that though some conquered families were not especially prosperous in Delhi and Kabul, in the Punjab their condition was quite respectable.[167] There was hardly any family of the defeated rulers left unaided by Ranjit Singh. He looked after the Sikh *sardars* and defeated rulers from other religions equally and with great benevolence. Lepel Griffin also reports that Ranjit Singh might have had many vices, but he was not remorseless or ruthless. After a triumph or the capture of a stronghold, he treated the vanquished with tolerance and consideration, and there were at his court numerous defeated chiefs to whom he had given suitable compensation.[168]

In pursuing his designs to build a great empire for himself, Ranjit Singh was ready to take on all who might threaten his ambitions, irrespective of religion or race. However, despite his love for power and money, he conducted himself very well throughout his reign. After the annexation of any territory, he would take over the administrative affairs himself. According to the records left by the former rulers, he would carefully appoint administrators to streamline revenue flow. Typically the ousted ruler was granted a *jagir* to manage his life, a larger one if he agreed to serve the interests of the Maharaja.

Although Ranjit Singh gave these Afghans *jagirs*, they continued to be a problem to him.[169] The Chattha *sardars* were old rivals, but when Ranjit Singh defeated them and confiscated their territory he granted them *jagirs*, including Jan Bakhsh, who had been a bitter enemy of the Maharaja's father. Subsequently, they served in the Sikh army,[170] and joined Ranjit Singh during the conquests of Kasur, Multan, Mankera and Kashmir.[171] The Raja Umar Khan of Chunian fought against the Sikhs. He died during the diplomatic dialogue with the Maharaja and his territory was annexed, but half of it was returned to his son. Unfortunately he, too, died six months later, and his brother and his cousin's brother were granted annual pensions of Rs.4,000 and 3,000 respectively.[172] Similarly Ahmad Yar Khan of Jhang received a huge *jagir*.[173]

The Tiwanas (a Punjabi caste) had a special place in the court of Maharaja, although Fateh Kahn Tiwana caused a great deal of trouble to the Lahore *Darbar*. When Fateh Khan Tiwana and Khuda Bukhsh Tiwana lost to Ranjit Singh, he took Fateh Khan, his siblings and his sixty horsemen with him. He also granted them *jagirs* in their own areas worth Rs.6,000 and employed the horsemen at a annual wage of Rs.300.[174] Khuda Bukhsh was appointed commander of a troop of horsemen. His father was designated a *chabook swar* (a title used for an officer in the *Khalsa* army) in attendance on Ranjit Singh. His good work earned praise and blessings from Ranjit Singh. Fateh Khan turned into the most trusted aide of the prime minister, Dhian Singh, and his family earned a large *jagir* worth Rs.12,000–15,000 when he passed away in 1832.[175]

There are numerous other examples of Ranjit Singh's great benevolence to the fallen Muslim rulers. The ruler of Sahiwal was granted a *jagir* worth Rs.14,400 in Jhang. However, he later went to Mankera and subsequently joined the ruler of Multan, Muzaffar Khan. After the fall of Multan, he went to Bahawalpur and died there in 1820. His elder son, Langer Khan, was then just 14 years old. Ranjit Singh invited him to Lahore and gave him employment in Multan along with a *jagir* worth Rs.1,200. He worked under Diwan Swan Mal for about ten years, and before the death of the Maharaja was given another *jagir* worth Rs.3,000 in Sahiwal.[176]

A number of other *sardars* were given *jagirs* by Ranjit Singh, including Sarfraz Khan of Pind Dadan, Sultan Khan of Jhelum, Mittha Tiwana of Tiwanas, Junjuas, Ghulam Khan, Ghulam Muhammad Khan, Salabat Khan, the Maliks of Attock and many others. The area of Kala Bagh came under the Maharaja's control in 1822. Malik Allah Yar, the chief of this area, was also appointed as a land revenue officer and acquired many other benefits from the Lahore *Darbar*. Sarfraz Khan of Kamalia was granted a handsome *jagir* of 300 villages, despite the fact that his family continued fighting the Lahore *Darbar*.[177] The Gardazis, Badozais, Makhdooms and Gilanis of Multan all received good grants from Ranjit Singh and the Lahore *Darbar*, as did the Laghari, Khosa and many other noble families of Dera Ghazi Khan.

The Maharaja would not tolerate any mishandling of the local people by his chiefs. This is why we find numerous examples of dismissal of the governors in the held territories. It was not uncommon for Ranjit Singh to invite the Muslim *qaries* (reciters of the Holy Quran) and listen to the Holy Quran. They were always rewarded generously.[178] The Lahore *Darbar* had an interesting blend of religious and social representation. Around one-fifth of the individuals were the fallen rulers and their dependants, mainly Sikh *misldars*, Rajputs, Afghans and Pathans. Sardar Fateh Singh, Mit Singh Padania, Sardar Attar Singh Dhari, Hukam Singh Attari and Hukma Singh Chimni represented the Sikh *misldars*. Others included the Pathan leaders of Kasur, Multan and Jhang. The families of the Nawab Muzaffar Khan, Sardar Sultan Muhammad Khan, the Barakzai and Saddozai chiefs were treated with great honour and respect. They not only received *jagirs* but also administrative assignments at the court of the Maharaja. Ranjit Singh had a very shrewd and clever mind. He knew that leaving them alone would encourage them to rise against him and his *darbar*. By offering them generous treatment, he was not only being benevolent but also preventing future troubles and conspiracies through appeasing the fallen enemies. This strategy also pacified the conquered community and people and helped him maintain peace and prosperity in his kingdom.[179]

Major Sir Henry Lawrence narrates the achievements of the Maharaja in Ranjit Singh's own words:

My kingdom is a great kingdom. It was small; it is now large. It was scattered, broken and divided. It is now consolidated. It must increase in prosperity and descend undivided to my posterity. The maxim of Taimur has guided me. What he professed and ordered; I have done. By counsel and providence combined with valour, I have conquered and by generosity, discipline and policy I have regulated and consolidated my government. I have rewarded the bold and encouraged merit wherever it was to be found. On the field of battle I exalted the valiant, with my troops; I have shared all dangers and all fatigues. Both on the field and in the cabinet I shut partiality from my soul and closed my eyes to personal comfort. With the robe of Empire I put on the mantle of care. I fed fakirs and holy men and gained their prayers. The guilty as the innocent, I spared. And those whose hands were raised against me have met my clemency. Sri Purakh Ji (God) has therefore been merciful to his servant and increased his power so that his territory now extended to the borders of China and the limits of the Afghans with all Multan and the rich possessions beyond the Sutlej.[180]

These words need no further explanation, portraying a true picture of Ranjit Singh and his policies. Lawrence provides a similar account of Ranjit Singh's generosity and kindness to non-Sikh communities and other religions.[181]

Elaborating the conduct and personality of Ranjit Singh, Alexander Burnes observes:

In a territory compactly situated, he had applied himself to those improvements, which spring only from great minds, and here we find despotism without rigors, a despot without cruelty and a system of Government far beyond the native institutions of the East though far from the civilization of Europe.[182]

Even Sir Lepel Griffin, a diehard critic of Ranjit Singh, writes:

With all the rapacity Ranjit Singh was not cruel or blood thirsty. After the victory or the capture of a fortress he treated the vanquished with leniency and kindness however stout their resistance might have been and there were at his court many chiefs despoiled of their estates but to whom he had given suitable employ.[183]

Ranjit Singh did not visit his conquered territories very often. However, he never allowed his governors and administrators to act unfairly with the local people. He held firm control over his representatives through various means, and had an exceptionally efficient intelligence system to keep a strict watch on his governors. A strong monitoring and reporting system existed in the Lahore *Darbar*. His governors and administrators would send regular and detailed reports containing all the required information about the territory.

Griffin further states that Ranjit Singh was a born soldier and leader, labelling him 'the beau ideal of a soldier, strong, spare, active, courageous and enduring'.[184] He subdued some twenty large states and several small territories.[185] It would not have been wise to keep their hostility alive and swelling, and he won the hearts of most of the defeated rulers mainly with his fair and kind treatment. Subsequently they were the main source of his strength during battles against the enemies of the Lahore *Darbar*. Most of his victories were the result of his policies of kindness and avoidance of unwarranted violence or cruelty.

Chapter 3

STATE POLICIES TOWARDS MUSLIMS: REALITY OR FAÇADE

Ranjit Singh frequently said: 'God had given me one eye to be able to see all the religions with one eye.'[1] Looking at the broader picture of his regime as ruler of the Punjab in the light of primary sources, it is evident that he not only frequently repeated this thought, but also tried to act upon it. Therefore, it is important to explore how far his thoughts and actions as a ruler impacted the condition of the Muslims under the Sikh regime. A number of historians have described his religious policies, but they paint him either as a great secular ruler or an extremist Sikh who was bent upon eliminating Islam in the Punjab.[2] However, I take the position that Ranjit Singh himself was a tolerant and secular ruler. The negative perceptions about him held by some historians, including Muslims, are mainly based on anecdotal and insufficient evidence. Moreover, some of his subordinates did mistreat the Muslim population. Therefore, in order to make a fair assessment of Ranjit Singh's various state policies including those on religion, administration, economics and education, this chapter revisits his reign in the light of primary and secondary sources, which hitherto have not been fully utilized by historians.

As already proposed, religious freedom, equal access to education and economic opportunities, dispensation of fair justice, and security of life and property are the mainstay of any benevolent state; a minority, however, would always like to keep its religious identity intact and still have access to all the facilities that other citizens enjoy. How true was this statement under the Sikh rule of Ranjit Singh? A close examination of his religious, sociopolitical, education and economic policies will lead us to a better understanding of Muslims' condition under his rule. We will see if his religious policies were sufficiently liberal to allow Muslims to practise their religion freely. We will also delve into his sociopolitical and education policies to ascertain if they were sufficiently open and tolerant to let Muslims exploit their potential for personal and professional growth. Similarly, an in-depth examination of his economic policies will let us see whether Muslims had access to equal opportunities for economic empowerment.

Socio-religious Demography of the Punjab

At the end of the Sikh rule, Punjab was home to about 10.5 million people[3] and the population of Lahore according to the census was 94,143.[4] Besides Sikhs, there were Kamboh, Arain, Pathan and Muslim Rajput citizens who owned ninety of the 150 villages in the district of Lahore.[5] The next big cities under Ranjit Singh were Peshawar with a population of 53,294, and Ludhiana with 47,191, mostly Kashmiris. Multan's population according to the census of 1855 was 24,973. These figures only include the city populations and not those of the suburbs.[6] The census of the northwestern province classified the population into two main groups, namely Hindus and Muslims, agricultural and non-agricultural. The subdivisions were given in the settlement census, and a summary of the castes was taken from this census. Census reports show that the Muslims were in a majority in western Punjab. Moreover, from Chenab to the trans-Indus frontier, in the northwestern and southern divisions – that is, in Jhelum, Multan, Layyah and Peshawar – the population was almost entirely Muslim.[7]

A British presiding officer posted to Lahore reports that in 1848 the Muslims were greater in number than the Hindus, by a ratio of three to two.[8] The trend continued from Lahore to the northwest and southwest, as far as the Indus, which was completely Muslim.[9]

Moreover, Ranjit Singh's court was diverse in its constitution, comprising people of different religion, nationality, race, region and colour.[10] The most respected and best-known races included the Jats,[11] Khatries,[12] Rajputs, Brahmans, Pathans and Syeds. The Jats made up 30 per cent and were mostly Sikhs. The Brahmans were 7 per cent and included sub-castes Gaur, Kaul, Joshi and Vaid. The Rajputs made up 11 per cent and were mainly located in Jammu, Punch and Rajauri as Katoch, Pathania and Dogra. The main Muslim groups included Kharal, Awan, Tiwana, Chattha and Sial. The Syeds and the Pathans represented 2 per cent and 4 per cent respectively.[13] Ranjit Singh's *darbar* also included nobles from foreign countries: French, English, German, Irish, Italian, American, Spanish, Greek and Austrian.[14]

Religious Policy

The history of Sikh–Muslim relations is full of complexity and ambiguities. Many unresolved mysteries engulf the realities of the relationship. Numerous allegations have been levelled against Ranjit Singh for maltreating the Muslims – for example: Muslims were deprived of their land, property and belongings;[15] they were treated brutally in Kashmir, Multan and in the northern areas;[16] the burden of taxation was heaviest on Muslims; before and during Ranjit Singh's rule, the Muslims always faced the brutality of the Sikhs;[17] Muslims were not allowed to perform *namaz* (prayer); *aazan*[18] was banned in most areas, and as the cow was as sacred to Sikhs as to Hindus, slaughtering cows was also forbidden to Muslims.[19] The treatment of holy places such as mosques and tombs is discussed below.

Closeness and unity between Sikhs and Muslims had never been in the interests of the Hindus or the British, who had always aspired to rule the Punjab, and a systematic campaign was applied to break the bonds between the two communities. As a result, historians and travellers such as S. M. Latif, Kanhaiya Lal, Lepel Griffin, M'Gregor, Hennery Laurence and many others levelled various allegations against Ranjit Singh for harming the Muslims;[20] this has obscured the realities of the Sikh–Muslim relationship during the Sikh period and fuelled the controversies and ambiguities between the two communities. This strengthens the need to re-examine these allegations against Ranjit Singh in the light of the available primary and secondary sources.

Buildings – Shrines and Mosques

The underlying hypothesis of this study is that the condition of the Muslims during the rule of Ranjit Singh was good and that the Muslims had full religious freedom, as did other religious communities. In the following pages an effort is made to highlight those measures of Ranjit Singh that historians have not previously discussed in their academic studies.

Ranjit Singh's tenure was benevolent to the Muslims and their places of worship and respect. According to Jacquemont,[21] Muslims had full liberty and there were many mosques throughout the Punjab.[22] Ranjit Singh, indeed, had great respect for all sacred places and people, irrespective of religion, caste or creed. He visited the shrines of the Muslims and the temples of the Hindus. He held Muslim and Hindu holy places as sacred as the Golden Temple. He granted generous gifts, estates and money to these shrines and holy places without considering religious affiliations. Lavish gifts were given for the repair and development of the Muslim holy places of worship. Despite his love of money, Ranjit Singh spent Rs.12 *lakh* annually on charity.[23]

Ranjit Singh's respect for other religions and their symbols, articles, art and architecture, particularly Muslim, can be judged from the following incident. When a Muslim calligrapher, who was in urgent need of money and wanted to sell his art piece, presented a copy of the Holy Quran to Ranjit Singh, the Maharaja treated the artist well and purchased his masterpiece, even though no Muslim ruler or rich individual had been willing to pay him the price he was asking. Ranjit Singh's close advisor Fakir Azizuddin praised the exquisiteness of the work, but even he could not purchase it at the high cost asked. Ranjit Singh took the *Nuskha-e-Quran* and gently touched it to his forehead with reverence and respect.[24] He added the Holy Quran to his private collection. Later, Fakir Azizuddin asked Ranjit Singh why he had bought a copy of the Holy Quran, and he uttered his famous phrase again, that God had given him a single eye with which to see all religions.[25]

Ill-treatment of mosques and tombs and other Muslim holy places is a further allegation levelled against Ranjit Singh. They were damaged or knocked down in many cities and performance of religious obligations was forbidden; mosques were even used as ammunition depots, *gurduwaras, dharamshala* (orphanage, poorhouse) and *sarayi*, and the famous Badshahi Mosque in Lahore was used for recreational and state functions.[26] Precious stones worth *lakhs* of rupees were stolen, gunpowder was stored in rooms around the Mosque, and three minarets were destroyed. Dance and musical performances were regularly held in Wazir Khan Mosque.[27]

An attempt has been made to verify these allegations through official documents available in the archives of Fakir Khana Lahore, the British Library, Archives of the Lahore Secretariate and other places, and they reveal a different picture of Ranjit Singh's religious policy, as illustrated by the following details. Ranjit Singh had a long list of Muslim sanctuaries, mosques, *fakirs*, scholars and others that he supported.[28] He granted land and paid stipends to many sanctuaries.[29] Muslim religious personalities and their mausoleums were given due support and respect, especially the custodians of Hazrat Data Ganj Bakhsh, *Rauza* (shrine) of Abu-al-Muali, Baba Farid Saidan Shah, Hazrat Sakhi Sarwar's *dargah* and Madhu Lal Hussain. In *Tahqiqat-e-Chishti* detailed information is given about the gifts and grants given to these shrines. The *mujawars* (custodians) of the shrine of Data Ganj Bukhsh were granted nearby wells, land and Rs.1,000 annually; however, the British reduced this to Rs.100.[30]

The wife of Kharak Singh built a well and lawn at the same tomb for the ease of visitors, while Ranjit Singh himself continued to support maintenance and repair work of the shrine.[31] In 1838, Ranjit Singh in person visited the mausoleum of Hazrat Ganj Bakhsh Hajveri through the Taxsali gate and offered Rs.125 as *nazar*.[32] Prince Nau Nihal and Rani Sada Kour donated additional land for the extension of the courtyard of the shrine.[33]

Ranjit Singh also visited the shrine of Hazrat Syed Yaqoob Zanjani in Lahore, which the British government later left unattended.[34] He increased grants of revenue and land attached to the famous shrine of Baba Farid in Pakpattan under the custody of *sajjada nashins* (successors of the shrine)[35] and directed the *jagirdar* of Pakpattan to ensure their continuity.[36] Moreover, on the marriage of Prince Nau Nihal, he granted more tax-free *jagirs* to both this holy shrine and Data Ganj Bukhsh.[37]

A parcel of land of 3.5 acres was donated as *waqf* (donation) to the shrine of Abu Ishaq situated just outside the *Mochi Darwaza*.[38] The holy shrine of Bibi Pakdamen also received a vast tract of land, which the British unfortunately reduced drastically.[39] The *khanqah* (monastery) of Hazrat Moj Darya received a monthly stipend of Rs.40 from the Maharaja.[40] He also took good care of the great graveyard of Miani Sahib in Lahore,[41] while the shrines of Shah Khairuddin Abu-al-Muali, Mosa Khokhar, Sheikh Tahir Bandgi, Sheikh Naimat ullah Sirhindi, Mian Mir, Pir Makki, Abdullah Shah Qadri and many other famous saints and Sufis regularly received grants and gifts from him.[42]

During *basant* (a festival of the Punjab region marking the start of spring), at the *chiraghan* (lights) carnivals at the shrine of Hazrat Madhu Lal Hussain, the army and the nobles were ordered to wear *basanti* (orange) dress. In fact, the whole city would turn orange and the dyers earned good money. Raja Dina Nath once gave Rs.5 to a dyer for his dress, increased to Rs.50 when the dyer complained about the amount. In the afternoon, the Maharaja would come out with his companions, all dressed in orange. Moreover, a month's salary was given to the army as a bonus,[43] and he donated Rs.1,100 and two expensive shawls to the shrine of Madhu Lal Husain.[44] Nauroz is the most important of all the Iranian celebrations, proclaiming spring and the start of the New Year,[45] and it is also recognized by Muslim high society and celebrated by the general population,[46] who whitewash their houses and wear new garments. It is generally believed that if this day is spent cheerfully, the entire year will pass happily.[47]

Ranjit Singh had a great regard for the Sufi saint Syed Ali Shah, who refused to accept a gift; therefore, the Maharaja deputed a Sikh orderly to look after the needs of the Sufi. After the death of Syed Ali Shah, Ranjit Singh continued his blessings on the custodian of his *khanqah*.[48] He granted 40 acres of land to support the shrine of Ismail Alias Wadda near the Shalimar Gardens at Lahore[49] and donated Rs.15,000 for the repair of mosques in Lahore.[50]

During his visit to Lahore, Moorcroft highly praised the grandness of the Mosque of Wazir Khan,[51] whose structure and building seemed quite new and original.[52] The Maharaja also saved the shrine of Shah Bilawal Qadri from the flooded River Ravi,[53] constructing a dam on the river; however, when his efforts proved in vain, the body of the saint was moved to a new shrine.[54]

When the Maharaja visited the shrine of Khawaja Bihari, the shining stones of the grave attracted his attention and he ordered them to be taken away. People warned him of bad consequences if he removed the stone but he ignored them. However, on his way back he fell off his favourite horse, Laili, and was seriously injured. On regaining consciousness, he went back to the tomb and asked for forgiveness, paying Rs.500 as a tribute. The annual income of a large *jagir* was also granted to the shrine. He often visited the holy shrine and paid generous sums to the *mujawars* of the Sufi saint.

Ranjit Singh was not alone in his generosity. Raja Dhian Singh, for example, built a well on the holy shrine of Shah Jamaluddin Qadri in Lahore.[55]

A controversy exists about the Sonehri Mosque situated in Lahore. It was built around a *bowli* (well) constructed during the time of Guru Arjun. After the Guru's death it was taken over by the state. In 1753, Nawab Bhikari Khan built a mosque near the *bowli* and some shops around it. The whole area was attached to the mosque. When Ranjit Singh captured Lahore, the Sonehri Mosque was under the control of the *Akali* Sikhs. In 1820, some of his Muslim officers approached him for the return of the mosque. General Allard and the Fakir brothers supported them. On hearing the real story, Ranjit Singh returned the mosque to the Muslims but the *bowli* remained in the possession of the Sikhs.[56] General Allard paid from his own purse for the rebuilding of the three tombs of the mosque.[57] William Barr, who visited India in 1839, describes the beauty of a mosque near the palace.[58]

Other members of Ranjit Singh's family also had respect for the Muslim holy places. One of the arches of the Sonehri Mosque crossed the *havali* of Prince Kharak Singh. He did not demolish the arch and instead carved his wall accordingly. Moreover, he constructed a balcony over his courtyard, which opened on to the mosque, from which he used to distribute money and other gifts to the Muslims. He paid Rs.10 every month to the *imam* for his services.⁵⁹

The non-intrusive style of government was a significant feature of Ranjit Singh's rule. He never forced other communities to adopt Sikhism. He married many Muslim women but never asked them to leave their religion; indeed, Moran, a Muslim, was his favourite wife, and he built an exquisite mosque for her in Paper Mandi, Lahore,⁶⁰ appointing Moulana Gulam Rasool and Moulana Ghulamullah as *imams*.⁶¹ Another wife was a Kashmiri Muslim, Badami Begum from Amritsar, and the famous Badami Bagh in Lahore was named after her.⁶²

The Maharaja also had great respect for Muslim relics, particularly those related to the Holy Prophet (PBUH) and his descendants. After the victory of Multan he was shown relics, which included shoes of the Holy Prophet (PBUH), a *nuskha* (copy of the Holy Quran), some religious compositions that Hazrat Ali, the fourth Caliph of the Muslims, used to read, and some hair, teeth and a *jubbah* (cloak) of the Holy Prophet (PBUH). These were all kept in the royal *toshakhana* (chamber in which objects of value or rare articles are kept) and were duly looked after and guarded. Mir Sher Muhammed Khan of Tehara offered Rs.125,000 for these Islamic artefacts but was refused. Instead, Ranjit Singh preferred to keep the relics with him; before his death he handed them over to the Fakir brothers as a gift,⁶³ and they are still preserved in the personal museum of the Fakir family. Mufti Ghulam Sarwer reports that Ranjit Singh showed the same respect for the Islamic artefacts as he did for Sikh relics and holy objects.⁶⁴

In Multan he also restored religious monuments and buildings; the city's nobles were mostly descendants of renowned Sufi saints such as Bahauddin Zakariya, Shah Rukn-e-Alam and Shah Shamas Tabriz.⁶⁵ In 1839 Fakir Azizuddin presented to the Maharaja a *fakir* from the *khanqah* of Multan, who requested the return of his *jagir* in Multan, and the Maharaja generously granted this together with Rs.500.⁶⁶

The shrines of Bahauddin Zakariya and Shah Rukn-e-Alam remained undamaged and intact throughout the reign of Ranjit Singh. However, later invaders and rulers of the Punjab mistreated them; during the British rule, the Punjab government requested the central government to sanction Rs.10,000 for their repair, but in vain. It was left to the rich and resourceful Mukhdoom Shah Mahmood to rehabilitate them.⁶⁷

It is worth mentioning that Hassan Shah, a *mujawar* of the *khanqah* of Baha-ul-Haq in Multan, received confirmation of his *jagir* from the Maharaja, agreed by the Nazim of Multan.⁶⁸ The situation was not very different in Kashmir, where hundreds of Muslim shrines received grants from Lahore.⁶⁹ Muhammed Shah Naqshbandi alone was granted five villages.⁷⁰

In Peshawar, every village had a mosque with an *imam*, supported by a small grant.⁷¹ At the time of the invasion of Peshawar, Ranjit Singh ordered Hari Singh Nalwa to protect the great ancient religious library of Hazrat Umar Sahib.⁷² He continued all the grants to which the *ulemas*, *syeds*, *qazis* and *fakirs* of Peshawar had previously been entitled. The *syeds* and *ulemas* of Bannu were also exempted from all types of taxation under Sikh rule.⁷³ The shrine of Sakhi Sarwar in Dera

Ghazi Khan was granted 40,000 acres of land in *dharmarth*.[74] The sheikhs of the *khanqah* of Pir Mittha of Wazirabad enjoyed some fifteen different dispensations including tax-exempted lands, daily allowances in cash, grants, grain from Gujrat, rice from Kashmir and salt from Pind Dadan Kahn. The Muslim grantees also enjoyed the support of the Sikh *jagirdars*.[75]

Jalandhar fostered a number of Muslim holy shrines with significant grants and contributions. Prinsep reports a number of *fakirs* in 1830 living well in their *takiahas* (platforms or places of shelter); most had also been granted some land.[76] The holy shrines of Imam Nasiruddin and Syed Ilmud Din were well-known places for the Muslims. In Sarayi Noor Mahel, the *dargah* (mausoleum) of Shah Malok of Haqqani was very famous.[77] A large portion of the Muslim population owned land in Jalandhar, Nia Shahar, Hadi Abad and Hoshiarpur.[78] Again, the Sikh rule was well known for its welfare-oriented policies for the *mafidars* (holders of revenue-free land)[79] and *jagirdars*. In Gujranwala alone, the early British administration confirmed over 16,000 revenue-free grants dating from Sikh times.[80]

For centuries, it had been a tradition to sanction grants and revenue-free land for religious purposes. Ranjit Singh fostered this tradition, sustaining, enhancing and expanding it. The vassal chiefs were free to give the *dharmarth* grants from their territories. The *jagirdars* of the Mughal era continued to enjoy their grants and *jagirs* during the regime of Ranjit Singh.[81] The *Khalsa Darbar* records contain numerous examples of grants coming down from the past. The *kardars* (revenue officers) were instructed again and again not to interfere with the old grants.[82] The early British records and gazettes also quote many instances of the continuation of the old grants and entitlements by the Sikh ruler in the districts of Lahore, Jhang, Multan, Amritsar, Rawalpindi and others.[83] In this, the Muslim grantees received the same treatment, as did the Hindus and the Sikhs.

The Muharram[84] processions were also allowed in the Punjab. They had been banned initially, but at the request of Prince Kharak Singh and Mirza Begun Baig the ban was lifted.[85] Although they were again banned on the persistence of some Sikhs in 1825, the Maharaja ordered Muslims to keep their *tazias*[86] at home. After two days, Prince Kharak Singh informed the Maharaja of the resultant anger and frustration among the Muslim army and the community. Ranjit Singh at once granted permission to restore the Muharram processions.[87]

On the direction of Ranjit Singh, Qazi Fakirullah announced the prayer of *Eid-ul-Azha* to be performed in the Badshahi Mosque, and was rewarded with an expensive Kashmiri shawl.[88] Moran, the Muslim favourite wife of Ranjit Singh, also presented a Holy Quran with every *para* (part) in a separate box to the mausoleum of Data Ganj Bakhsh.[89] Bokan Khan, in charge of the Maharaja's stables, and the famous Muslim *topchi* (cannon operator) Ghose Khan also built mosques in different places. On the death of Ghose Khan, Ranjit Singh spent some days at the shrine of Shah Abul Muali.[90]

There is a very interesting insight into Ranjit Singh's personal beliefs: whenever he found himself in serious danger, he immediately turned to the Muslim saints for salvation. On 7 February 1839, he visited the grave of Hazrat Mian Mir, the famous Muslim Sufi saint who had been the spiritual mentor of Prince Dara

Shikoh and also a very dear friend of Sikh Guru Arjun. Mian Mir also laid the foundation stone of the *Darbar Sahib*. Ranjit Singh visited the shrine of Data Ganj Bakhsh during the same year.[91] On two occasions he attended *Eid-ul-Fitar*[92] and *Muharram* congregations just like a Muslim.[93] In the month of Muharram, his family joined the congregation and processions like Muslims, and every year Prince Kharak Singh distributed milk, water and food to the participants of procession.[94]

Given his fair and wise treatment of them, Ranjit Singh was loved by all the religious communities including Muslims and Hindus. All used to pray for his health and long life during important religious occasions.[95]

Some historians also condemn Ranjit Singh for banning *aazan*.[96] However, Fakir Waheeduddin states that *aazan* was not permanently banned in the reign of Ranjit Singh. The *Akali* Sikhs did try to stop it and pressurized Ranjit Singh accordingly. He agreed to the ban, but then the Muslims approached him via Fakir Azizuddin to reverse his decision. When he refused, Fakir Azizuddin asked for an alternative arrangement, so Ranjit Singh gave the *Akalis* the duty of waking up the Muslims and letting them know the timing of their prayers. The Sikhs accepted the task, but within a week showed themselves unable to perform this duty. As a result Ranjit Singh allowed *aazan* in Lahore.[97]

The perception of the Muslims at that time was that although Ranjit Singh was born a Sikh he was a secular, benign and great ruler. It was never religion that motivated him, but his desire for greater power and control over the Punjab. A major portion of his army was Muslim. He could never take the risk of alienating them all by proscribing their religion. At times he did falter, but he recovered quickly. For example, he initially disallowed *aazan* but realizing the consequences, reversed the decision. Mughal Emperor Akbar the Great also for some time banned slaughtering cows, to ensure social and religious harmony. If some of Ranjit Singh's acts appear to reflect hostility to the Muslims, there were also many acts of generosity and benevolence – for example, the governors of Kashmir were removed mainly for their ill-treatment of the Muslim population.

Muslim Historic and Cultural Centres

Maharaja Ranjit Singh was invited to attack Lahore by both the Muslims and the Hindus of that city. The Muslims received pledges to rebuild famous Muslim buildings, which had been destroyed by the Bhangi Sikhs, and Ranjit Singh kept his promise. He was greatly disheartened to see the dilapidated condition of the Shalimar Gardens. The canal, which supplied water to the garden, was filled with silt and bricks. The walls and buildings within the garden were totally rundown, overgrown by weeds. Ranjit Singh sanctioned huge grants to renovate and rebuild the garden and the canal.[98] He rebuilt the Shalimar Gardens along with Shahla Bagh (garden) and Gulabi Bagh.[99] These gardens were greatly praised by foreign travellers such as W. G. Osborne, Baron Hügel, William Barr and Lord Auckland.[100] Osborne, for example, poetically describes the beauty of Shalimar Gardens, noting that all the fountains were working, the walls were in good condition and covered with flowers. The roads around the water channels were built of handsome black stone. Hundreds and thousands of fruit trees were blooming all over the garden.[101] Hazoori Bagh in the fort of Lahore was also rebuilt.[102] Badami Bagh was studded with almond trees and Hazoori Bagh with different fruit trees including mango, orange and guava. Twenty-six gardens were built around the road from the fort of Lahore to the Shalimar Gardens, and Ranjit Singh generously rewarded those who maintained them. He not only restored the gardens of the Mughals but also created several new gardens, this time not reserved for the nobles but open to the common man to enjoy the scenic beauty.[103] William Barr describes groups of people visiting these gardens and enjoying the evening.[104]

There is evidence that the Maharaja was not responsible for the destruction of the tomb of Jahangir. Initially the Durrani rulers damaged it, when Nadir Shah and Ahmad Shah Abdali attacked Lahore; they removed the precious stones from the walls of the tomb.[105] During the period of Ranjit Singh, Sultan Muhammad Khan visited Lahore as a guest and he took away yet more precious stones and marbles from the tomb.[106]

The city of Lahore was plundered many times by invaders, both Muslim and non-Muslim.[107] However, when Ranjit Singh captured it, he did much to restore its former beauty and grandeur. In addition to the gardens and tombs, he restored the Shahi (imperial) Fort to its former glory and strength and rebuilt the Walled City, many buildings of which had been burnt or destroyed,[108] assisted by ministers including Dina Nath, Fakir Azizuddin and Jamadar Khushhal Sing. In fact, Lahore remained the centre of all social and festive activities during his reign.[109] The beauty of the Shahi Fort and the tomb of Jahangir especially impressed M'Gregor, who visited Lahore in 1835.[110] Four years later Lord Auckland, the British envoy, visited Lahore with his family and assistants; all were completely overawed by the magnificence of the Shalimar Gardens.[111] Ranjit Singh had planned this visit very carefully to impress Lord Auckland with the grandeur and strength of the Sikh domain. He decided to take him first to the *Darbar Sahib*, then to Lahore itself to see the historic places of the Mughals, including the Badshahi (imperial) Mosque and Wazir Khan Mosque.[112] In their accounts of visits by foreign envoys, especially the British, historians claim that the grandness and exquisiteness of the Lahore *Darbar* always stunned visitors. On this occasion, Ranjit Singh did not want to miss the opportunity to impress the British governor, and would never have taken him to see such places if these had been in ruins. This is sufficient evidence that the Muslim buildings and monuments were well looked after during Ranjit Singh's reign. Concerning the religious attitude of the Maharaja, Jacquemont confirms that he was a 'Sikh by profession, and a skeptic in reality'.[113]

Akalis

Any discussion of the relationship between the Sikhs and the Muslims or any other community remains incomplete without exploring the phenomenon of the Sikh

Akalis. The *Akalis* or *Nihangs* formed an independent and distinct class of Sikhs. The word *akali* means immortal and was used for *Nihangs*, a particular order of Sikhs, which claimed its origin from Guru Gobind Singh. They were fanatic warrior priests. They had assumed the office of guardians of the *Darbar Sahib* at Amritsar and acted as enforcers of Sikh morality and preservers of the original ordinances of the faith.[114] They were always at the front of religious rituals. Their hatred for other communities was not hidden, and they remained a constant source of tension for Ranjit Singh. They were as dangerous to their friends as to their enemies, and did not hesitate to take on Ranjit Singh himself. They once attacked M'Gregor when he was returning from hunting, frightening him and asking for money. Afterwards, despite assurance from the Maharaja, M'Gregor did not dare go outside his residence without a guard and protection.[115] Alexander Burnes reports several unfortunate incidents caused mainly by this group, including burning an entire village and inflicting harsh punishments on other communities.[116]

Even when the *Akalis* attempted to kill Ranjit Singh, out of some political exigency or probably fear of their religious power (the common Sikhs respected them because of their association with the last Guru), Ranjit Singh did not crush them, although he could easily have done so. With his astuteness, he successfully managed to channel their energies to his benefit.

Emily Eden writes that the *Akali* Sikhs were uncontrollable enthusiasts and that Ranjit Singh was really confused about them, deciding to create a special regiment of *Akali* Sikhs. She reports that they caused havoc while offering a guard of honour to the English representative general, chanting slogans against Ranjit Singh, Sikh *sardars* and Englishmen and swearing soon to take over Calcutta.[117] When she and her sister wished to go to the bazaar in Amritsar, Ajit Singh Sindhianwala and Lehna Singh Majithia were deputed to protect them from the uncontrollable *Akalis*.[118]

M'Gregor also described them as uncontrollable fanatics, wild with a mix of cunningness and cruelty. When and wherever they saw Europeans they would start abusing them. They had a very frightening appearance, especially with naked swords in their hands.

Akali Phula Singh was the leader of the gang who attacked General Metcalf. He later joined the Sikh army and won many battles for the Maharaja. Following their unsuccessful attempt on the general, Phula Singh and his companions forced their way into the *darbar*, where he took out his sword and threatened to take revenge on the foreigner. Ranjit Singh dealt with their aggression diplomatically and offered himself in place of the British diplomat. After a long discussion, he was able to appease them and send them away, later granting gifts to all of them.[119]

Consequently Phula Singh became very popular and his group grew bigger and bigger, with 4,000–5,000 warriors. They mainly remained busy looting wealthy people and fighting with other communities. Complaints against them reached the Lahore *Darbar* and Ranjit Singh tried to stop them by giving them money and *jagirs*. Phula Singh refused to join the Maharaja's army, but Ranjit Singh continued to ignore their wrongdoings and bribed them until his gifts finally worked and Phula Singh, along with his fellows, joined the army. It was certainly the sensible policy of the Maharaja that tamed the savage *Akali* leader. In fact, Ranjit Singh was known for his talent in finding the right people for the right job. He understood the aggression that boiled deep within the *Akalis* – aggression that could best be used on the battlefield.[120]

Given that the conquest of Lahore was largely due to Muslim support, paving the way for establishing his rule in Lahore, Ranjit Singh not only offered Muslims high posts in his *darbar* but also granted them almost complete religious liberty. The exception is that out of fear and his policy of appeasement of the *Akalis*, he sometimes enforced some restrictions against the Muslims, which were taken away sooner or later. In February 1809, when the *Akalis* attacked the ambassador of the East India Company, some Muslims were martyred. Ranjit Singh himself apologized to the East India Company.[121] The *Akalis* had a special position in the Sikh army and their war tactics were very proficient. For this reason Ranjit Singh feared them, although he did take strict action against their criminal activities. But again this was solely political expediency and religion had no role to play in the whole episode.

The Muslim population had a special place in their hearts for Ranjit Singh. In 1826, during his sickness, mosques had regular congregational prayers for his recovery.[122] During his funeral ceremony, Muslims took part and kept on reciting the Quran and praying for blessing upon him with *duroods* (prayers).[123] His religious policy highlights the fact that political power includes the idea of service to the people, their wellbeing, and protection of their lives, goods and self-esteem.

Osborne believes that whatever wrongs were done to the Muslims it was largely because of a group of illiterate and extremist Sikhs who opposed them. Khushwant Singh and others report that, on the whole, Sikhs, Muslims and Hindus lived together and celebrated each other's religious festivals.[124] Modern-day scholars agree that some of the aides of Ranjit Singh had myopic vision and did not follow his example. During this period a number of *gurdwara* and temples were built, not due to his personal efforts but to the efforts of others. In fact, he was somewhat careless about religion.[125]

Economic Condition, Policies and Opportunities

Although more interested in agriculture, Ranjit Singh did not ignore trade and commerce. He spent time improving trade and economic policies of his kingdom. He knew that he could not build a strong state without a strong economy. The Muslims were in a majority in the Punjab, and it was impossible to ignore them. However, a particular group of historians and researchers have pointed out that Ranjit Singh did not give equal opportunities to the majority Muslim population.

Under Ranjit Singh, the industrial sector was divided into state-owned enterprises and privately-owned industry. The defence industry manufactured the cannons, ammunition and various articles of warfare for the army. This was a highly sensitive industry, which was under state control and directly supervised by Fakir Nuruddin and Mian Qadir Bukhsh. Fakir Nuruddin was assisted by a host of experts, mostly Muslims, such as Qaida Khan and Mistri Afzal Khan.[126]

The revenue of the state was collected mainly from tributes, *nazrana*, customs duties and land revenue. There was no regular system of budgeting other than that based on income and expenditure. Although there are not many reliable sources available, a wider view can be taken from the work of Henry T. Prinsep, listed as follows.[127]

Source	Annual income (Rs. in millions)
Land revenue and tributes	12,403,900
Custom duties	1,900,600
Moharana	577,000
Total	14,881,500

Shahamat Ali gives a second estimate of the annual income of the Sikh kingdom.[128]

Source	Annual income (Rs. in millions)
Khalsa	19,657,172
Jagirs	8,754,590
Khiraj dars	1,266,000
Customs duties	550,000
Total	30,227,762

The Punjab was a Sikh state where all had full and equivalent rights regardless of rank or race. Some historians have regarded the reign of Ranjit Singh as a secular one in which all religious minorities were allowed freedom.[129] Sikhs, Muslims and Hindus were all represented in his cabinet and state administration.[130] The Sikhs gained many benefits from his reign,[131] as did the other religions and people of all communities. In return, Ranjit Singh had the trust and power of his people.[132]

As has already been seen, the doors of government were open to non-Sikhs as well, according to their legitimacy and fitness for a task. Religion had never been the deciding factor for Ranjit Singh when offering economic or employment opportunities; employment solely depended on one's competence and calibre. Initially the most senior officer of the Maharaja's cabinet was Mian Ghause Khan; on his death, his son, Sultan Mahmood Khan gradually rose to his father's rank. In the illustrious *darbar* of Ranjit Singh, nobody else could equal the status of Fakir Azizuddin, who used to be given the most delicate, intimate and sensitive assignments.[133]

Case of Kashmir

As discussed in Chapter 2, Kashmir fell into the hands of the Sikhs in 1819, but before the Sikh period the Kashmiris had suffered under the cruel rule of the

Afghans.¹³⁴ G. M. D. Sufi writes about the condition of the local people, who were mostly Muslims:

> The Afghans signalized their stay by roughness and harshness. Their chief victims were the bold Chaks and the Shias. The Sunnis did not fare better. It is said of the Afghans that they thought no more of cutting off heads than of plucking flowers.¹³⁵

Under the reign of Ranjit Singh, eight governors were appointed to control Kashmir affairs.¹³⁶ The short periods of office resulted from the complaints of the local people of their brutality, and especially the dissatisfaction and unease of the Muslims. After hearing the complaints of the Muslims, in 1833 Ranjit Singh sent the French officer General Allard to Kashmir with the direction to investigate the complaints and assess the governance. In the light of his findings, Ranjit Singh introduced reforms and appointed Colonel Mahan Singh, who proved to be a good administrator and improved the welfare of the people.¹³⁷

Shawl making was one of Kashmir's main sources of revenue.¹³⁸ Ranjit Singh could not afford to see it weakened, but the revenue rapidly decreased until its revival in 1825. Ranjit Singh was well aware of the rights of the workers in this industry. The hosiery industry United Punjab was initially set up by Muslim Kashmiri migrants who had left their homeland in 1830s.¹³⁹ They introduced a new variety of woollen shawls in the Punjab that made the brand very popular across the country. Some writers have noted that the Indian elite and the British officers liked these woollen brands. The popularity of the shawls among British officers helped to introduce the products to the Western market. The industry also produced traditional *loongi* and *patkas* and provided the Army with uniforms and badges.¹⁴⁰ However, some accounts suggest that Muslims did not own the hosiery industry on a large scale and their status was of workers. Nevertheless, it is important to mention that all the production and management was in the control of Muslims and they used their experience to help the hosiery industry to flourish in Lyallpur. V. N. Dutta writes that the hosiery industry of Delhi suffered from the outmigration of Muslims as they largely maintained the sector in United India. Similarly, Pippa Virdee writes that the hosiery industry of Ludhiana suffered for the same reason.¹⁴¹

Kashmiri shawls were sent to the Lahore *Darbar*, and it is reported that during the period of Ranjit Singh, the workers received full benefit from their work. When Kirpa Ram was the governor of Kashmir, he introduced different styles of shawl – some were even named after him, such as *Kirpa Ram's Doshala*¹⁴² – as well as different types of Kashmiri carpets.¹⁴³ The first factory for Kashmiri shawls was established in Amritsar; because of the harsh behaviour of Jamadar Khushhal Singh, the Kashmiris left Kashmir and set up their businesses in Amritsar and Lahore. This confirms that the maltreatment of local Kashmiris was the outcome of the personal policies of the individual governors and not because of Ranjit Singh's *Sarkar-e-Khalsa* and its policies. Had this been under the command of Ranjit Singh, the Kashmiris would likely not have chosen Lahore or Amritsar as their business and living abodes. Ranjit Singh also encouraged the shawl industry by providing grants and loans in cash and kind (wool) to the weavers.[144] C. M. Wade's report, published in 1832, states that the final cost of some shawls was Rs.500, of which the weaver received 53 per cent.[145]

The Maharaja also encouraged the cultivation of saffron, reducing the government's share of the income from agriculture and providing facilities to bring more land under cultivation.[146] William Moorcroft, who visited Kashmir five years after its annexation, paints the other side of the picture, writing that the people were living in abject conditions and were migrating to the plains of the Punjab for a better livelihood.[147] Muslims dominated the shawl industry in Kashmir.[148] The streets of Islamabad were full of beggars. G. T. Vigne, who was in Kashmir from June to December 1835, also describes the pathetic condition of the people of Shupiyan and Islamabad during the Sikh regime.[149]

These were some of the facts and obvious charges against Ranjit Singh claimed by some historians and especially English writers. Before we make up our minds about the economic condition of the Muslims and the role of Ranjit Singh, it is important to take a deeper look into these allegations.

Pandit Birbel, who himself went to Lahore to invite Ranjit Singh to attack Kashmir, was punished by the Sikh governor on the charge of misappropriation of revenue. It was one of the reasons that he ran away from Afghan rule. He died in jail and the Maharaja confiscated all his property.[150]

Vegnie narrates the story of Moti Ram, a very cruel person who was replaced by Hari Singh Nalwa for his failure during the famine of 1820–1. He in turn replaced Hari Singh Nalwa during his second tenure because of Nalwa's oppressive rule.[151] It was important that Hari Singh Nalwa was replaced, despite the fact that his tenure was the most fruitful in terms of revenue collection and administration.[152] Therefore, we should understand that had revenue collection been the only objective of Ranjit Singh, Hari Singh Nalwa would have continued in his post. He was removed for his aggressive policies against the people of Kashmir.

During the reign of Prince Sher Singh, a terrible famine hit Kashmir, which reduced the population from 80,000 to 20,000. During that period, Jamadar Khushhal Khan collected the revenue from the people and presented it to the Maharaja. The Maharaja was angry with Jamadar for taxing the people of Kashmir during difficult times. Subsequently all the money was returned and distributed among the Kashmiris. Special convoys of food and grain were dispatched to Kashmir and Colonel Mahan Singh, governor of Kashmir for some seven years, did his best for the welfare of the Kashmiris. There are several accounts of his justice and fair treatment. He tried to establish trade and industry again in Kashmir, which largely benefitted the Muslims, and to do his best to mitigate the ravages of the famine. He also advanced interest-free loans for improvement in agriculture.[153]

It seems illogical to continue taxing people in order to accumulate more and more wealth, especially over an extended period of time. It has already been mentioned that Ranjit Singh kept on replacing the governors who maltreated the people administratively, economically and socially, forcing many of them to migrate to other parts of the Punjab for better employment. This means at least that other parts of the Punjab were considered safe economically as well as socially. Although the Sikh government received taxes from the people, it also took care of their welfare.

During the governorship of Diwan Chunni Lal, the strong *sardar Kumedan* Gurmukh Singh was appointed as the head of revenue collection and administration. Gurmukh reduced the governor to a nonentity who had implicated Khwaja Muhaiy-ud-Din, a respectable citizen, in a cow-killing case and treated him badly on false evidence. When Ranjit Singh heard reports of their cruelty, he recalled them to Lahore.[154] He even appointed a committee of three representing the Hindus, the Sikhs and the Muslims, which, however, could not achieve its desired objectives.[155] Therefore, we cannot blame only Ranjit Singh for this. In fact, the governors and the prevailing system of Kashmir remained mainly responsible for the failing economic condition of the people.

Another key factor in the rundown economic condition of the Muslims was the sequence of famines that hit Kashmir one after the other, while Muslims enjoyed good financial and economic health in other parts of the Punjab. Ranjit Singh tried to control the natural calamities of repeated famine and disease, yet could not fully do so. He always tried to help the valley of Kashmir. On one hand, he never hesitated to punish the dishonesty, cruelty and maladministration of his governors; on the other, he established colonies of Kashmiris in the Punjab to help them in their time of difficulty.[156]

Economy of Multan

Analysing the economic development and condition of Multan, a Muslim-majority province, Mufti Ghulam Sarwar reports that Multan had great economic and industrial potential. It was known for its fine silk, carpets, different types of coloured cloth and pottery. Its products were even exported to other parts of the subcontinent and, with the encouragement of the Maharaja, outside India. Multan was also very well known for its delicious and juicy mangoes and dates, which were often sent as gifts to other parts of the Punjab and India, as well as for its shrines and Sufi saints.[157] Multan cotton was very famous during the Maharaja's time, exported to Sindh and other parts of India. Just as Peshawar was famous for the blue coloured *lungis* (sarongs),[158] so Multan was known for its dyeing.

For the promotion of Multani silk, Ranjit Singh regularly gave silk products to his guests of honour, foreign courtiers and other visitors. Subsequently it became fashionable to wear Multani scarves and sashes.[159] On some occasions, the Maharaja even bought these articles in bulk for trading purposes, and once between thirty and thirty-five boatloads were sent to foreign markets for the promotion of the industry.[160] In order to encourage an industry that was dominated by the Muslims, only moderate duties were imposed on its export to Khorasan and other parts of India. Multan was an even bigger centre of trade than Bahawalpur. At that time, about forty moneychangers were working in the city of Multan.[161]

However, the British did not look after the industry well, which subsequently lost its potential.[162]

Economic Potential of Other Parts of the Punjab

Lahore was the biggest centre of trade, with food items and other goods exported to Central Asia. Similarly, Peshawar was famous for its *gur* (hard brown sugar), *shaker* (soft brown sugar) and dried fruits. Salt was cheaper during the period of Ranjit Singh. Jhang's cotton was known for its superior quality and Sialkot was a leading centre of paper manufacturing.[163]

As Ranjit Singh's territory expanded, various mints were set up in Multan, Peshawar, Kashmir and Derajat. The Punjab turned into a vibrant centre of economic activity. Its marketable products were mainly pashmina shawls, fleeces, silk, cotton, weapons, and a number of horticultural and mineral items. Ranjit Singh once informed Dr Murray that the entire contents of the arsenal were made in Lahore.[164]

Walter Hamilton viewed Amritsar and Kashmir as grand centres of exchange for shawls and saffron.[165] All these things were additionally traded to other parts of India, and shawls from Kashmir, Amritsar and Gujrat to Europe. Silk and coarse Punjabi cotton fabrics were sent to Afghanistan and Turkistan. The *lungis* of Peshawar, Dera Ghazi Khan, Multan and Khushab were known for their export quality.[166] Rawalpindi was acclaimed for its grain and fabric. Similarly Attock was well known for its timber and Pind Dadan Khan was a major exchange centre for salt.[167]

The trade routes before Ranjit Singh's time were not safeguarded, and caravans were frequently looted. The Maharaja drew up a robust and unique strategy and action plan for the protection of the traders, with posts set up at regular intervals to protect the convoys. Mohan Lal identified five different routes between Dera Ghazi Khan and Khandar via Rojhan, Ghause Pur and Shikarpur.[168] Amritsar, Lahore, Multan, Rawalpindi, Peshawar and Dera Ghazi Khan were centres for export. The two main routes were first – and most famous – through Amritsar, Lahore, Multan and Dera Ghazi Khan, and second through Amritsar, Lahore, Wazirabad, Rawalpindi, Peshawar and Kabul. A third was from the hilly zones of Ladakh and Kashmir.[169] All the urban communities and towns were guaranteed safety on these trade routes.

The *khojas* and *parachas*, the Muslim merchant community, were the main traders and industrialists. They were converts of the Khatris and Aroras. The term *paracha* is said to have been a derivative of *parcha* or 'cloth', one of the main items of their trade. *Khoja* was really nothing more than the Persian *khwaja*, and denoted simply men of wealth and decency.[170] *Parachas* and *khojas* appeared to be good competitors for each other. The *parachas* were active and resourceful manufacturers whose business stretched to Turkistan and Afghanistan.[171] They traded in cloth, silk, tea and indigo. Many of them kept small shops and some of them farmed. The *khojas* were expert in the leather trade. They were common in Lahore and Sialkot as industrialists and suppliers of leather goods.[172] They were good traders and businessmen who sold products against credit, especially in the villages.[173]

It was customary that if a trader was robbed during the course of his business, the Maharaja made good his loss. He made the roads and trade routes so safe that even two persons alone could travel with their luggage without fear. The looting of trade convoys became very uncommon.[174]

Land Revenue, Agriculture, and Farming Policies and Prospects

Ranjit Singh made serious efforts to increase the cultivable area for better agricultural produce and revenue in the Punjab. The government lent money, mostly interest-free, to the farmers for repairs and digging wells and to buy better seeds, implements and bullocks.[175] Cultivators were exempt from the grazing duty. The *nazims* and *kardars* were told to develop an infrastructure for better farming in their regions.[176] Leases were also given to the farmers in Multan to build wells to bring more land under cultivation.[177]

Ranjit Singh granted a huge tract of land to Elahi Bukhsh when he offered to develop it, directing him to increase its cultivable area and look after it well, and a handsome amount was promised for improving the village.[178] A number of canals were dug from the rivers Chenab and Sutlej to irrigate Multan and surrounding areas, and the desert was turned into a rich cultivated area. Diwan Swan Mal, the administrator of that area, did much for welfare and agriculture. The people were given liberal and easy loans to build wells and dig canals or to repair old ones. People who wanted to cultivate barren areas were given concessions on their taxes.[179]

In order to understand the revenue policies of Ranjit Singh, we need to explore his relations with his people, especially the Muslims. In 1801, he appointed Qazi Nazimuddin as head of the Muslims in Lahore for revenue. Mufti Muhammad Shah assisted him in revenue matters.[180] The policies and programmes initiated and subsequently pursued by the Maharaja profited all segments of society. The state strategy was to incentivize farmers to bring more and more land under cultivation with the aim of increasing agricultural produce and subsequently revenue. The lot of the lower class of Punjabis was a great deal more agreeable than at any other time in recent memory. Similarly, there was significant increase and improvement in trade and business during this period, as a result of which an increase in urban development was seen in the Punjab.

The demographic outlines and boundaries become more expressive and clearer in the light of the data collected by the British administrators of the Punjab in order to have a better understanding of the territories held by Ranjit Singh. Of the leading tribes and castes in terms of ownership of land, the Baloch were influential in Dera Ghazi Khan, Dera Ismail Khan and Mankera. They were also prominent in Muzaffar Garh, Shahpur, Jhang, Multan and Montgomery (Sahiwal). West of the Indus, they had preserved their ethnic identity with distinct language and society. However, in other places they had mingled with the locals.[181]

The Pushtu-speaking Pathans mostly lived in Bannu, Kohat and Peshawar. They were also well represented in Sindh Sagar Doab, Kasur and Bari Doab.[182] In Sindh Sagar Doab, there were also Awans in the western and central salt range. The Junjuas were mostly in the eastern salt range. The Gakhakars mainly occupied Rawalpindi and Jhelum. The Tiwanas were dominant in Shahpur and the Khokhar were mostly in Shahpur and Jhang. The Sials lived in Jhang and the Kharals in Montgomery. The Gujjars were also significant as landowners and cultivators. They were mostly in Sindh Sagar Doab, Chaj, Gujranwala, Hassan Abdal and Jhelum. The Arain and Kamboh were also farmers. These were all the areas where the Muslims were present in greater numbers and owned most of the land.[183] The statistics show that under Ranjit Singh the Muslims mainly occupied the agricultural sector and produced its revenue. They had significant opportunities to grow economically and politically.

Ranjit Singh was meticulous about the welfare of the people. Bhai Govind Ram told him about the corn harvest in Dera Ghazi Khan, where there was distress among the people because of the high price of corn. The Maharaja immediately ordered the garrison officer to sell the stores of corn to ensure availability of grain to the people. He also introduced a price control mechanism in Peshawar to check hoarding and black-marketeering. General Avitabile ordered the shopkeepers to sell their goods at fixed prices, under a fine of Rs.5.[184]

The *sahukars*, who were mostly Hindus, lent money to people to buy seeds, cattle and land, charging very high rates of interest. Ranjit Singh not only kept an eye on these *sahukar* retailers and lenders, but they were advised to take only 20 per cent interest annually from the lender. If any *sahukar* tried to charge higher interest than that prescribed by the government, the *kardar* took him to task. This indeed improved cultivation and agricultural produce, and therefore state revenue.[185]

Ranjit Singh instructed his officials to collect the revenue from the people while keeping in mind their welfare. In 1833, Diwan Swan Mal, in charge of Pindi Bhattian and Hafizabad, was instructed to pay due regard to the people and their prosperity while collecting revenue for the state.[186] In 1838 a general declaration was issued to all the governors advising them to improve the condition of their people and especially the *zamindars* in all matters, and to show no cruelty to any of them.[187] These were Ranjit Singh's general instructions to all state officials to keep the welfare of the people and the state at the forefront. He never allowed his troops to damage crops during wars and invasions. A number of occasions are reported in the *Umdat-ut-Tawarikh* when the Maharaja accepted the requests of the *zamindars* and changed his route to avoid such damage. In 1809 Fateh Khan, the local chief of Sahiwal, complained to the Maharaja that the encampment of royal troops had damaged his crops. The Maharaja accepted this and immediately left the area and crossed the River Jhelum with his troops.[188] He also ordered Kunwar Nau Nihal Singh, who was heading to Peshawar with his troops, to remain careful about the cultivated land and crops. When the *zamindars* of the town of Kukran complained against the Misr Sukhraj regiment for the loss of their crops, Kunwar waived his 50 per cent land revenue.[189]

The first census of the Punjab was carried out in 1855. Non-agricultural employment occupied 44 per cent of the total population.[190] The huge size of the population was in itself a great economic opportunity in terms of the consumption of agricultural goods. Crops including wheat, cotton and sugar were staples and essential trading products. The Bedies (sub-caste of Khatris) of Wyrowal and Goindwal transported sugar and cotton to Multan and in return brought dye for the markets of Amritsar and Jalandhar.[191] Rice, ginger and dyes from the hills were carried to the plains and cotton from the plains to the hills.[192] External trade in agriculture was primarily with Afghanistan and the Central Asian states, and mostly in the hands of influential traders such as the Lohanies, Khojas and Shikarpuries.[193]

Educational Policy

Education is a powerful means of escaping from poverty and improving one's economic condition. A quick look at his educational policies will give us an insight into the extent to which Ranjit Singh was generous and liberal towards the Muslim community. Although he had no formal education himself, he understood its significance. Like Akbar the Great, he could not read or write in any language, although his exposure to various languages and people taught him the art of reading people and handling state affairs. He was able to understand even the most complex political, business and war strategies and decisions to be made on behalf of the state.[194] Throughout his reign he supported and encouraged the education sector. The Punjab had nearly 4,000 schools, catering to the needs of each and every community. Approximately one *lakh* and 20,000 students were registered in these schools.[195] By and large they were akin to religious schools, as *gurduwaras*, mosques and temples, and Ranjit Singh very generously helped the custodians of these educational institutes. There was not a mosque, a *dharamshala* or a *gurudwar* that was without a school. These were mostly in the villages for the religious education of young citizens. There were hundreds of schools that taught Persian, which were common for all regardless of caste or creed.[196] The Muslim schools and *madrassas* (traditional religious schools) worked successfully and without restrictions from the state, meaning that Muslim students had complete freedom to study and to progress in life and society.

Ranjit Singh never tried to promote the Gurumukhi script[197] in place of Persian or Urdu, and there was no common or formal form of teaching. Education was given on a needs basis. For instance, Persian was essential to obtain an executive job. Similarly Sanskrit, Arabic and Gurmukhi were keys to religious education and employment.[198] Persian was the official language and the language of literature. It was frequently taught in schools, which received donations and land for their management. The teachers were invariably Muslims. Classics such as *Gulistan*, *Boostan* and works of *Saadi* were the typical courses.[199]

Ranjit Singh supported contemporary trends in enhancing and standardizing education. During the last days of his rule, he started encouraging the learning of

English. There is evidence that he also obtained the services of a Christian teacher to establish English-medium schools in Lahore. However, promoting Christianity or the teachings of the Bible was strictly forbidden in the curriculum of these schools.[200] On the other hand, Muslims and Hindus were all allowed to have a religious as well as a vocational education.

Education had mainly been delivered in the mosques from the early period of Islam, and continued during the Sikh period. Persian was the official language not only for Muslims but also for Sikhs and Hindus. A number of *maktabs* (informal schools) and other schools were run under the administration of the Muslims. A very famous writer, Leitner, who worked on indigenous education in the Punjab, very interestingly describes the Persian, Quranic and Arabic schools in the province. Under Ranjit Singh, to get an administrative post it was essential to have full knowledge of Persian. *Moulvis* or educated women ran schools in their homes.[201] Leitner also gives a detailed list of the syllabus, which included the *Sikandar Nama* of Nizami and the letters of Abul Fazal.[202] He further reports that these schools were capable of delivering education from primary grades for reading Arabic to the higher grades for reading and understanding Arabic works, especially on medicine.[203]

Hashim Shah, a literary person, received a *jagir* for his scholarly services despite the fact that he fought against the Sikhs in Shah Ahmad's *jihad* movement.[204] Ranjit Singh also invited Dubir-ud-Doulah, the grandfather of Syed Ahmad Khan, for his knowledge of economics and mathematics. However, he refused to join the *darbar* because of his failing health, returning the money sent to him to travel from Delhi to Lahore.[205] This shows the keenness of the Maharaja for scholarship and scholarly people, no matter which religion they belonged to or what they had done in the past. He respected them without any communal or religious affiliation. The most scholarly and well-respected among them were Hashim Shah, Ahmad Yar, Qadir Yar, Fazal Shah, Ghulam Rasool and Imam Bukhsh. This period saw the growth of a collection of *qissas* (romantic fictional stories) with many new topics coming from both Indian and Arabic sources. The Sikh *sardars* at court were also educated. Lehna Singh was a mathematician and an engineer.[206] Kunwar Nau Nihal Singh, Ajit Singh and Lehna Singh studied the higher concepts of mathematics and astronomy under the well-known Akhvand Ali, who was specially called from the Frontier to Lahore. Lehna Singh, Ajit Singh and Attar Singh also had a good understanding of Arabic. There were many Muslim tutors who were very good teachers and received *jagirs* and incomes for their talent and hard work.[207]

Ranjit Singh did not attempt to bring about changes in set and established ways of doing things – for example, Persian continued to be the court's official language. However, he brought about simplicity and candidness in state administration. This arrangement somehow never conflicted with the dispensation of state business.[208] As the language of the Lahore *Darbar*, Persian was very popular with both Muslims and Hindus. Among the Hindus, Khatris had an exceptional interest in learning Persian in order to secure service in revenue management.[209] Mufti Ghulam Sarwar gives a list of the people who were from the ruling class of Lahore. Among them, the family of the Fakir brothers were famous for their literary status and services. Several *maktabs* and schools were run under their supervision.[210]

It is similarly significant that Muslims adopted Punjabi culture and work and made an impact on Punjabi literature. A review of the literature produced during this period discloses a strong affinity in the Muslim writings to secular anxieties, which may be somewhat understood in the context of the decaying Mughal power. But this trend reveals both a process of Punjabization of their literature and the rise of a new type of literature written for pleasure and the amusement of the common man.[211]

As far as higher education was concerned, there were more than thirteen Quran, Arabic and Persian schools in the Punjab.[212] The higher-standard schools taught mathematics, logic, philosophy and medicine. The Maharaja provided students who came from far away with free food and books.[213]

At Batala, there was a large and well-known school run by the Qadri family. It drew students from other countries, such as Iran. This institution was given a big *jagir* which was later seized in the British period.[214] An identical school was established in Sialkot under Moulvi Sheikh Ahmed, a well-known literary man. There was an outstanding school of Bara Mian in Lahore, which was no less than a college, and was generously supported by the Sikh government. There was another institution in the Moran Mosque under Khalifa Sahib. Students from Persia and Arabia received education in many disciplines. Khawaja Suleiman had a successful school at Sangrosa in Dera Ghazi Khan district, attended by students from Khorasan and other parts of Hindustan.[215]

Farid-ud-Din, Elahi Bukhsh, Mufti Imam Bukhsh and Syed Israr Shah Gilani were very famous for their poetry,[216] and Ustad Pir Bukhsh and Mian Fazal-ud-Din for their calligraphy.[217] It is striking that neither Ranjit Singh nor the *darbar* ever ordered any work commemorating his military victories or his memoirs, although Punjabi poets and various authors wrote for him out of their own interest. The Lahore *Darbar* asked Munshi Sohan Lal to write *Umdat-ut-Tawarikh* and Moulvi Ahmed Yar *Shahnama* in Persian. Ranjit Singh's courtier Diwan Dina Nath's son, Diwan Amar Nath, wrote *Zafar Nama Ranjit Singh* in Persian. Sikhs had the tradition of telling their history in poetry in the period of Ranjit Singh. Rattan Singh Bhangu in 1841 wrote his *Prachin Panth Parkas*. Another amazing element was that Punjabi was established as a literary language as a result of the ingenuity and creativity of the writers of those days that flowed out of the love for the common Punjabi and his chores.[218]

Ranjit Singh allocated one-tenth of his state revenue for charity, a striking illustration of his personality and government, highlighting its Sikh character. The fifth Guru had recommended that Sikhs commit *daswandh* or one-tenth of their income towards a religious cause for the general public, but it is nevertheless exceptional that Ranjit Singh's government acted likewise.[219]

In conclusion, it is clear that Ranjit Singh had a great respect for learning and education. Although his government was a military association, he gave significant support to the system of native education and literature by making grants of land and money for the upkeep of these educational institutions. It is not an overstatement to say that he not only supported the existing institutions but made positive contributions to the field of education, giving grants regardless of religion or caste. English, Hindi and Persian were taught to the royal family. This also confirms that Muslims had equal access to education and educational institutions, as teachers and students. Ranjit Singh gave freedom and opportunity to the whole Muslim population to acquire new skills and knowledge for improving their living standards.

Justice System

One of the pillars of state is its judicial system. Ranjit Singh's system of justice has been criticized because, apparently, it mainly served his financial needs and those of the state. However, I do not totally agree with these allegations.

Judicial and penal systems covering both public and private crimes were largely based on responsibilities and not on rights. Punishments were given in terms of fines, and capital punishment was non-existent. At the public level, custom and tradition served as law. At the central level it was the duty of the ruler and his administration to check numerous groups and ensure social, religious and political harmony. Ranjit Singh strictly followed the customary concept of monarchy as the father and guardian of the people,[220] which was necessary to command their respect. To win their goodwill and trust, justice and fair treatment were essential. Ranjit Singh was keen not only that justice should be provided but also that it should be seen, be free, quick, equity-based and people-oriented (unlike modern times, when the justice system seems so complicated and expensive that a common man cannot benefit from it). G. L. Chopra rightly points out that Ranjit Singh's judicial system appeared very raw and rudimentary, but was feasible and responded well to local needs.[221]

The Punjab had no coded law except the Islamic *Shariah* Laws, which governed the Muslims. All other Punjabis were governed by tradition and custom.[222] The idea of equity in that age and of judicial procedures was basic and straightforward. Town *panchayats* (councils of five elders) heard petty and common cases. Until the introduction of English Coded Laws, the *panchayat* framework worked very well in the Punjab. The *kardar* of *taluqah* (revenue administrative unit) used to recover the fines with the assistance of members of the *panchayat*. Criminal cases were tried in the courts of the *kardar*. In the examination of burglary cases, *khojis* (experts in tracing footprints of criminals) were engaged. There were, however, no systematic procedures for recording evidence, etc.

In fact, there was no specific list of offences or set of punishments and penalties. The fine was the most popular and common mode of punishment, although caning or lashing was sometimes inflicted in addition. For some heinous crimes, in rare cases limbs such as hands, ears or noses were chopped off as punishment. As discussed earlier, capital punishment was banned under Ranjit Singh. This is why he severely reprimanded his governors when, in a few cases, they inflicted the death sentence.[223] The Maharaja and his *darbar* acted as the superior court where decisions of the *kardars* could be contested.[224]

While referring to some primary sources belonging to a Bhandari family in Batala, J. S. Grewal states that during the Sikh period people had the discretion to go either to the *shariah* courts or to decide their matters according to custom. In the towns, matters were in the hands of the *qazi*, but in the countryside they were mostly decided in line with existing custom. There are a number of instances where deeds between Muslim and Muslim, Muslim and non-Muslim, and even non-Muslim and non-Muslim were executed by the *qazis* in the court of Batala.[225] Therefore, the *shariah* courts decided matters for Muslims as well as for non-Muslims,[226] and all the laws introduced by the Muslim *qazis* were applicable to Muslims and non-Muslims.[227] While the laws of *shariah* were supreme in deciding matters for the Muslim community, the Brahmins, Khatries, goldsmiths and Hindus also abided by these courts as much as did the Muslims.[228]

Ranjit Singh was accessible to all and used common sense to redress their complaints on the spot. However, he employed Europeans and other foreigners and made best use of their potential. He tamed the wild energies of the *Akalis* for his own benefit. He kept his people together by his fair treatment. The archives of the Fakir Khana library narrate the story of a Muslim woman from Peshawar who came to the court of the Maharaja for justice as she had been molested by some of his soldiers. The Maharaja listened to her grievance, and then offered her his sword to kill him. The woman refused to do that and insisted he punish the real culprits. An identification parade was held and she recognized the five soldiers, who all begged for forgiveness. However, Ranjit Singh made it clear that only the woman could forgive them, and she remained adamant in avenging her honour. Given that capital punishment was not allowed, she decided that the faces of the offenders should be blackened and they should be paraded through the streets of Lahore. The Maharaja was not satisfied with this punishment and offered to impose the death sentence for this heinous crime. However, the woman was satisfied with his sense of justice and the soldiers were sent to prison for the rest of their lives.[229] This story shows the justice of Ranjit Singh for all communities; in fact, anyone could stop his carriage and ask for justice. In a similar vein, at times he imposed punishment by cutting off a hand, maintaining his belief that punishments should discipline people and not take their lives.[230]

Eventually, Ranjit Singh started taking a greater interest in his judicial system, and was critical of the performance of his judicial officers and their dispensation of justice. In 1828 he appointed Bahadar Singh Hindustani to prepare the Civil and Criminal Code. Prince Sher Singh was also given judicial training.[231]

G. L. Chopra accepts that, considering the social and political state of the nation that he led, Ranjit Singh was most certainly a tolerant and cool-minded ruler.[232] He once reprimanded one of his generals for killing a *koel* (songbird) when she was chattering, and no one was allowed to harm a swan, a parrot or a sparrow.[233]

Regardless of all his power and authority, Ranjit Singh still believed in equality and fairness among all communities. Fakir Syed Waheeduddin cites two directives of Ranjit Singh: first to guarantee equity among individuals, and second to decide the matters of various communities according to their relevant laws.[234]

Despite lacking formal educational training, Ranjit Singh was a sharp statesman and a talented administrator. He guaranteed that the Sikh government was just to all. No final order could be passed without his permission. He kept a complaints box in which any distressed person could make an appeal regarding the administration. The keys of the box always remained with him. He himself held a *durbar* daily to listen to complaints and appeals, and took instant and relevant action accordingly. The administrators, therefore, were scared of these appeals, although they inspired confidence in the general public. He issued orders to bring all the wrong directions or orders of the state officials to his notice, which he would then himself annul or direct the relevant official to modify them. He even authorized Fakir Nuruddin to review the orders of the Maharaja himself, and further directed him to ensure that no highhandedness took place in the kingdom and to supervise fair dispensation of justice and legal rights of the people. He authorized the judges to decide matters according to the relevant laws of *shariah* and the *shastars* (divine order of Hindus) and to report delinquents to enable him to decide accordingly.[235] An extract from the letter in the footnote shows his deep interest in the welfare of his people.[236]

By adopting such a style of government Ranjit Singh had *de facto* made himself and his civil and military bureaucracy answerable to the community. It was his common practice to go into public places to hear the grievances of the people, which brought him closer to the community. There are numerous examples where he reversed the decisions of his administrators. When Avitabile (his French officer) penalized some locals in Peshawar with an inhumane fine and a lashing, he sent General Ventura to ensure the return of Avitabile and make good the losses of the unfortunate locals.[237]

In addition to going around his kingdom to inquire about the condition of the people, Ranjit Singh had an independent spy system to keep an eye on state matters. Above all, he used to ask the opinion of foreign visitors and travellers about the condition of his people and administration – for example, Burnes and Vigne, who travelled to Kashmir in 1836, and Court, who visited Peshawar in 1836 and 1838.[238] W. G. Osborne, a British officer who visited the Lahore *Darbar*, describes it in the following words:

> He (Ranjit Singh) rules with a rod of iron, but in justice to him it must be stated that except in actual warfare he was never been known to take life, though his own life has been attempted more than once and his reign will found free from any striking acts of cruelty and oppression than those of many more civilized monarchs.[239]

Conclusion

Jean-Marie Lafont describes the Maharaja's fairness and unbiased personality in his own words:

> Being questioned as to why he spent Rs.10,000 for a holy book Quran for which he, being a Sikh, had no use, the Maharaja is believed to have replied: God

intended me to look at all religion with one eye, that is why he took away the light from the other.²⁴⁰

Maharaja Ranjit Singh knew well that good relationships with the Hindu and Muslim populations had to be maintained and strengthened to perpetuate his rule in the Punjab. This was not possible without significant freedom to practise their religions and access economic opportunities. The multi-ethnic and multicultural executive and military structure of the state reflected the overall policy of fairness and liberality. This in turn encouraged feelings of belonging and oneness among the population.

Ranjit Singh did not announce Sikhism to be the state religion, nor did he make any conscious endeavours to spread Sikhism. He believed in equity, opportunity and human nobility, not through any characterized proclamations or religious promises or strategy claims but through practical deeds. The most striking feature of the policy of Ranjit Singh was the equal respect shown to all faiths. He did not treat the Sikhs as a privileged class and did not place any barriers in the way of his non-Sikh subjects, nor did he ever interfere with the religious and cultural life of other communities. They were allowed to freely practise their religions without payment of discriminatory tariffs. His policy was free from bigotry or any of the narrowness and racial arrogance inherent in the traditional Hindu system of caste.

Ranjit Singh was well aware of the rights of his subjects. In many of his letters, he ordered Fakir Nuruddin to take special care of his people, stating that whosoever committed a crime or destroyed anyone's house or land should be punished.²⁴¹ Although Western writers describe him as a despot, even they agree that throughout his life he never committed unwarranted cruelty. Certainly, he was not barbarous or bloodthirsty by nature. His humanity was remarkable. He always treated his fallen enemies with kindness. Available evidence in the archives of the Fakir Khana library shows how concerned he was for the rights of his people.

In the process of inter-community cooperation, the sense of co-existence and acceptance adopted by Ranjit Singh played an important role in maintaining peace and harmony in the kingdom. The Maharaja represented the inter-communal partnership that united the people of the Punjab and led to a common Punjabi culture, community and character.

Ranjit Singh always credited God with his success and glory. His life and kingdom can be studied for learning the art of administering people and utilizing their energies. Chief Murray pays the most fitting tribute to the Maharaja when he compares him to Mehmet Ali and Napoleon. Given his level of education, the complex environment and his minority status, his accomplishments stand far ahead of these men's achievements. With his personal traits and qualities that were free from traces of aggression and oppression, he stands on an even higher pedestal.²⁴² Baron Charles Hügel, who visited India during this time, writes:

> Never perhaps was so large an empire founded by one man with so little criminality; when we consider the country and uncivilized people with whom he had to deal, his mild government must be regarded with the feeling of astonishment.²⁴³

His administration was based on humility, simplicity and good governance. Anything that was good for the state was dear to him and he would hardly do anything that could harm it. He kept *Akalis* with him not out of religious association but out of political and military exigencies. His political sagacity and taking on board all shades of opinion enabled him to govern his state with ease, which is why there was hardly any large-scale agitation against his administration.[244]

Being a great administrator, Ranjit Singh was able to maintain peace in most parts of his kingdom. He monitored his governors and administrators through a robust spy system. George Keene, a visitor to the Punjab, reports that he had a calm, safe and happy journey during his visit to the Sikh kingdom. Numerous Muslim individuals from the Cis-Sutlej states moved to the Maharaja's domains where their rights and benefits were better ensured. Even Afghan rulers such as Shah Shuja sought refuge with Ranjit Singh. The Maharaja gave his subjects all the basic rights and fundamental opportunities embedded in any constitution in the modern world.[245]

Chapter 4

SARKAR-E-KHALSA: STATUS AND ROLE OF HINDU, MUSLIM AND EUROPEAN COURTIERS

This chapter throws light on the strength, composition and workings of the *darbar*, and the civil and military administration of Ranjit Singh. As discussed earlier, the Maharaja was a benevolent ruler who cared for his subjects irrespective of their religion, caste or creed. He had a vision to run the state with some rules and regulations and, like Akbar the Great, he believed in broad-based harmony and cooperation among all communities, to create a peaceful and prosperous society. Although an authoritative ruler, he commanded the respect and loyalty of his *darbar*, which comprised nobles and officials from many nationalities and religions: Sikhs, Muslims, Hindus and even Christians.

In the state machinery, the Hindus and Muslims held more of the key positions than did the Sikhs. It has already been established that the Maharaja cared only for the greatness of the state and welfare of the people; his policies were driven by a secular approach and not by a bigoted or myopic religious one. Under Ranjit Singh, the Sikh state practised secularism, which is still uncommon in much of today's world.

Darbar *of Maharaja Ranjit Singh*

The Lahore *Darbar* was the central institution of the Sikh state. Highly personalized, it was a creation of the Maharaja, nominally a devout Sikh, who was clearly the most powerful figure in it. All the state affairs – political, foreign and domestic – were completely subservient to his will. He did not follow the Mughal tradition of sitting on the throne, but held the *darbar* in his own way, sitting on a chair or even, more informally, on the carpet, which some courtiers did not appreciate. He ignored their disapproval, however, and continued the practice. He wore a simple turban, and simple plain silk or cashmere clothes, reserving colourful robes for special occasions. He rarely wore jewellery, although during the visits of foreign dignitaries he wore a string of pearls or diamonds along with the famous Koh-e-Noor diamond on his arm.[1]

Although the Maharaja was indifferent to personal showiness, 'he liked to be surrounded by magnificently robed ministers and fine looking *sardars* majestically accoutered and armed'.[2] Prince Kharak Singh, Sher Singh and Raja Hira Singh[3] were the only persons who had the privilege of sitting on chairs in the *darbar*. The *darbar* itself stood on golden pillars, and expensive Kashmiri carpets covered the entire floor.[4] The court colour was yellow or green and most of the officials wore yellow garments of Kashmiri silk or wool. There was no firm gradation of ranks. In fact, the level of trust placed in him by the Maharaja usually determined the position of a courtier.

His group of the advisors sat on the floor to the right of the Maharaja, headed by Fakir Azizuddin, and the army officials sat on the left with Raja Dhian Singh, the prime minister, at their head.[5]

Composition of the Darbar: Courtiers

Ranjit Singh's courtiers represented various creeds, diverse races and different traditions, comprising Europeans[6] as well as Muslims, Sikhs and Hindus. Fakir Azizuddin, the foreign minister, Nuruddin, the home minister and Ghause Khan and Elahi Bakhsh, military generals, were all Muslims. Dhian Singh Dogra, the prime minister, Gulab Singh Dogra, governor of Jammu, Suchet Singh and Hira Singh who held key posts, Khushhal Singh, the chamberlain, Dina Nath, minister of civil administration, Ganga Ram, Tej Singh and Lal Singh were Brahmin Hindus. Other Hindus were Diwan Mohkam Chand, Moti Ram, Ram Dial, Diwan Bhawani Das, Diwan Devi Das and Diwan Karam Chand.[7] The Sikhs included Lehna Singh, the Sandhianwalay *sardars*, Hari Singh Nalwa and Sham Singh.

The sociopolitical background of the aristocracy of the Lahore *Darbar* was heterogeneous. About one-fifth of the members were subjugated chiefs and their dependent relatives, who were mostly Sikh *misldars*, Rajputs, Afghans and Pathans. Sardar Fateh Singh, Mit Singh Padania, Sardar Attar Singh Dhari, Hukm Singh Attari and Hukma Singh Chimni represented the families of Sikh *misldars*. Other nobility hailed from the families of the Pathan rulers of Kasur, Multan and Jhang.[8]

The Maharaja was a devoted Sikh in theory, known as the Drum of the *Khalsa*,[9] and his government was based on the ideals of the *Khalsa* or 'commonwealth' of Guru Gobind Singh. However, in practice his was a secular government. I take the position that if we closely study the primary and secondary sources of the period, it can be concluded that the Sikh state under the Maharaja was *de jure* a religious but *de facto* a secular one.

Ministers and Executives

The Maharaja's policies of recruitment for civil and military posts were based strictly on merit.[10] His appointments of ministers, generals and administrative officers all reflected his neutrality and merit. Moreover, his dispensation of matters relating to religion also speaks volumes for his secularism. His *darbar* used Persian script, spoke Punjabi and followed the Hindu calendar of Vikramdtya along with the Islamic calendar (AH).[11]

The Sikhs somehow were less engaged in the civil administration of the Sikh state. However, for non-Sikhs, there was no barrier or constraint on any community in joining any state department or walk of life. Personal ability, competence and hard work were the main criteria for selection to the state service. Similarly, state donations were meant for all religious denominations. These facts clearly establish that under Ranjit Singh the nature and character of the Sikh state was secular and neutral. As we have already seen, he himself engaged with all the religious communities of the Punjab. He respected people and tribes for qualities such as bravery, statesmanship, financial acumen and diplomatic skills and not for their religious affiliation.[12]

Given existing military imperatives, the defence industry was an important state enterprise, headed largely by Muslims. Major ordnance factories were set up at Nakodar, Shahdarra, Peshawar, etc. Fakir Nuruddin supervised the workshop at Nakodar and Subha Singh and Jawahir Mal Dogra the factories at Shahdara, while Fakir Nuruddin was in overall charge of the state ordnance factories.[13]

In examining the various departments of Ranjit Singh, it is clear that he always tried to choose the right person for the right job, irrespective of religion. He deliberately chose the Majha Jats for the army for their bravery and fighting skills, and the Hindu Banias for the revenue and secretarial departments for their accounting, documentation and business skills and their experience with the Mughals.[14] Roughly one-fifth of the members of the *Khalsa Darbar* had already served under the Mughals; these were mostly Rajputs and Pathans. Under Ranjit Singh, top-ranking Muslim officers included two ministers, one governor and several district officers, and forty-one senior army positions including two generals and many colonels. About ninety-two Muslims served in the judiciary, police and justice department, remaining loyal to the Sikh state even after his death.[15] This lends support and is evidence of the secular policies of Ranjit Singh, who was always far from establishing a Sikh dictatorship over other religions.[16]

Syeds, qazis, sheikhs, ulemas and *mullahs* constituted the Muslim religious class. With their knowledge of the *fiqh* (Islamic knowledge of laws) and the Quran, they commanded significant respect among the community. The *syeds* and *sheikhs* belonged to the upper sections of Muslim society and were respected for their knowledge of religion and miracles. The *syeds* spread across the Punjab and were also landowners and farmers.[17] The Sikh government granted them many favours and concessions.

Lepel Griffin confirms that Ranjit Singh was a kind ruler who did not believe in hostility.[18] He never preferred one religion to another; instead, he believed in ability and competence as a measure of respect and position. Therefore, he had no special feeling for Sikhs or eternal hatred for non-Sikhs. He simply needed competent people to work for him, whether they were Sikhs, Hindus or Muslims. He did not meddle with their religious beliefs, there were no segregating taxes, and his approach was free from extremism or any sort of restricted viewpoint and the racial pomposity natural in traditional Hinduism.[19]

General Administration

The land revenue system continued under Ranjit Singh as it had been under the Mughals. He was shrewd enough to find the right persons to administer his revenue system, appointing the experienced Hindu Khatris and Brahmins who had already worked as revenue ministers with the Mughals.[20]

Ranjit Singh held supreme authority, personally appointing and guiding his officials in the discharge of their duties. He initially appointed Ramananda from Amritsar and Bhawani Das, who had earlier seen service as revenue officers under Shah Shuja of Afghanistan.[21] Diwan Dena Nath was also appointed to this post. Under their administration, the revenue department improved significantly. Misr Bali Ram was in overall charge of the treasury,[22] while Bhai Ram Singh along with Bhai Govind Ram and Fakir Azizuddin assisted in treasury and diplomatic affairs. Fakir Azizuddin conveyed royal instructions to the state functionaries. The *kardars* looked after the general administrative affairs of state in each district, although matters relating to the military, settlement of the revenue and audit of the accounts were entirely decided by the Maharaja.[23]

The *Khalsa* armed force prepared by the Europeans comprised all religious groups. The cavalry was mainly Sikh, the artillery under General Elahi Bukhsh had a majority of Muslims, and the infantry had a mixture of Dogras, Gurkhas, Sikhs and Muslims. In short, this heterogeneous Punjabi fighting force held Ranjit Singh in high regard as their commander and as an individual.[24]

For any ruler to command respect and love, fair and benevolent treatment of his subjects seems imperative. In this sphere, and in comparison with his contemporaries, Ranjit Singh excelled.[25] He ensured good administration of justice, and regular courts were held throughout the state, providing fairness to all communities, whatever their religion. The justice system was based on the lines of the Mughal courts. The old *muhallah dari* system was reintroduced, whereby an influential person in a *muhallah* (locality) was responsible for resolving petty matters between people. Imam Bukhsh had custody of the office of the *kotwal* and Sadullah Chishti was his representative.[26]

Hindu Courtiers and Officials

A substantial number of Hindus served in the administrations of the Maharaja and his successors. They were mostly Brahmins and Khatris, with some Rajputs, Gurkhas and Purbias. Khatri officers included Diwan Mohkam Chand, his son Moti Ram and grandsons Ram Dayal and Kirpa Ram, Diwan Bhawani Das and his brother Diwan Devi Das, Diwan Swan Mal and Diwan Karam Chand. The Brahmins included Diwan Ganga Ram, Diwan Dina Nath, Diwan Ajudhia Prasad, Misr Diwan Chand, Misr Beli Ram and his sibling Misr Rup Lal. Brahmins held high and strategic positions, especially in the army, where they were war strategists and commanders. Some of them also served as governors and administrators. A number of other Hindus held senior positions in the Lahore *Darbar*, many of whom had been immigrants who faced discrimination and repression in their own states as commoners. They were welcomed for their talent and offered positions worthy of their skills and experience. Diwan Mohkam Chand had escaped from the persecution of Sahib Singh Bhangi of Gujrat. Diwan Ganga Ram and Diwan Bhawani Das took refuge in Lahore after escaping from the oppression of their rulers. Similarly the Misr brothers, Diwan Swan Mal and Misr Diwan Chand, belonged to humble families. Diwan Bhawani Das, Diwan Ganga Ram, Diwan Dina Nath and Beli Ram headed the revenue and finance branches of the state of Lahore. Diwan Mohkam Chand, Misr Diwan Chand and Ram Dyal occupied top military offices. Diwan Swan Mal, Diwan Moti Ram and Misr Rup Lal also served as provincial governors.[27]

Diwan Mohkam Chand

Diwan Mohkam Chand was one of the most famous courtiers of the Maharaja, a Hindu nobleman who had risen from a non-military background to become general and military commander. He was born into a Kochhar Khatri family; his father, Baisakhi Mal was a well-known merchant in Kunjah (Gujrat).[28] Before joining the Maharaja's court and service, he had worked as a *munshi* (accountant) under Dal Singh Gill of Akalgarh until the latter's death in 1804.[29] Sehju, the widow of Dal Singh, did not like Mohkam Chand. She requested him to examine the accounts of Dal Singh's properties but he did not like this task and left. Subsequently he sought employment with Sardar Sahib Singh Bhangi of Gujrat, who appointed him as Diwan.[30] However, after a few years, Mohkam Chand lost the trust of Sahib Singh and was imprisoned.[31] Sahib Singh Bhangi ordered his execution, but Mohkam Chand managed to escape with the help of the ruler's wife, Chand Kaur.[32] He entered Ranjit Singh's service in 1806, and his hard work and dedication won his trust.[33] Rising to the rank of general, Mohkam Chand proved himself to be a great tactician who won many battles and territories for the Maharaja.[34]

From 1806 to 1814 Mohkam Chand was not only responsible for all the key conquests of the Maharaja; he was also a loyal friend of the ruler and his closest aide. The Maharaja had the greatest regard for his military skills and in 1812 bestowed upon him the title of Diwan and Fateh Nasib.[35]

Diwan Mohkam Chand was an able and strong administrator, whom the Maharaja regularly consulted on various state affairs. On the occasion of Metcalf's visit to Lahore in September 1808, he assigned Mohkam Chand along with Fateh Singh Ahluwalia to receive the English envoy at Kasur.[36] Historians report an interesting conversation between Charles Metcalf and Mohkam Chand: the latter commented that the British had not seen Sikh bravery on the battlefield, to which Metcalf readily responded that the Sikh had not yet seen British courage.[37] The Maharaja was left to diplomatically handle this confrontation. During 1808 and 1809, Ranjit Singh had to decide whether to wage war with the Cis-Sutlej states or maintain peace with them. With the shrewd advice of Diwan Mohkam Chand, he devised a smart two-pronged strategy: while Mohkam Chand prepared for war, the Maharaja initiated peace talks. However, Mohkam Chand was not in favour of the agreement between the British and the Cis-Sutlej Sikhs.

When Mehtab Kaur, wife of the Maharaja, died, Ranjit Singh was in Amritsar. Owing to disagreements with his mother-in-law he decided not to attend the funeral, but it was Mohkam Chand who persuaded him that he should.[38]

Diwan Mohkam Chand died in Phillaur and was buried in a garden there.[39] He had been the owner of a *jagir* worth Rs.642,161 a year.[40] He left behind an able and renowned son, Diwan Moti Ram, and grandsons Diwan Kirpa Ram and Diwan Ram Dyal, who also served the Sikh state in high positions. In August 1831, when Captain Wade visited Lahore, the Maharaja shared with him his good memories of the loyalty and talent of Mohkam Chand.[41] Two years later he commented: 'Today I am remembering the intellect, conviction and gentlemanly confirmations of Diwan Mohkam Chand.'[42] Murray sums up the personality of Diwan Mohkam Chand: 'The Diwan was liberal, upright, and high-minded. He enjoyed the confidence of the troops placed under his command and was popular and much respected amongst the entire Sikh community.'[43]

Diwan Moti Ram

Diwan Moti Ram was the only son of Diwan Mohkam Chand; whenever the Maharaja assigned Mohkam Chand a special task away,[44] Moti Ram looked after the *doab* (the territory between the Sutlej and Beas).[45] He was a man of amazing capacity. After his father's demise he succeeded to his *jagirs*, and the title of Diwan was also bestowed upon him.[46] He participated in the final battle of Multan in 1818.[47] The Maharaja appointed him as the first governor of Kashmir, and he served twice from 1819 to 1826.[48] However, he was called back for his repressive policies against the Kashmiris and reprimanded by the Maharaja, despite his standing, when the welfare of the people of Kashmir, predominantly Muslim, was at stake. Nevertheless, he was among the most regarded and capable officers of Ranjit Singh, as well as an intelligent and effective administrator and politician.

Ranjit Singh sent Diwan Moti Ram on many political missions. In 1826, when Lord Amherst visited Shimla, Diwan Moti Ram along with Fakir Imamuddin and Vakil Ram Dayal went there to receive him on behalf of the Maharaja.[49] He was also a member of the delegation that called on Lord William Bentinck at Simla.[50] In December 1831, the Maharaja granted him the areas of Kunjah, Haveli, Kabula, Pakka Sudda and Pakpatton Sharif.[51]

Unlike his father, Moti Ram could not retain the trust of the Maharaja, and gradually lost his sway and the influence of his family, even having his *jagirs* confiscated. Dejected and humiliated, he went to Banaras and died there in 1837.[52] Ranjit Singh had nevertheless had great regard for the Diwan and once commented that although he was not like his father, yet he was superior to others.[53]

Diwan Kirpa Ram

Diwan Kirpa Ram was the younger son of Diwan Moti Ram. He held various appointments including governor, *nazim*, *diwan* and administrator.[54] He led the *Khalsa* army on many battlefields, showing great strength in the battle of Mankera along with Misr Diwan Chand.[55] In 1823, he defeated the Afghan army led by Muhammad Azim Khan of Kabul at the battle of Naushehra.[56]

Despite his military success, Diwan Kirpa Ram was better known as an able administrator and governor. He remained *nazim* of the Jalandhar *doab* when his father, Diwan Moti Ram was governing Kashmir.[57] The Maharaja appointed him governor of Kashmir in 1826 and he ruled the province better than his father.[58]

When Diwan Moti Ram lost favour with the Maharaja, Kirpa Ram asked to be allowed to join his father in Banaras, but his request was not granted. Greatly humiliated, in December 1834 he went to Jawala Mukhi, managing to cross to the British region over the Sutlej and join his father at Banaras.[59]

Misr Diwan Chand

Misr Diwan Chand was another of Ranjit Singh's ministers. A Brahmin from Gondlanwala town in Gujranwala district,[60] he rose to the rank of chief of the *Khalsa* ordnance and army. He had previously worked as *munshi* under Nakai chief Nodh Singh in Modikhana. Nodh Singh reprimanded Diwan Chand for not being able to properly account for Rs.90, making him stand in the sun with a musket on his shoulder. This incident reached the ears of the Maharaja, who paid the missing amount and had him released.[61] Ranjit Singh then included him in his administration, initially deputing him to the *topkhana* (arsenal) of Mian Muhammad Ghause Khan in 1812.[62] At that time, he was still in his teens.[63]

Diwan Chand was a dedicated and hard worker who performed his duties diligently. Through his sheer hard work and loyalty, he was appointed as *naib* (deputy) in charge of weaponry. In 1814, after the demise of Mian Ghause Khan, he was made head of the *topkhana*.[64] The Maharaja remained dependent on him for various military victories, and he is famous for his role in the conquests of Multan and Kashmir.

Following the advice of Ali-ud-Din Mufti, the Maharaja ordered a review of the revenue records and income of the farmers of different regions, and a huge amount was reported to be outstanding against the farmers. The farmers asked Misr to speak to the Maharaja on their behalf, requesting exemption. While the Maharaja admired Misr's kindness, he advised him to be vigilant in case it should cause loss to the state exchequer. This incident disheartened him[65] and he died on 19 July 1825 after two days' sickness.[66]

The Maharaja had an extraordinary regard for Misr because of his contribution to consolidating and developing the Sikh state. Once he gave him a costly *hukkah* (Indian traditional smoking apparatus) and granted permission to smoke in his presence.[67] On his demise, the Maharaja was deeply upset, and said that Misr had been an extraordinary individual of his times with no match to his loyalty.[68] Misr died a rich man with Rs.11 *lakh* in cash, and precious pearls, jewellery and other valuables.[69] He was a talented general, a brilliant chief and a dedicated worker. His younger brother Sukhdial succeeded him after his death.

Diwan Dina Nath

Dina Nath, a civil officer and advisor to the Maharaja, wielded immense influence at the Sikh court for well over three decades. Shahamat Ali observed: 'He was a shrewd, sensible man and possessed great statistical and financial information regarding every part of the Punjab.'[70] He was originally from Kashmir, and during Shah Jehan's rule some members of his family had held good positions at the imperial court.[71] His father Bakhat Mal had served under Perron, the Maratha Deputy at Delhi.[72]

Diwan Ganga Ram was a close relative of Dina Nath and head of the state office at Lahore. He invited Dina Nath to Lahore and attached him to the state office in 1815, where he worked with great enthusiasm and dedication and soon attracted the attention of the Maharaja, especially for his excellent arrangements for rewarding heroes of the battle of Multan.[73] He also reorganized all the land records of Multan, which the first *nazim*, Sukh Dayal, had let fall into chaos.[74]

With his sheer talent and political acumen, Dina Nath soon rose to the heights of success and influence in the state's affairs. Following the death of Diwan Ganga Ram in 1826, he took over as administrator of the royal seal and head of the military records division. He also assumed the responsibilities of head of the finance office after the death of Diwan Bhawani Das in 1834.[75]

In addition to all these portfolios, he headed twelve other offices of general and military business of the Lahore *Darbar*. Indeed, he was among the most influential ministers of the Maharaja who, in 1838 bestowed on him the title of Diwan. Ranjit Singh relied on his advice and always consulted him on important state matters. Shahamat Ali reports that Dina Nath received Rs.20 a day as remuneration for his services. He also had a *jagir* of Rs.6,000 and enjoyed several other benefits which accompanied his positions, especially in Kashmir and Multan.[76] He also had *jagirs* worth Rs.9,900 in Amritsar, Dinanagar and Kasur districts.[77]

Later, during the rule of Maharajas Kharak Singh and Sher Singh, Diwan Dina Nath remained neutral.[78] During the fight between Mai Chand Kaur and Kunwar Sher Singh, he sided with neither.[79] He retained his influence even under Hira Singh, who became the prime minister of Dilip Singh, the last Maharaja of the Sikh state, who trusted *pandit* Jalla, a political rival of Diwan Dina Nath. Even the strained relationship between Gulab Singh and Hira Singh could not weaken his powerful position in the *Khalsa* state.[80]

Dina Nath founded and led the *mutsaddi* group.[81] He was also one of the trusted persons of Rani Jindan, with whom he had many similarities. Both stood firm against the rigours of time and successfully passed through them.[82]

Diwan Dina Nath also witnessed the treaty between the Sikhs and the British following the first Anglo–Sikh War in 1846.[83] He played an important role in the

Council of Regency and in 1847 was given the title Raja of Kalanaur with a *jagir* worth Rs.2,000 annually for his services to the Regency Council.[84] His shrewdness also won him the trust of the British. Therefore, after the fall of the Punjab, Raja Dina Nath retained all his *jagirs*. His eldest son, Amaranth, was granted a *jagir* worth Rs.4,000 annually during the lifetime of his father. After the death of Amaranth, all his wealth descended to his heirs forever, in line with the principle of primogeniture.[85]

In discussions with the British, he communicated with confidence, which was rare among his fellows.[86] Griffin portrays Dina Nath as

> The Talleyrand of the Punjab and his life and character bear a strong resemblance to those of the European statesman. Revolutions, in which his friends and patrons perished, passed him by; dynasties rose and fell, but never involved him in their ruin; in the midst of turmoil when confiscation and judicial robbery were the rule of the state, his wealth and power continually increased. His sagacity and farsightedness were such that when, to other eyes, the political sky was clear he could perceive the coming storm, which warned him to desert a losing party or a falling friend.[87]

Misr Beli Ram

Misr Beli Ram was a Brahmin who hailed from Kahan village near Kitas in Jhelum.[88] His father, Misr Diwan Chand (see above) came to Lahore with his family in 1809. Misr Beli Ram and his four brothers, Rup Lal, Ram Kishan, Megh Raj and Sukh Raj, were employed in the *darbar* of Ranjit Singh. In fact, when Misr Beli Ram joined the Sikh administration, he was only 11 years old, and helped his uncle Basti Ram in the treasury. Despite opposition from the Dogra brothers and Dhian Singh,[89] he succeeded his uncle after his death in 1816, aged 19.[90]

The Maharaja had given an elephant, a *doshala* (shawl) and a sword to Misr Rup Lal, Beli Ram's brother, and this was the reason for the dispute.[91] Misr Beli Ram served Ranjit Singh with great dedication and received a *jagir* of Rs.60,000 and agricultural land worth Rs.200,000 income annually. He remained in possession of this *jagir* until after the death of the Maharaja.[92]

European Officers

The Lahore *Darbar* had a number of French and other foreign notables and officers. However, not much is known about their role in shaping the foreign policy of the Lahore *Darbar*. The following paragraphs examine how influential were they at the court of the Maharaja? How well were they paid? Were they allowed to carry out private business? Most importantly, how and what did they think about Ranjit Singh?[93]

Ranjit Singh was worried about the expanding power of the British in the Indian subcontinent. He was aware of the fact that only a trained army could stop their growing influence, and so he began to employ European officers to train his army. The *Fauj-e-Khas* was a model unit trained under their command. Many Europeans served in the army of the Punjab, the most famous being Generals Jean-François Allard, Jean-Baptiste Ventura, Paolo Di Avitabile and Claude August Court.

Ventura, Italian by birth, and Allard, French, came to Lahore in 1822 to seek employment in the Sikh army. Both had served under Napoleon in the imperial army of France, losing their positions after Napoleon's defeat at Waterloo and now, in fact, political exiles. Ventura had been the bodyguard of Prince Eugene and had fought alongside Napoleon in Russia. Allard had fought in Italy, France and Spain during the Napoleonic campaigns of 1814 and 1815.[94] After the fall of Napoleon, Allard had planned to go to America, but on the advice of Ventura they set off for Egypt. Diverted by an outbreak of plague, they went instead to Constantinople and finally reached Iran, where they were employed by Shah Abbas to train his army.[95]

However, due to the political pressure of the British officers in Iran, they had to leave that country in 1821, reaching the Punjab and the court of Ranjit Singh in March 1822.[96] In fact, they had already heard about the Maharaja of the Punjab and his wisdom. Being a cautious ruler, Ranjit Singh carefully probed the antecedents of the two European generals before admitting them to the Sikh army,[97] and it took some time and the facilitation of Fakir Azizuddin before both the generals were hired.[98] On the advice of Fakir Azizuddin, the generals wrote to the Maharaja himself, asking for employment in training the *Khalsa* army, and it was this letter that ended the doubts of the Sikh ruler.[99] Both generals served him well and contributed significantly to the Sikh army.

By the time the European generals joined the Sikh army, Ranjit Singh had already annexed most of the territories in the Punjab, so some members of the Lahore *Darbar* thought their appointment unnecessary. On the contrary, the two officers improved the skills and performance of the Sikh army. The Maharaja was a man of vision, who recognized that conquering a territory was easier than governing and controlling it. Caught between the two Muslim states of Afghanistan and Sindh, and the British, he wanted to have a strong army.

Ranjit Singh was already much impressed by George Thomas,[100] who had defeated a large Malwa Sikh army with only a small number of men, and by a similarly small number of trained soldiers who had defeated the *Akali* assailants at a Muharram procession.[101] All these incidents were in his mind when he hired the European generals in 1822 to train his troops. Their salaries were not determined until he was satisfied with their performance. The Sikh army had to undergo such rigorous training that some soldiers left altogether.[102] Three months after joining the imperial service, the generals arranged a parade of the four companies of cavalry trained by Allard and four battalions of infantry trained by Ventura. The Maharaja was very pleased to see the discipline of his army and decided to create the *Fauj-e-Khas* or the French legion. This army proved their worth until 1846, when they surrendered to the British.[103]

Ranjit Singh especially respected Allard for his vast experience in Europe, and he sought his advice on many matters. When the number of European officers in civil and military administration was increased, Allard was considered as the senior, helping to settle many affairs of state.[104] Both Allard and Ventura started their service with the monthly pay of Rs.500, but soon their salaries were increased by the granting of *jagirs*. Ventura's troops were the best-trained in the *Fauj-e-Khas*, and in 1832 he was appointed governor of the Derajat and promoted to the rank of general along with six Indian officers. He married an Armenian Jewish lady in 1825 at Ludhiana, and they had a daughter. He went on leave to France in 1837, but returned on the illness of the Maharaja and was sent to Peshawar to join the British forces to help Shah Shuja.[105] Captain Wade, a British agent in the Punjab, once commented that Ventura was the only man who had a firm control over the Sikh soldiers,[106] but despite his strong personality his men were not ready to fight in alliance with the British army. He left the Sikh army after the death of Sher Singh and returned to France, where he died in 1858.[107]

The British Archives hold two important reports revealing the state of affairs in the Sikh state. Dr Murray, although apparently sent to Lahore to treat the Maharaja, was instructed by the British to send back details of the military training and its strength. He attended several parades of regular infantry and was surprised by the precision of the firing. On another occasion, he observed the parade of Ventura's battalions, and the discipline of the Sikh army surprised him greatly.[108] Consequently, he reported the superiority and the style of the Punjabi army.[109] Dr Murray's reports were highly informative for the British, although he had only met Ventura for fifteen minutes in the presence of Maharaja Ranjit Singh. He never met General Allard, but communicated with him through letters. The British government pressurized Dr Murray to get more information regarding the military preparedness of the Punjab, recognizing that the *Khalsa* army was as good in terms of military training as were the British troops.[110] The effort put into training the Sikh army[111] greatly worried the British envoy at Ranjit Singh's court.[112]

Allard and Ventura worked hard with the Sikh army and infused great discipline and skill into it, although these did not come very easily. The army went through a rigorous training programme before becoming *Fauj-e-Khas*, making the generals unpopular. The most serious incident occurred in 1826 when Ventura and Allard faced a serious mutiny, which almost claimed their lives. Ranjit Singh acted swiftly and with his typical political sagacity. He camped at Anarkali with his own bodyguards, arrested the ringleaders of the rising and amicably negotiated the whole matter.[113] Such a firm and quick response was a stern warning to the opponents of the officers, and it also increased the confidence of the officers themselves. Nevertheless, the Maharaja would never agree to their demand for enforcement of the death penalty for serious offences in the army.[114] These developments strengthened the position of the European officers in the eyes of their soldiers, and the Sikh army never again revolted against them.

Jacquemont reported strong bonds between the Sikh soldiers and the European officers, although he attributes this to the fact that the soldiers' promotion depended on the goodwill of Ventura and Allard. Interestingly, both of them were particularly kind to the Muslim soldiers and officers, who held many key positions in the artillery. In fact, from an early period the Muslims were the first to employ firearms, cannons and hand grenades in their conquest of the subcontinent, and they maintained their superiority in this field.[115] Sultan Mahmood and Elahi Bukhsh were famous generals of artillery under Ranjit Singh. The *Fauj-e-Khas* and Allard's cavalry also counted many Muslims in their ranks.[116] In 1839, part of the Muslim Punjabi contingent from the French brigades assembled at Peshawar to capture Kabul, commanded by Sheikh Basawan of the *Fauj-e-Khas*.[117] As stated earlier, the famous Sonehri Mosque was given back to the Muslims at the request of General Allard and its beautiful domes were recoloured with his donation.[118]

The *Akalis* were always a trouble to the Maharaja, especially during festivals. They crossed the border and spread anarchy on both sides of the river Sutlej, and Captains Murray and Wade, British envoys to the Lahore *Darbar*, never lost a chance to create tension between the Sikhs and the British over even small incidents. Ranjit Singh was always concerned about handling the *Akalis* and maintaining law and order in these areas. In 1824, Murray again advised his government to protest about the mischief of the *Akalis*. This time, the Maharaja responded swiftly and sent troops to Phillaur. The unexpected entry of the *Fauj-e-Khas* impressed the people on both sides.[119] Allard provided Jacquemont with an escort of Muslim horsemen on his way to Kashmir. These horsemen were well trained by the European officers and were capable of taking on the fanatic *Akalis*.[120]

The main campaigns of the *Fauj-e-Khas* included the battles of Naushehra, Dera Ismail Khan, Kangra and Peshawar. In 1829 they advanced from Lahore to Attock to stop the followers of Syed Ahmad from crossing the Indus; Allard's strategy prevented Syed Ahmad from entering the Punjab to call the Punjabi Muslims to *jihad*. General Court and his forces played an important role in the annexation of Peshawar. Again in 1837, these troops stopped Dost Muhammad Khan's *jihad* – an attempt to seize Peshawar for Afghanistan. The *Fauj-e-Khas* actively participated in the conquest of Kulu and Mandi in 1841.[121] In fact, trained by the European officers, the *Fauj-e-Khas* never lost a battle in twenty-three years.[122]

Within a short period of time, Ranjit Singh completely transformed an unruly crowd of looters and guerilla warriors, crying *maro, waddo, lutto*,[123] into a well-organized army. However, this was only possible because of the efforts of the European generals.[124]

Although the European officers were very close to Ranjit Singh, even their positions were not permanent and their pay and position totally depended on their performance and the pleasure of the Maharaja.[125] Strangely, he never allowed them to go on leave, expecting them to consider the Punjab as their home. Those who wanted to leave had to resign, although they were rehired if they returned within a reasonable time. Paid leave was granted only in very special and rare cases.[126]

Allard had been away from France for many years, and he requested leave of a few months. The Maharaja was reluctant to let him go and sent Jamadar Khushhal and Bhai Gurmukh to prevent him returning to France, although he was finally forced to grant him leave on half pay.[127] Allard was received in France with great honour and was invited to dinner by King Louis Philippe, who appointed him ambassador of France to the Punjab. He returned with many expensive gifts for the Maharaja, who was very pleased to take him back. Allard died in 1839 and was buried in Lahore with military honour.[128]

Ranjit Singh was enthusiastic about modern technology and scientific inventions. Once he heard about a steamboat and asked Ventura to build one for him, sanctioning Rs.40,000 for this purpose; Ventura spent less than Rs.2,000 and the rest was given to him as a reward.[129] One day he asked Ventura if he could make anything to keep water cool without ice in summer. Ventura constructed a well during winter, filled it with water from a nearby stream, and closed the mouth of the well with an airtight seal. When it was opened in the hot season, the water was still cool.[130]

In 1827, two more Europeans entered the service of the Maharaja: Court and Avitabile.[131] Court had been an infantry officer in Napoleon's army. After leaving France, he joined the Iranian forces of Shah Mirza Muhammad Ali, but left for the Punjab in the company of the Italian Avitabile. They were well received by the Maharaja.[132]

Court was appointed ordnance officer of the *Khalsa* army. He supervised the manufacture of guns at the Shahdarra and Lahore foundries.[133] In 1827, he redesigned the cannon department into three wings.[134] Pleased with his services, the Maharaja increased his salary to Rs.25,000 a year and in 1836 promoted him to general. Hennery Lawrence considered him to be the most respectable of all the French officers.[135] He was present at the Peshawar campaign, where his timely help saved the Sikh army from humiliation. His main work was organization of the artillery and the manufacture of cannons, which seriously damaged the British forces during the Anglo–Sikh wars.[136]

Court taught the *Khalsa* army how to use iron to make the cannon ammunition shells, as the Sikhs had only used brass. The Maharaja rewarded Court with Rs.30,000 when the Sikh artillery exploded its first iron shell. Despite the immense respect of his soldiers, he never mixed with them.[137] After the death of Ranjit Singh his brigade turned against him, but his life was saved with the help of General Ventura. He resigned from the army, but when Sher Singh became the ruler of Lahore, he invited him to resume his duties in Peshawar. Again the hostility of the army forced him to leave and he settled in Grasse with his Kashmiri wife, where he died in 1861.[138]

Among the European officers, the career of Avitabile was the most audacious and complex. After several voyages and a journey through Turkey he entered the service of the Shah of Iran. After five years he left the Shah and returned to Naples, but soon tired of the gentleman's life and decided to go to India. He had heard that his former companion Ventura had a very good life at the court of Ranjit Singh and wrote asking for a post in the Lahore *Darbar*. Avitabile arrived in Lahore with many gifts for the Maharaja, along with Court. Both were taken into the *Khalsa* army in 1827.[139] He was appointed at Rs.700 salary a month, which was increased to Rs.12,000 and later Rs.50,000 a year.

Avitabile, who had been taken on at the recommendation of General Ventura, soon came to the notice of the Maharaja for his administrative qualities, and he was made governor of Wazirabad and Peshawar. Renowned for his vociferous barking while training his platoons, Avitabile used a seal depicting a dog on a letter he sent to the Maharaja. This created much hilarity in the *darbar*, and Jamadar

Khushal Singh said that in training the units he had turned into a dog, for he followed them shrieking like this creature. However, his severe punishments for disobedience were less popular at court and he was the most carefully watched European officer.[140] He was relieved from service in 1843 and returned to Naples, where his wife poisoned him to death.

The Lahore *Darbar* kept the Europeans under strict control and encouraged them to marry and settle in the Punjab, wearing turbans and beards like the Sikhs and not eating beef or smoking in public.[141] This is the reason that Allard, Ventura and Court married Punjabi girls and settled down after leaving France.

The civil, military, foreign, judicial and educational services of the *darbar* were not strictly delineated. Although the primary duty of the European officers was the military training of the army, the nature of the *darbar* did not permit them to confine their work to this sphere. There were many incidents of military officers being given administrative duties, especially in problem areas such as the borders with Kashmir and Peshawar. In fact, they had significant influence in political affairs, without restriction during the lifetime of Ranjit Singh. On their side they gave him their complete loyalty. Allard, who was the most senior, had great regard and admiration for the Maharaja, and with the passage of time the friendship between them developed, as can be seen from their private correspondence and the public and private reports of the general on his visit to Paris. Ranjit Singh's reluctance to let him leave the Punjab has been mentioned above.[142]

As soon as both Allard and Ventura had joined Ranjit Singh, they were given a number of duties. Wade wrote a letter to the British government in 1823 describing the influence of these two officers.

> The French gentlemen possess at this moment a degree of influence with the Raja to which none else can pretend. The Raja listens no one's advice in opposition to them. If fines and penalties are to be levied from any of the courtiers, the farmers of the revenues, or *jagirdars*, the French officers are entrusted with their execution and levy the money. All the officers of the court declare that French men have brought some spell on the Maharaja for whatever they suggest is immediately adopted.[143]

There were many reasons why Ranjit Singh had such confidence in them, not least being his strong belief in their ability and their loyalty. Another reason may be that these officers had no personal interests or family in the Punjab, depending solely on the Maharaja for their positions.

A number of incidents are related in the *Umdat-ut-Tawarikh* concerning their duties, which they fulfilled responsibly. In 1832, Ventura was given orders to arrest Asad Khan, and he effectively secured his obedience. In 1833, Diwan Waisakha Singh was ordered to pay Rs.5 *lakh* but only managed Rs.211,000; he was released on the surety of General Allard, who paid the balance without delay. In October 1833, Ventura successfully seized the whole state of Jawala Singh, and on 31 December 1835, he again had to manage the land of the Garjakhia in the district of Lahore, worth Rs.21,000.[144]

These actions were not always easy for these officers, and they sometimes shrewdly used their own judgement in obeying instructions. For example, when Allard in 1834 was again sent to extract Rs.100,000 from Waisakha Singh, he first asked what job would be given to the Diwan. The Maharaja assured Allard that when the money was received he would give him a post.[145] In the same year, when Avitabile was ordered to confiscate the estates of the chiefs of Jasrota, he asked to be allowed to bring them before the Maharaja; only then would he carry out whatever orders were given to him.[146] These examples demonstrated Ranjit Singh's trust in the officers, whom he sent to confiscate territories, carry out administrative tasks and collect the arrears from persons who owed him money.

Other casual duties were also given to them, such as solving a dispute between *zamindars*. In 1838 Ranjit Singh had to interfere in a matter between the *zamindars* Munj Kakra and Taj Singh, and he sent General Court to solve the problem, who decided the matter in favour of Taj Singh. Some months later, travelling through these areas, the Maharaja was stopped by the *zamindars*, who complained that Court had been unjust. The Maharaja refused to blame General Court, saying that he was impartial because he was a stranger at that time to both parties.[147] The officers also solved a dispute between Lehna Singh Majithia and Misr Rup Lal.[148] Such incidents were common because of political manoeuvring; however, the European officers were disinterested in such disputes, as they had no political affiliation with the Punjab. Ventura was even appointed as a *qazi* and governor of Lahore in 1837. Hügel described his influence at court as the third place in the Lahore *Darbar*.[149] The Maharaja had complete confidence in the diplomatic intelligence of his European officers.

In addition to the good salaries paid to these officers (see above), they were given extra allowances for their special duties, including expensive shawls, pashminas and robes of honour. In *Umdat-ut-Tawarikh* a number of instances are given of the distribution of large or small amounts – for example, Allard was awarded Rs.50,000 and shawls worth Rs.30,000 when he left Lahore for another posting. Ventura was given Rs.5,000 for his recovery of arrears and treatment of Ludhiana. Both took leave in Europe on half pay and they were also granted *jagirs*, wells and land for their services.[150]

In summary, Ranjit Singh had realized that he could not fight the trained army of the British, whose secret of success was good organization and training on modern Western lines. If he wanted to be anything more than a minor ruler, he must establish a strong army, for which he hired European officers. In addition to training his army in the Western style, these officers also contributed to the security of his state by helping to bring about the treaty with the British under which they agreed not to cross the Sutlej.[151]

Muslim Courtiers and Officials

The Muslim clergy continued to enjoy a position of privilege and power. Not long after the control of Lahore in 1799, Muslim judges were appointed to hear Muslim civil and common cases. In the Lahore *Darbar*, *qazi* Nizam-ud-Din was designated as religious head of the Muslims, with full power in religious matters.[152] Ranjit Singh appointed Muslim *qazis* and *muftis* (religious scholars) to dispense justice: *qazi* Nizam-ud-Din to decide on disputes relating to marriage and divorce,[153] and *muftis* Muhammad Shahpuri and Sadullah Chishti to decide on matters relating to property and deeds. Common cases such as home loans, deals and contracts became the responsibility of *mufti* Muhammad Shah. Many Muslims were appointed as *kotwal* or police officers.[154] Ranjit Singh would mostly assign Muslim officers to guard the borders of the Punjab. Every foreigner entering Punjabi territory would require permission from these officers.[155]

As described earlier, Muslims held many key positions in the administration of Ranjit Singh as ministers, governor, judicial and police officers, generals and foreign diplomats. These individuals remained loyal to his successors after the demise of Ranjit Singh.[156]

Fakir Brothers

The famous brothers in the *darbar*, Fakir Syed Azizuddin, Fakir Syed Nuruddin and Fakir Syed Imamuddin, had deep and close connections with the Maharaja, occupying respectively the posts of foreign minister, home minister, and the Maharaja's physician, as well as various other important positions at different times.[157] These three brothers helped Ranjit Singh to establish his kingdom on sound foundations, and they remained with him until the last day of his life. They were among his chief counsellors and assistants, not only in public but also behind the scenes. They have left valuable versions not only of the activities in and around the court but also of the day-to-day life of Ranjit Singh and his court.

Jacquemont wrote about them:

> Among his most intimate councillors are three Muhammadan brothers, who conceal their wealth under an outward appearance of poverty and seek to atone for their intrusion by the humility of their behavior. All of them bear the title of 'Fakir', as do their sons. They know Arabic and have read the medical books in that language, hence their reputation for deep scientific knowledge. The eldest, whom I met near Amritsar, is more or less the minister for foreign affairs; it is he who writes all the dispatches from Ranjit to the British government. Another is the trusted agent at Govind Garh. The third, whom I meet every day, is sometimes appointed governor of the city, when Ranjit does not take him away with him. These brothers have a cipher, which they use in correspondence among themselves and this artifice, hitherto, I believe, unknown in the East, gives them a reputation for great cleverness.[158]

The family traced its origin from a famous holy man, Jalaluddin. It is written in the records of the Fakir family that he converted Halaku Khan to Islam, married one of his daughters and travelled to the Punjab.[159] Because they were residents of

Bukhara the family was called Bukhari, but from the time of Ranjit Singh assumed the title of Fakir because of their humility. It is narrated in the diaries of the Fakir Khana family that one day the Maharaja, who used to address Azizuddin by the name Shah Ji (it is still the practice to call *syeds* Shah), was so pleased with the services of the brothers that he told him he wanted to give them a name which would remain forever with the family. On the suggestion of Azizuddin he gave them the name Fakir, along with the gift of two prestigious shawls.[160]

Fakir Azizuddin was a physician, linguist, ambassador and foreign minister at the court of Ranjit Singh. He was a Muslim, one of numerous non-Sikhs, at the secular court.[161] It was as a physician that he first met the Maharaja, who was inspired by his medical expertise and facility with languages (Arabic, Persian and English) to grant him a *jagir* and a position at court. He never lost the regard and confidence of Ranjit Singh, who rarely took a decision without consulting him. It was through his wise advice that the Maharaja was well disposed to the British, on the basis of fairness and equality. In 1808, when British troops moved to the river Sutlej, intending to push him north of the river, the Maharaja was angry enough to fight; however, Azizuddin, with extraordinary negotiating skill, discouraged him from this risky course, and skilfully directed the two forces towards a kinship which withstood numerous tests and which demonstrated his own worth to his ruler. His negotiations with the British culminated in the agreement of Amritsar in 1809, and in 1820 he held talks on behalf of the Sikh ruler with David Ochterloney. Before long the British understood that they were confronting a man who could negotiate smoothly in seven languages, including English and French. From 1810 until 1838 he was given a great number of diplomatic assignments and tasks as a translator.[162] Illustrating Ranjit Singh's trust in him, it is written in the handwritten diaries of the Fakir family that the Maharaja promised him that whenever he conquered a territory, he would receive a *jagir* from that territory.[163]

Fakir Azizuddin reflected his admiration of his ruler when, on meeting the British Governor-General George Eden, first Earl of Auckland, he was asked which one of the Maharaja's eyes was missing. Fakir Azizuddin replied: 'Maharaja is similar to the sun and the sun has only one eye. The grandeur of his face is such that I have never been able to look close enough to discover.'[164]

Fakir Azizuddin proved especially skilled in dealing with the arrogant Afghans, who continued to cause problems. In 1813, he was given leave to settle the colonies of Attock. With enormous effort and skill he arranged the transfer of Attock Fort to the Sikhs, and in return the Afghan governor Jahandad Khan accepted a *jagir*. His dealings with the Pathans are another example of his ambassadorial skills. When Dost Muhammad Khan invaded Peshawar to regain the city from Ranjit Singh, Azizuddin was sent with some Sikh representatives to settle the matters with the Afghans. He received an aggressive welcome with shouts of *kafirs*. There followed a heated debate on religious and political matters, but he outshone the Afghans with his superior knowledge and his similarly great gift of persuasive speech. Dost Muhammad Khan listened with great consideration and clapped more than once. One of the Maharaja's courtiers asked him why, being a Muslim, Fakir *Sahib* was supporting the infidels. He opened the letter of Dost Muhammad

Khan to Ranjit Singh, and explained that it clearly showed that Dost Muhammad Khan was fighting for territory and not for Islam, and that as a Muslim it was his duty to be faithful to his master.[165]

During Ranjit Singh's reign, Fakir Azizuddin almost alone was in charge of foreign relations for the Sikh kingdom. In 1815, he held several negotiations with the leaders of Mandi and Rajauri, and later the Nawab of Bahawalpur. In 1823, he was sent to Peshawar to collect tribute from Yar Muhammad Khan Barakzai. After the death of Raja Sansar Chand of Kangra in 1824, his son, Anirudh Chand, defaulted on an instalment of *nazrana*, and it was Azizuddin who went to Nadaun and persuaded him to pay tribute to the Maharaja and his successors.[166] In 1827, he set out to Shimla on a goodwill mission to approach Lord Amherst, the British representative general. Again, in April 1831, another delegation from the Lahore *Darbar* met Lord William Bentinck; although the Sikh General Sardar Hari Singh Nalwa led it, he had imperial instructions to follow the advice of Diwan Moti Ram and Azizuddin.[167] This led to a meeting between Ranjit Singh and Bentinck in October 1831. Fakir Azizuddin, through Captain Wade, went as translator and led discussions that prompted the drawing up of the Tripartite Treaty of 1838 supporting Shah Shuja on the throne of Kabul. Seven years later he again went as translator when the Maharaja met Lord Auckland, generally considered to have resulted in extending the life of the *Khalsa* state.[168] Indeed, Fakir Azizuddin was described in British intelligence reports as 'the oracle of the Maharaja', and on one occasion even 'his master's mouthpiece'. The British consistently met their match when it came to keeping authorized records of state. His grip on Arabic, Persian, English and French made him among the most expressive men of his day.[169] In the parade of the returning mission from Shimla, Azizuddin, in his *howdah* (seat on elephant),[170] must have reflected on the good fortune that had taken him from humble beginnings in the old city of Lahore to the icy climes of Shimla, from an apprenticeship as a *hakim* (doctor) to the representative of the Sikh *Darbar*, welcomed by the British *Lat Sahib* to sit beside him.[171]

Fakir Azizuddin was a man of knowledge, not a fighter by profession, although Ranjit Singh's confidence in his skills sometimes resulted in his being given military duties. He was sent to seize Gujrat from Sahib Singh Bhangi, to strengthen the fort at Attock, to capture the fort of Phillaur from Diwan Kirpa Ram, and to take charge of Kapurthala, Jandiala, Hoshiarpur and Fateh Singh Ahluwalia's lands. He was sometimes left in charge of Lahore when Ranjit Singh went on military expeditions.[172]

His captivating manners and perfect ministerial behaviour made Fakir Azizuddin a perfect advisor and confidant of Maharaja Ranjit Singh. For example, when Raja Sansar Chand of Kangra came to see the Maharaja to speak to him in private, Ranjit Singh directed him to speak instead to Fakir Azizuddin.[173]

As he was a Sufi, conventional Muslims considered him an unbeliever, although he looked on all religions equally. On one occasion Ranjit Singh asked him whether he favoured Hinduism or Islam. 'I am', he answered, 'a man sailing along a compelling waterway. I turn my eyes towards the land; however I can recognize no distinction in either bank.'[174]

Ranjit Singh's appointment of Sardar Hari Singh Nalwa as governor of Kashmir was questioned by Fakir Azizuddin on the grounds that, extraordinary general though he was, as a leader he was rash and rude. So strongly did Azizuddin feel that he added that if Hari Singh was to go to Kashmir as representative, ploughs should be sent with him to level the thriving towns of the Kashmir valley to the ground. Without a moment's delay, Ranjit Singh withdrew his decision and appointed a more thoughtful individual to Kashmir.[175] On individual family matters, the Maharaja placed equal trust in the advice of his loyal Fakir. In 1816, he inquired whether Diwan Moti Ram would be able to deal with the possessions of Kunwar Kharak Singh, and Azizuddin gave a thoughtful reply, saying that time would be required to check his ability to manage things.[176] By 1817, Azizuddin was in a unique position, and his brothers highly valued.

Dr Murray reported on the influence of the three Muslim brothers in 1826. He was received by them and was taught how to present himself in front of the Maharaja. Fakir Imamuddin went with him to court and prevented him from doffing his hat in the Western way of respect, explaining that it was not a Sikh tradition to uncover the head, as this was a sign of social nakedness. Fakir Nuruddin told him that Azizuddin, who was departing to present precious gifts personally to the governor general, had been instructed to return immediately as he had to be in constant attendance on the Maharaja at night, and was consulted even in the most trivial matters.[177]

Fakir Azizuddin's career as a distinguished ambassador, a convincing speaker, an expert planner and a fluent orator reached its peak in 1838. This was during the last days of Ranjit Singh, when he was paralysed, had completely lost the power of speech and could only communicate with his eyes; Fakir Azizuddin was the only person who could understand him, serving him with his full loyalty and love.[178] Emily Eden, the sister of Lord Auckland, described Fakir Azizuddin as the comfort of Ranjit Singh's life, and wished that everyone could have similar comfort in their life.[179]

Imamuddin, the second brother of Fakir Azizuddin, was for many years in charge of the fort of Gobind Garh. After establishing his power in Amritsar, Ranjit Singh constructed this famous fort, named after the tenth Guru of the Sikhs, Gobind Singh. It had belonged to the Bhangi Sardar Gujjar Singh and was rebuilt in 1809 under the supervision of Fakir Imamuddin who, although not a member of the *darbar*, held an important position at military and administrative levels.[180] The fort's construction was well planned, as part of the protective line of the kingdom: 'Whosoever will pass the Govind Garh fort will hold the keys of the kingdom.'[181] Throughout the reign of Ranjit Singh, Fakir Imamuddin held the key position of protector of the fort and governor of the areas around the city. He was also in charge of the treasury, the magazines, royal stables and the arsenals in the fort.[182] Although Sikh generals criticized him, the Maharaja would never hear a word against him.[183] Because his post meant that he was away from the Lahore *Darbar*, he played an active role as a bridge in the correspondence between the British and the Maharaja. In 1827 he was sent to Shimla on a complementary mission.[184]

Fakir Nuruddin was the home minister and also royal physician, almoner, administrator of the royal palaces and gardens, one of the three guardians of the royal treasury, head of the stores at the fort, a judge, keeper of the Maharaja's judicial integrity, and master of ceremonies in charge of royal splendour and ritual. When guests arrived, they had to be received with the appropriate amount of *zeafat* (food) and a suitable level of generosity. If transport was needed, elephants and horses had to be got ready. If a full *darbar* was to be held, the pashmina tents had to be fitted out, expensive rugs freshened and the gifts given and received displayed and accounted for; overnight guests had to be accommodated, and reports on all this work given to the Maharaja.[185] With the passage of time it became second habit for Nuruddin speedily to arrange such functions. His true achievement, however, was being able to complete his every duty in line with the customs held by the court.[186]

Among his many other tasks, Nuruddin was required to select the charitable gifts of the Maharaja to the poor. He was in charge of the dispensaries in Lahore and all the other big cities, where indigenous medicines were given to the people.[187] Because of these multifunctional duties he became so close to Ranjit Singh that although he was not a member of the council, he had great influence on him. The Fakir family's records illustrate other instances of this closeness. His son, Prince Sher Singh, had an eye on one of the Maharaja's favourite horses, Dooloo. He tried to ride it on several occasions but without success. One day he took it from the stable and did not return it, and his father ordered that all the prince's possessions should be taken away and he himself exiled. Before the orders could be executed, Fakir Nuruddin intervened on behalf of the prince. When the Maharaja complained to him about Sher Singh, Fakir Nuruddin gave a witty reply and Ranjit Singh not only cancelled the punishment but also gave Dooloo to the prince, with the royal trappings.[188]

Another exceptionally important duty of Fakir Nuruddin was the provision of the Maharaja's food, prepared under the supervision of *Hakim* Bhishan Das and tested by a team of professionals before being poured into special dishes that could detect poison. The food was then locked in special containers under the supervision of Nuruddin, and fastened with his own seal. Ranjit Singh never ate anything that did not have the seal of Fakir Nuruddin.[189]

Nuruddin was a copy of his brother Azizuddin in terms of versatility, persuasiveness, clean discussion, refined behaviour and comprehension of political matters.[190] William Barr in February 1839 praised him in these words: 'He was a short, elderly, and rather plainly dressed man, with an intelligent and somewhat amiable cast of the countenance and the perfect gentleman in his manners.'[191]

By 1838, the three Fakir brothers had achieved a uniquely unassailable position in the Sikh court. Moorcroft was especially complimentary about them, recognizing them as men of extreme sophistication and extraordinary intellect.[192]

Conclusion

When Maharaja Ranjit Singh came to power, he wanted all his subjects, including Hindus and Muslims, to feel themselves part of the Sikh kingdom. Hence, he created an environment in which his people believed that they had equal rights, no matter what religion or community they belonged to. He gathered around him a pool of able and talented people from all religions and communities, the most notable of whom have been described above. His *darbar* was secular in character, and merit and personal qualities were the main criteria for appointment and increased status and position. In selecting the right man for the right job, he also assessed the traits, characteristics and customs of the community or tribe the incumbent belonged to. On this basis, he entrusted the revenue and financial departments to Hindus who had been in the service of the Mughals. Similarly the Jats were best suited to the *Khalsa* army. Those individuals from the landed aristocracy and upper classes, whose personal stakes made them carry out their obligations sincerely and enthusiastically, were generally sent on diplomatic missions.

According to Machiavelli,

> The first opinion that is formed of a ruler's intelligence is based on the quality of the men he has around him. When they are competent and loyal he can always be considered wise because he had been able to recognize their competence and to keep them loyal. But when they are otherwise, the prince is always open to adverse criticism, because his first mistake has been in the choice of his ministers.[193]

Maharaja Ranjit Singh's most prominent quality, notwithstanding his valour and insight, was his ability in selecting individuals, keeping close those persons whom he could trust for their wisdom and loyalty, whether Hindu, Muslim or European. They proved themselves as true professionals and worked according to the requirements of the Maharaja.

Despite many reservations and objections by influential Hindus and Sikhs, Ranjit Singh appointed the Fakir brothers to important positions. These administrative decisions confirm that Ranjit Singh was a secular ruler. He wanted able and competent people around him to run his kingdom. Religion was hardly a criterion in deciding state matters or policies. These were the individuals who remained loyal to the *Khalsa* state even after death of Ranjit Singh in 1839.[194]

Chapter 5

SIKH–MUSLIM RELATIONS IN THE POST-RANJIT SINGH PERIOD (1839–49)

Sikh power in the Punjab underwent an unpredictable and rapid decline from 1839 to 1849. During these years four rulers, namely Kharak Singh, Nau Nihal Singh, Sher Singh and Dilip Singh, held power, but none of them could prevent the fall of the Sikh Empire caused by both internal and external threats. After the demise of Ranjit Singh in 1839, a war of succession started among his heirs.[1] Internal disputes and political hostilities severely weakened the state. The British East India Company cunningly exploited this opportunity and waged wars against the Sikhs to realize their long-held dream of taking over the Punjab.

Unlike Ranjit Singh, his successors lacked political sagacity and leadership qualities. They were more interested in securing their rule than strengthening the state.[2] The Punjabis were divided and the court split into a number of groups. The Dogra Hindus stood up against the Sikhs and started challenging their power. However, Muslims mostly remained indifferent to all these developments during the early years of the decade. The army grew bigger and the state's resources to feed them meagre. As a result, the army became uncontrollable and their allegiance to the state subsequently faded away as they sided with anyone who could pay them.[3]

The successors of Ranjit Singh eroded the very foundation of the Sikh state with their lust for power. They not only destroyed their political status but also their magnificent heritage and themselves as well. However, even in this crisis and struggle for the survival of Sikh rule, the Muslims remained loyal citizens and showed no sign of revolt; similarly, the state did not deprive the Muslims of their fundamental rights. However, the British and their Hindu allies were successful in capitalizing on the situation and were able to capture and merge the Punjab into the British Raj. Therefore, it is important to investigate how the Sikhs adopted their communal policy, particularly towards the Muslim community, during this period, and how the Muslims reacted to the declining Sikh rule in the Punjab and their policies. This chapter will discuss the causes of the downfall of the Sikh rulers, the main political developments of the period, the Sikh state policy towards Muslims and the response of the Muslims to these developments.

Sikh Rulers (1839–49)

On his death in 1839, Maharaja Ranjit Singh passed on to his successors a prosperous, peaceful and tolerant Punjab. For forty years he had ruled the Punjab with a balance of ambition and patience. His ambition expanded the *Khalsa* Empire from Dera Ghazi (DG) Khan to Peshawar and Kashmir and his patience won him the support of the *Akali* warriors. His foresight kept the British away from the Punjab and his fair conduct earned him the allegiance and loyalty of the Muslim majority. Despite the intricate sociopolitical history of the two communities, he skilfully handled the relationship between Sikhs and Muslims. He made mistakes – at times bad ones – but he corrected most and learned from them.

Ranjit Singh had made inroads into Afghanistan and annexed Peshawar and Kashmir to the Punjab. With his military genius and political acumen, he slowly yet steadily subdued almost all his opponents including Muslim, Hindu and Sikh rulers in the Punjab. He treated the defeated rulers intelligently and fairly and continued the practice of rewarding competence and loyalty with *jagirs*, gifts and ranks. He created a heterogeneous society run by an administration that included Sikhs, Hindus and Muslims. He invested in relationships and in return earned the allegiance of all the communities. With the help of his European generals, he created a formidable army that at one time awed the British forces.

Yet within a few years of his death, all the hard-earned and cherished victories of the 'Lion of the Punjab' were wasted by his unscrupulous successors, and subsequently the Sikh kingdom fell to the British. In contrast to the reflections of many historians, I maintain that the Sikh monarchy founded by Ranjit Singh was 'Napoleonic in the suddenness of its rise, the brilliancy of its success and the completeness of its overthrow'.[4] However, it was, indeed, shattered into pieces within ten years of his death.

Numerous factors were responsible for the decline of the Sikh rule in the Punjab. However, I identify three key reasons. First is the disputed succession of Kharak Singh to the throne, which was not accepted or supported by many, including his own wife and son. In fact, Ranjit Singh himself seems to be mainly responsible for this uncertainty around the succession. Despite his being the eldest son, the obvious succession of Kunwar (Prince) Kharak Singh was not formally announced until the Maharaja was on his deathbed.[5] This ambiguity and uncertainty encouraged the ambitions of the prince's rivals, and Kharak Singh faced serious opposition and intrigues on his accession. From the first day, the Dogra brothers and his own son Nau Nihal Singh were conspiring against him and weakening his rule. Moreover, Ranjit Singh had done little to train the prince to run the *Khalsa* state after his death. Making no significant contribution to the strengthening of the Sikh kingdom, Kharak Singh was no match for the political and administrative wisdom and even physical strength of his father, his rival Sher Singh, his brother, or Nau Nihal Singh, his son. In short, the selection of Kharak Singh as ruler of the Punjab was not a wise decision.

The second reason flowed from the first. The dispute around the succession weakened the Sikh hold on the state and resurrected a deeper political issue: the old antagonism between various courtiers, chieftains and families, mainly Sikhs and Hindus, who were holding important positions in the kingdom – for instance, the enmity between the Dogra brothers and the Sundhiawala *sardars*, and the rivalry between Chat Singh and the Dogra brothers that ultimately claimed the life of Chat Singh. A detailed discussion of these rivalries and the resulting negative impact follows.

The weakening of state authority also gave birth to the third key reason for the fall of the Sikh kingdom: the rise of the army as a major political player in the state. As the intrigues and disputes among various groups intensified, the significance of the army rapidly grew. Every group wished to have the army on its side against the rival group, and consequently it assumed a pivotal role in deciding both the succession and the fate of the kingdom. This antagonism not only politicized the institution but also badly weakened it. An army which had been formidable and a source of pride and strength became a saleable commodity as its members fought only for those who could pay them. This situation hastened the fall of the Sikh Empire.

Kharak Singh (1839–40)

Ranjit Singh left seven sons from different wives. Kharak Singh, born in 1801 to Maharani Raj Kaur of Nakai *Misl*, was the eldest.[6] He was granted the principality of Jammu in 1812, and in 1839 was appointed by his dying father as heir to the Sikh throne with the title of *Tika Sahib Bahadur*.[7] Physically, intellectually and morally he was a weak person and, despite his being the eldest son, historians do not consider him to have been the best choice for the throne of the Punjab. Unlike his father, he had few leadership qualities. He was an addict and hardly able to handle the affairs of the state.[8] His wife, Chand Kaur and son, Nau Nihal Singh knew his weaknesses and therefore asked him to step down in favour of Nau Nihal Singh, but he refused. As a result, his own family started conspiring against him and soon made him powerless; he was still *de jure* king while Nau Nihal Singh was the *de facto* ruler of the Punjab. These intrigues finally claimed the life of Kharak Singh, who was poisoned to death; his wife and son were said to have been involved in this plot. I am unable to understand what exactly made both the wife and son of Kharak Singh conspire against him when they were both effectively enjoying the powers of the king. Kharak Singh's rule of one year had proved to be an eventful time full of intrigues and rivalries.

Soon after becoming ruler, Kharak Singh assured his courtiers, including Sikhs, Muslims and Hindus, continuance of all the ranks, *jagirs* and privileges bestowed upon them by his father.[9] In fact, after the death of Ranjit Singh, Raja Dhian Singh Dogra, the prime minister, called a meeting of courtiers and nobles to discuss the future of their *jagirs*, privileges and offices. The meeting was attended by an exclusive group of courtiers and nobles that included Sikhs such as Ram Singh, Bhai Gobind Ram and Jamadar Khushhal Singh; two of the Fakir brothers; Dhian Singh and his son, Raja Hira Singh Dogra; Diwan Dina Nath and Misr Beli Ram.

They prepared a *shahi farman* (imperial order) for the signature of the new Maharaja assuring continuation of all of their privileges and *jagirs*.[10] The courtiers claimed to hold their *jagirs* on a hereditary basis, a right that had previously been enjoyed by very few nobles. They also claimed the right to act as a council of permanent ministers to run state affairs. In order to ensure the loyalty of the nobles and courtiers to safeguard his rule against the rival princes aspiring to capture the throne, Kharak Singh accepted these demands.[11] Dhian Singh and others, especially new appointees, therefore supported him against his opponents, but he nevertheless failed to win the support and confidence of his family, as described above.[12]

The distrust between Kharak Singh and his stepbrother Sher Singh gradually increased. Sher Singh attended the last rituals of his father after being assured by Kharak Singh that he would not be arrested.[13] Although nothing untoward happened at the funeral ceremony, mistrust continued between the two brothers.

Unlike his father, Kharak Singh had little interest in affairs of state. Ranjit Singh had always handled state affairs himself, trusting no one and hence delegating power only with caution and close supervision. He never left everything to even his closest aides, including the Dogra brothers, and most courtiers were seen to comply with his orders.[14] However, Kharak Singh changed everything by his laxity and unprofessionalism.[15] He also started to build his own team under the leadership of Chat Singh Bajwa, his childhood teacher.[16] Chat Singh replaced Dhian Singh, which turned Dhian Singh against both of them.[17] Chat Singh also penalized the favourites of Dhian Singh, Wazir Singh being one of them.[18] Wazir Singh lost all his property and was imprisoned, which increased the Dogra brothers' hatred for the Maharaja and Chat Singh.[19]

Consequently, the Dogra brothers started to conspire against Kharak Singh and Chat Singh, spreading the rumour that they were intending to sell the Punjab to the British. They misled Kharak Singh's son, Nau Nihal Singh, who also turned against his father.[20] In order to get rid of Chat Singh, the Dogra brothers planned his assassination, and Suchet Singh Dogra along with Gulab Singh killed him on 9 October 1839,[21] a mere five weeks after the accession of Kharak Singh, while he was asleep in the Maharaja's palace.[22] However, Dhian Singh Dogra remained unaware of this assassination plot.[23] Chat Singh's property, worth about Rs.60 *lakh*, was also confiscated.[24]

The assassination of Chat Singh pushed Kharak Singh into the background, away from the mainstream political scene of the Punjab, and Prince Nau Nihal Singh assumed the *de facto* role of the Maharaja of the Punjab. Kharak Singh was finally dislodged and imprisoned and his son replaced him. Kharak Singh died of slow poisoning on 5 November 1840.[25]

Kharak Singh was the incapable successor to a capable father. He failed to understand the political and administrative undercurrents of the *darbar* and his handling of the internal and external affairs of the state proved to be a complete fiasco. It is pertinent to mention here that none of the Muslims, whether courtier, noble or general, had any role in the fall of Kharak Singh. It is also clear from the records that hardly any of the Muslim nobles holding any position of significance at court were deprived of their posts in the administration or army during his short reign. The Muslims therefore continued to enjoy the privileges and positions conferred upon them by Ranjit Singh.

Nau Nihal Singh

When Kharak Singh failed to control the various rival groups of chieftains, Prince Nau Nihal Singh took control of state affairs during the lifetime of his father. However, his official reign lasted for only a single day, as probably he died on the same day as his father. Unlike his father, Nau Nihal Singh was a strong and resourceful administrator. His grandfather Ranjit Singh liked him very much, and he also had the support of the *Khalsa* army.[26] He fought many battles for the Sikh army and also remained governor of the northwestern areas of the Punjab at the time of Ranjit Singh's death. At the age of 16, in April 1837, he married Sahib Kaur, daughter of Sardar Sham Singh Attariwala (1790–1846) of Attari in Amritsar.[27]

Initially Nau Nihal Singh had good relations with Dhian Singh; however, he very soon wearied of him and his brothers and wanted to be rid of them. He found his man in Tej Singh, the nephew of Jamadar Khushhal Singh. Tej Singh and the prince together started removing from office sympathizers of the Dogra brothers. Malik Fateh Khan Tiwana, who was a close aide of Dhian Singh and the *jagirdar* of the Mittha Tiwana area in the Chaj *doab*, was imprisoned for not paying revenue arrears. It is pertinent to highlight here that Malik Fateh Khan Tiwana was not removed for being a Muslim but for being an ally of Dhian Singh.[28]

On the advice of Tej Singh, the Prince took away the hill region *jagirs* of the Dogra brothers.[29] In 1840, he and Tej Singh also planned to disband the army garrisons that were under the influence of the Dogra brothers and replace them with their own.[30] Dhian Singh was angry and responded with further intrigues.[31] The Lahore *Darbar* was divided into two groups, one led by Sardar Tej Singh, Attar Singh Sindhianwalia and Jamadar Khushhal Singh and the other by Dhian Singh with support from his brother Raja Gulab Singh Dogra and Fakir Azizuddin.[32] However, before this rivalry could develop into an armed conflict, both Kharak Singh and Nau Nihal Singh had died.

Returning from his father's funeral rituals, Nau Nihal Singh was injured when granite blocks fell on him as he was passing through *Roshni Darwaza* (the gate of the Hazuri Bagh at Lahore Fort). Dhian Singh took him into the fort under his strict supervision, and not even his mother was allowed to see the prince on the pretext of medical advice.[33] He was not hurt very badly and was able to walk by himself, yet Dhian Singh insisted on a *palki* (carrier) to carry him to his personal chamber; two days later he declared that Nau Nihal Singh had died from severe injuries.[34]

The British doctor who treated him confirmed to the British author McAuliffe that Nau Nihal Singh had only minor injuries to his head; however, when he visited him on the following day, his head was badly crushed and he had no pulse. Nau Nihal Singh died at the age of 19, presumably a victim of the intrigues of the Dogra brothers.[35] According to the historic records and the report of the British doctor, he had survived the first attempt and was murdered on the second. This inference is supported by the fact that even his mother and wife were not allowed to visit him after the first accident.[36]

It is also worth mentioning that during the whole of his *de facto* tenure nothing significant happened against the Muslims. Although Fakir Azizuddin sided with Dhian Singh, he continued to hold his position in the *darbar*. Malik Fateh Khan Tiwana was penalized for being a confidant of Dhian Singh but, as already explained, his religion had nothing to do with his mistreatment. Tej Singh and his allies even maltreated and opposed Dhian Singh, who was one of the most important persons in the Lahore *Darbar*. They were more concerned and preoccupied with intrigues to take over Dhian Singh and his aides. How could prince Nau Nihal Singh and Tej Singh offend and ill-treat a community that was in the majority and significantly well placed, especially when Dhian Singh was conspiring against them? It can be safely concluded that Prince Nau Nihal Singh and Tej Singh were more concerned about the means to perpetuate their rule than maltreating the Muslims and other minorities.

Rani Chand Kaur

Despite all these intrigues, Dhian Singh Dogra could not realize his designs. Another son of Ranjit Singh, Sher Singh, was proclaimed as Maharaja of the Punjab, but none other than the mother and wife of Nau Nihal Singh challenged this.[37] His mother, Chand Kaur, claimed the regency in the name of Nau Nihal Singh's widow, Sahib Kaur, who was pregnant and would be the mother of the unborn legal successor.[38]

Dhian Singh supported Sher Singh while his brother Gulab Singh, Khushal Singh, and Bhai Ram Singh were in favour of Chand Kaur, the widow of Kharak Singh. After prolonged meetings, all the groups agreed to declare Sher Singh as the vice-regent and Chand Kaur as the regent.[39]

Realizing his deteriorating position in the Lahore *Darbar*, Dhian Singh retired to Jammu. However, before leaving Lahore, he secretly sent a message to Prince Sher Singh to be ready to seize the throne. Army officers who were in favour of the prince were also alerted. They were promised a rise in salary and other rewards for supporting Sher Singh.[40] Under these circumstances, Sher Singh declared himself ruler and marched to Lahore, where he was expecting the support promised by Dhian Singh. However, in the absence of Dhian Singh, Gulab Singh shocked Sher Singh by refusing to surrender to him. Gulab Singh's loyalty to Mai Chand Kaur upset Sher Singh, and Gulab Singh assumed command of the forces within the fortress. While Gulab Singh emerged as the guardian of the Lahore government, Sher Singh found unexpected support from Raja Suchet Singh and General Ventura. Their allegiance to Sher Singh strengthened his army, which swelled to 70,000 with the promise of an increase in salary and rewards.[41] Sher Singh bribed the gatekeepers and was able to enter the city.[42]

Sher Singh attacked the fort from the *Hazoori Bagh* Gate and was able to blow it up. However, Gulab Singh's soldiers shot down his men and the attack was repulsed. Despite many attacks, Sher Singh was able to make no inroads into the city of Lahore until Dhian Singh finally arrived. Sher Singh gave him an imperial reception, but it was only after several days that his forces were able to enter the fort and drive out the Rani's forces.[43]

Under these circumstances, Rani Chand Kaur appealed for peace and was finally sent off with a respectable *jagir*, while her Sandhanwalia chieftains went to the British territory across the Sutlej. Sher Singh ascended the throne on 20 January 1841 and immediately appointed Dhian Singh his prime minister.[44]

However, the settlement could not last for very long. Allies of Sher Singh and Rani Chand Kaur were again face to face. According to their plan of action, Raja Gulab Singh Dogra stood with the Rani, while his brother Dhian Singh supported Sher Singh, thus ensuring their success, influence and the preservation of all privileges, whatever the outcome of the struggle. Very soon Rani Chand Kaur also started conniving with the Sandhanwalia, the British and the Sikh army. Enraged by this, Dhian Singh Dogra assassinated her with the help of her maidservants, supposedly from Jammu,[45] as he had replaced Rani's maidservants with his own hill women.[46] These maidservants first tried to poison the Rani and eventually killed her with sharp stakes on 11 June 1842. Some historians also report that they dropped a heavy stone on her and crushed her to death.[47] As under the other rulers, nothing important or bad happened to minorities or the Muslims during this period. Nobody had time for such unscrupulous dealings during the era of chaos and anarchy, where all were occupied in finding ways to stay in power and dislodge their opponents.

Sher Singh

Sher Singh (1807–43) was the son of Maharani Mehtab Kaur, the first wife of Maharaja Ranjit Singh, and his claim to the throne was being the son of the first wife of the Maharaja. He officially became Maharaja on 27 January 1841, after the death of Nau Nihal Singh, but was later declared vice-regent of the Punjab under the regency of Chand Kaur.[48] However, he had to struggle hard to finally regain the throne, with the help of Dhian Singh Dogra, as described above. Sher Singh was daring, ambitious and very popular with the army but he was not a shrewd politician.[49] On the contrary, his prime minister, Dhian Singh Dogra was a clever and intelligent minister,[50] his dominating persona and political awareness always a threat to the rulers. Just like Kharak Singh and Nau Nihal Singh, Sher Singh soon felt threatened by Dhian Singh and started avoiding him. Consequently he started gathering around him people who were against the Dogra brothers.[51] Dhian Singh paid in the same coin and started strengthening his own group by recruiting some 6,000 fresh soldiers, predominantly non-Sikhs from Jammu and other hill states.[52] He further rewarded supporters such as Malik Fateh Khan Tiwana, who received new *jagirs* and many of whose relatives were appointed *kardars*.[53] Dhian Singh also gave employment to those officials who were expelled by Sher Singh and his group.⁵⁴

At the same time, *sardars* who had old enmity with Sher Singh and Dhian Singh fled Lahore and joined the British. These were mainly the Sandhanwalia *sardars*, including Ajit Singh, Lehna Singh and Attar Singh.⁵⁵ However, the clandestine enmity between Dhian Singh and Sher Singh brought them closer to Sher Singh, who had lost influence in the Sikh *Darbar* after the death of Rani Chand Kaur.

With the help of Clerk, the British governor general's political agent at Ludhiana, the Sandhanwalia *sardars* were able to negotiate reconciliation with Sher Singh and returned to Lahore in October 1842. Sher Singh returned their *jagirs* and they were allowed their old ranks in the *darbar*. After winning the trust of Sher Singh, they planned the assassination of both Dhian Singh⁵⁶ and Sher Singh.⁵⁷

In order to secure the support of the Sandhanwalia *sardars*, Sher Singh gave them good ranks in the army. However, one day when he was inspecting his troops, Ajit Singh Sandhanwalia treacherously shot him while showing him a new gun. Sher Singh died saying '*aah ki daga*' (why this treachery). In the meantime, Lehna Singh Sandhanwalia killed Pertap Singh, the 10-year-old son of Sher Singh. The Sandhanwalia brothers, Ajit Singh and Lehna Singh, also killed Dhian Singh Dogra and hung his body in pieces all around the city of Lahore.⁵⁸

The killing of Sher Singh, his son and Dhian Singh enraged the Sikh army. They butchered both Sandhanwalia brothers along with their supporters.⁵⁹ Thus Sher Singh's reign ended as it had emerged, in violence. If analysed closely, it is clear that within three days, 15–17 September 1843, about a thousand people died. A maharaja, a prince, a prime minister and a number of nobles of the Lahore *Darbar* were among those who lost their lives during these three days. However, essentially nothing changed. At the end of this sad and violent saga, a Dogra, Hira Singh, was the prime minister of a Sikh maharaja, Dilip Singh. The equation of political power remained the same except for the addition of the army as a powerful variable – or, more probably, a powerful constant. However, during this reign of bloodshed, Muslim nobles conducted themselves very intelligently and maintained their respect and positions in the Lahore *Darbar*. Everyone knew that Fakir Azizuddin was a close friend of Dhian Singh, but neither Sher Singh nor even the Sandhianwalas maltreated the Fakir brothers.

Dilip Singh

Following the unfortunate death of Sher Singh, Raja Hira Singh Dogra announced Ranjit Singh's 5-year-old son Dilip Singh as Maharaja, with himself as prime minister.⁶⁰ All, including the army and Sikh nobles, supported Dilip Singh's succession to the throne. His mother Maharani Jindan was made regent.⁶¹ Hira Singh's first orders were to confiscate all the property of the Sindhianwalias and their followers, and to kill Bhai Gurmukh Singh, Misr Beli Ram and Misr Ram Kishen for supporting the assassination of his father Dhian Singh.⁶²

Hira Singh Dogra and his Brahmin advisor Jalla were now in control of the whole administration, and Maharaja Dilip Singh and Rani Jindan were no more than *de jure* heads of state.[63] Suchet Singh Dogra, the uncle of Hira Singh, opposed Jalla and pressed Hira Singh to dismiss him, but Hira Singh disagreed. Subsequently Suchet Singh came to Lahore with his general Rai Kesari Singh and stayed at the shrine of Mian Wadda outside the city. Hira Singh Dogra was infuriated and attacked Suchet Singh and Rai Kesari, killing both of them.[64] However, Hira Singh later regretted the death of his uncle and gave him an honourable funeral.[65]

Very soon, two groups emerged in the Punjab: one the *Sarkar Khalsa* at Lahore and the other in Batala under Bhai Bir Singh, a religious leader.[66] Many Sikh *sardars*, such as Majhitias and Attariwalas, although loyal to the *Sarkar Khalsa* at Lahore, were also in contact with Bhai Bir Singh. Attar Singh Sandhiawalia, who had earlier fled to Thanesar, also joined Bhai Bir Singh, who welcomed and promised him the throne of the Punjab. Princes Kashmira Singh and Peshawara Singh, sons of Maharaja Ranjit Singh, also joined Bhai Bir Singh. Finally the *sardars*, who were against the Dogras, came together under the leadership of Bhai Bir Singh.[67]

During a gathering of these *sardars*, in a fit of anger Attar Singh Sandhiawalia shot a Sikh officer named Attar Singh Kalkattia, creating complete disorder in the meeting. As a result the army killed almost all the guests and Bhai Bir Singh himself; Attar Singh Sandhiawalia and Prince Kashmira Singh were also killed. Major Croft, who had been appointed by the *Sarkar Khalsa*, led the battalion responsible for this slaughter. This battalion became known as *Gurumar*, murderer of the Gurus. Hira Singh Dogra, as prime minister, accepted his mistake and apologized to the Sikh community and the army for the deaths of their leaders.[68]

Meanwhile, a devastating earthquake hit Amritsar and Lahore in April 1844, believed by the general public to be a bad omen. Under these circumstances, Hira Singh Dogra and his close aide *pandit* Jallah fled to Jammu but were chased, and were killed by the army on 21 December 1844.[69]

After the death of Hira Singh, Maharani Jindan was left alone and unaided. She felt threatened by the unruly *Khalsa* army.[70] However, she conducted herself well with the help of her brother, Sardar Jawahir Singh. Nevertheless, the army grew stronger and more violent. For instance, in April 1845, the army *panchayat* forced Raja Gulab Singh Dogra to Lahore to pledge his loyalty and Rs.7 *lakh* was required as guarantee against this pledge.[71]

In July 1845, Prince Peshawara Singh stood up against the Lahore *Darbar* and took over Attock with the help of the local Muslim tribes, declaring himself ruler of the Punjab. Sardar Jawahir Singh knew that only Malik Fateh Khan Tiwana and Sardar Chattar Singh Attariwala could defeat Prince Peshawara Singh. In fact, both had once been close friends of the Dogra brothers. Malik Fateh Khan was a close aide of Dhian Singh Dogra and Sardar Chattar Singh Attariwala, the *nazim* of Hazara, was an old friend of Gulab Singh Dogra. Jawahir Singh secretly convinced Fateh Khan Tiwana and Chattar Singh Attariwala to kill the Prince, thinking that the Dogras would be held responsible for the murder.[72] However, army *panchayats* learned everything beforehand and in September 1845 Jawahir Singh was found guilty and executed by the *panchayat*.[73]

In utter despair, Rani Jindan resorted to Lal Singh, her lover,[74] and Tej Singh, an incapable courtier. She appointed Lal Singh as her prime minister and Tej Singh as commander of the army. The army endorsed these appointments. Disappointed by the unruly *Khalsa* army, the *darbar* decided to embark on a very risky venture. Alexander Gardner[75] described the solution to handling this mammoth as 'throwing the snake into the enemy's bosom'. He described the *Khalsa* army as 'evilly-disposed, violent yet a powerful and splendid army'.[76] It was decided to oppose the *Khalsa* army against the British and thus weaken it. The Maharani and likeminded courtiers believed that the supremacy of the *darbar* would be revived if the British were successful. They also believed that if the *Khalsa* army were successful, the Sikh kingdom would expand as far as Delhi.[77] In December 1845, the *Khalsa* army under the command of Tej Singh fell on the states across the Sutlej in violation of the signed treaty, effectively inviting the British to invade the Punjab.

It is interesting to note that Peshawara Singh took over Attock with the help of local Muslim tribes, and therefore it is naïve to think that the Muslims of Attock were maltreated in any way. Moreover, despite this assistance from local Muslims, hardly any historian has mentioned any retaliatory action against any Muslim noble in the Lahore *Darbar*, and indeed the Fakir brothers continued to hold their positions in the *darbar* even after the fall of Attock.

Council of Ministers: Muslims' Role and Representation

Maharaja Ranjit Singh had delegated power to Muslims, Hindus and Sikhs to discharge state functions; Dhian Singh Dogra led the Hindu group, and the Fakir brothers the Muslim group. He did not enforce the *Khalsa* code of conduct on anyone. Dhian Singh Dogra, who was actually a Hindu, was made prime minister of the *Khalsa* state, and his whole family was eventually involved in state administration. The Fakir brothers and other Muslims held portfolios of foreign and internal affairs, medicine, science and the army under the *Sarkar Khalsa*.

The Sikh group comprised nobles from all over the Punjab, including Dhanna Singh Malwai, the Majithia brothers, the Sandhawalia brothers, Ahluwalias, Ramgarhias, the Virks of Sheikhupura, and the Bajwas of Narowal. This group was mostly involved in the defence of the state. Sikhs dominated the cavalry, but the artillery was under the command of Mian Ghause Khan, a Muslim. Ranjit Singh had kept a fine balance among all three groups. His rewards, privileges and promotions were meant only for capable and loyal people; religion, communal or familial affiliations were hardly considered.

After the death of Ranjit Singh, the council of ministers and the nobility of the *darbar* were also divided. The Dogras group included Gulab Singh, Dhian Singh, Suchet Singh and Dhian Singh's son Hira Singh, who was a favourite of the Maharaja. The other group included the Sikh *sardars* Sandhanwalia, Attariwalias and Majithias.

There was another group, not allied to any other, who did not take any part in of the intrigues of the *darbar*. The Fakir brothers were the most prominent among them. They continued their service to the Lahore *Darbar* as advisors on various matters, especially foreign affairs and medicine. As advisor on foreign affairs, Fakir Azizuddin was deputed to meet Mr Clark at Ferozpur to sort out matters relating to Afghan tribes. The brothers' influence continued during the reigns of Kharak Singh and Nau Nihal Singh. Dhian Singh respected them and always consulted them on important state matters. Maharaja Sher Singh assigned Fakir Azizuddin to get help from the British in handling the Sikh army.[78] Fakir Azizuddin was excused from attending the *darbar* every day during Sher Singh's period, due to an injured leg. He nevertheless felt threatened by the anarchy of the Sikh army and the intrigues of the Lahore *Darbar*.[79] He lost the confidence of Sher Singh, who believed that he was a friend of Dhian Singh, no longer close to Sher Singh.[80]

Following the death of Sher Singh, Fakir Azizuddin stopped taking an active part in the politics of the Punjab, due largely to his poor health. His eldest son, Fakir Shahdin, worked as *wakil* (ambassador) in Ferozpur until his death in 1842. Fakir Chiraghudin, another son, replaced his brother in the post and continued even during the British period.[81]

Fakir Azizuddin's brother, Fakir Imamuddin, was governor of the fort of Govind Garh. He continued as such until his death in 1844. His son Tajuddin replaced him as governor of Govind Garh and continued until his death in 1846.[82]

Fakir Nuruddin, the third brother, was also a trusted courtier of the Lahore *Darbar*. Understanding the significance of the British power, he and Fakir Azizuddin always strove to maintain amiable relations between the British and the Sikh Empire. The Sikh army respected him greatly, and when Rani Jindan sent him with Diwan Dina Nath and Sardar Attar Singh to negotiate with the army, he was the only one whom the army did not insult. He was also an important member of the council established to administer the Punjab under the regency of Maharaja Dilip Singh in 1846. He was a wise person and worked for the welfare of the state. His son, Fakir Zahooruddin, taught Dilip Singh.[83]

Similarly the *jagirdar* of Mamdot, Jamaluddin Khan, who hailed from the ruling family of Kasur, fought for the Sikhs against the British during the war of Mudki. The British approached him to help them against the Sikh army and also promised to reward him well, but he refused. His cousin Fatah-ud-Din also fought for the Sikhs and gave his life.[84] In line with the policy of the Fakir brothers, Dina Nath, who was a revenue officer, also continued his service without becoming embroiled in the court intrigues.

The continuing service of the Fakir brothers as ministers and governors confirms that even after the death of Ranjit Singh, Sikh rule remained benevolent and fair to the Muslims and minority groups. They always received due respect in the Lahore *Darbar*. Even the unruly army had great respect for these nobles; indeed, Dhian Singh undertook special measures to strengthen and protect the Muslim contingent, although this was for his own political reasons. Again, after the demise of Ranjit Singh, there is virtually no significant evidence to prove maltreatment of any Muslim contingent in the Sikh army.

Sikh Army: An Unruly Power

Earlier, Maharaja Ranjit Singh had ensured that the army had no role in the state administration. During his lifetime, the British did not dare to confront the Sikhs, and he closely watched the British military developments and engaged European generals to train his army to take on the British. After his death, the civil and military administration deteriorated and the local governors became uncontrollable. They stopped paying revenue and taxes to the Lahore *Darbar* and hence the state ran short of resources. As a result, it failed to pay the soldiers for their services; some units were not paid for more than two years. Therefore, the military started looking for other avenues of livelihood to support their families, and the practice of plundering, looting and working for others gradually crept into the army.[85] This turned the army into a tool with which to mollify opponents, making it a powerful force and an important player in struggles for the throne.[86]

The non-payment of taxes by various states meant that even the *jagirdari* troops were not being paid on a regular basis.[87] During Sher Singh's rule the army set up *panchayats* on the pattern of traditional village councils.[88] These *panchayats* had direct access to the Maharaja for addressing their concerns. They were also used to penalize officers who were no longer favourites of the *darbar* or who had lost influence with the army. During this time, recruitment to the army was also politicized. Troops were frequently recruited without the permission of the *darbar* during 1839–46. The Dogras, for instance, strengthened Rajput and Muslim contingents, and as a counter-move the anti-Dogra group bolstered contingents of Sikh Jats.[89] As a result, the kingdom turned into a military state – something totally unknown during the days of Ranjit Singh. The army had consumed roughly 41 per cent of the state revenue during the late 1830s when its total strength was around 80,000. However, with the increase in numbers, expenses also increased.[90] By 1844 the army was 123,800 strong, consuming two-thirds of the state revenues.[91] Ironically, the biggest threat to the state came from none other than its own army, which was supposed to defend it.

The rule of Sher Singh was marked by violence and chaos. With the Sandhanwalia clan as contenders to the throne, the army became uncontrollable.[92] In order to calm them down, Sher Singh raised the soldiers' pay and also allowed them to recruit their relatives to the army.[93] As described earlier, due to this unruly behaviour, Rani Jindan and others decided to bring the Sikh army to face the British forces.

Impact on Khalsa Sarkar

With the weakening of the Lahore *Darbar*'s authority during the 1840s, the separatist forces became active and the governors of distant provinces started to claim independence. Muslim tribes, the Yousaf Zai and the Balochis spread between Jhelum and Indus, revolted against the Lahore *Darbar*.[94] The chieftains of Rawalpindi, Peshawar, Attock and northwestern areas also rose against the *darbar* and refused to pay taxes.

Dogra Sardar Gulab Singh, who had been appointed governor of the province of Jammu by Ranjit Singh, started expanding his territory as far as Kashmir and Ladakh, annexing Ladakh itself. Gulab Singh also gained Kashmir for rendering services to the British, who had it from the Sikhs. All this happened due to the weak and incapable centre of the *Khalsa Sarkar*.

Ultimately, the intrigues of the Dogra brothers, vested interests and the inability of the Sikh rulers precipitated the fall of Maharaja Ranjit Singh's *Khalsa Sarkar*. The result of these devastating developments all across the Punjab was disintegration of the *Khalsa* state, and establishment of a Hindu state in Multan, a Dogra state in Jammu and an independent trans-Indus frontier with a very small Sikh state in the centre.[95] However, well before the final internal disintegration, war with the British changed the whole scenario in the Punjab.

British Interest

Although completely contained during the rule of Ranjit Singh, the British began planning to take over the Punjab after his death. Incapable Sikh rulers, treacherous *sardars* and the weakened *Khalsa Sarkar* helped the British to accomplish this very easily. Wider geopolitical developments also played an important role in the downfall of the Sikh government in the Punjab, further helping the British takeover. Although the British failed to instal Shah Shuja in Kabul,[96] the Afghans were too engrossed in their internal affairs and were confined to the Khyber Pass.[97] With the takeover of Sindh in 1843,[98] the British found the perfect opportunity to take over the Sikh state and complete their conquest of the subcontinent.[99]

The instability of the Lahore *Darbar* and the anti-British viewpoint of the *Khalsa Sarkar* provided this opportunity. In 1844, a veteran of the Peninsular Wars against Napoleon, Henry Harding, was appointed governor general of India. He was known to have a determined personality, although initially he showed some hesitation in taking on the Sikhs. However, after the assassination of Hira Singh, he decided to confront the Sikh state,[100] as he believed that it now had no chance of revival.[101] He also connived with Gulab Singh, who promised not to support the *Khalsa Sarkar* and instead to help the British if needed.[102] Gulab Singh, once a trusted general and ally of Maharaja Ranjit Singh, now stood against the *Khalsa* state, using the wealth he had looted from Lahore during the anarchy of Sher Singh's rule. While he assured the Lahore *Darbar* of his full support, he secretly connived with the British for the fall of the Sikh government in the Punjab.[103] He had his own plans to expand his territory to Tibet.[104]

The first Anglo–Sikh War opened with the Battle of Mudki in December 1845. The battle revealed that despite the reputed degeneration of the *Khalsa*, once in battle they were still formidable, and the British had to fight hard for victory. Fuelled by their hatred of the British, the Sikhs were ruthless and their artillerymen, trained well in Western techniques of warfare, caused heavy casualties to Gough's men. The British fared no better at Ferozeshah; with their army at his mercy, Tej Singh perceived Gough's attempt to withdraw as a flanking manoeuvre and himself withdrew to safety, allowing the wearied British to escape being massacred.[105]

In subsequent battles at Aliwal (January 1846) and Sobraon (February), the Sikhs lost their critical advantage in artillery, as successive defeats saw most of their cannons fall into British hands.[106]

Meanwhile, the British plotting at the *darbar* bore fruit. At Sobraon, Tej Singh, who was now secretly corresponding with Harding, was informed of a surprise British attack at dawn. Fleeing his camp, he destroyed the bridge over the Sutlej, leaving his men trapped between the British and the river. In the ensuing battle, 10,000 Sikhs were cut to pieces. Britain and the Company had won the war.[107]

Situation in the Punjab Countryside after 1839

The decade 1839–49 was an eventful period. Many intrigues and conspiracies, alliances and confrontations were made and unmade. However, the picture of the socio-economic, cultural and religious landscape during all these years remains obscure, and information sparse, due largely to preoccupation with the political turmoil. The gazetteers, archives and reports focus on the political and military developments of the Punjab. However, a broad perspective can be taken from the available evidence. As might be expected, the tumultuous events in the capital had a profound impact on the stability and prosperity of the countryside. After 1839 the authority of the *darbar* in the countryside, particularly at the periphery of the kingdom, underwent a sharp decline. In 1839 minor insurrections broke out in the tributary Rajput states of the lower Himalayas and in the vicinity of Tank on the far side of the Indus.[108]

On the near side of the Indus the Baloch rebelled in 1842, and the Ghebas in 1845.[109] In 1843, and again in 1845, the pastoral tribes of the lower Sutlej and Ravi took advantage of the political situation at Lahore to resume their old predatory habits.[110] Several chieftains in the countryside used the opportunity provided by events in the capital to settle old scores with rival families.[111] None of these disturbances remained unchecked for long, but while they lasted they posed a serious problem for the provincial administrators. This was because of the mutinous state of the provincial garrisons during this period. On numerous occasions between 1841 and 1844 the troops stationed on the kingdom's borders refused to follow orders until they received the same pay increases that had been extracted from the central authorities by the troops at Lahore.[112]

With the rise of the army to political power, the *zamindars* of the central Punjab, especially the Manjha, found protection against the *kardar* in their soldiering kinsmen. Diwan Ajudhia Parshad, a contemporary *darbar* official whose sympathies were obviously with the *kardars*, left an account of the situation in the central districts after Jawahir Singh's execution by the army.

The *kardars* took advantage of the political instability throughout the kingdom to extend their own power and wealth. They did this in a number of ways. First – and most obviously – many of them simply fell behind in their revenue remittances and waited until the *darbar* threatened them with punishment before sending any instalments to Lahore. As early as August 1843, during the reign of Sher Singh, the annual loss to the state from districts under *darbar*-appointed *kardars* was reported to be in the vicinity of Rs.20 *lakh*.[113] In some cases, the *kardar* bribed members of the *panchayat*, the village council, to support his illegal demands from the *zamindars*.[114] In other cases, he enlisted the support of local notables – religious leaders in particular – by alienating in their favour the greater portion of *inams* (gifts) that were normally reserved for *zamindars*.[115] Generally, the *kardar* got away with these illegitimate demands because the central administration's auditing of district accounts had become defective. Most *kardars* maintained false records, or no records at all, and *patwari* (revenue official) establishments were often permitted to run down.[116]

In the early 1840s, Diwan Swan Mal, for example, had strengthened his fort and built up his own troops at Multan with a view to declaring his independence from Lahore should a suitable opportunity present itself. With this in mind, he had placed a number of his own relatives into administrative offices in and adjacent to Multan. In September 1844, however, a soldier assassinated him. His son, Diwan Mul Raj, took over as *nazim*. The *darbar* demanded of Mul Raj a *nazrana* of Rs.10 million for the acknowledgement of his succession. At this time the two Sikh battalions stationed at Multan by the *darbar* were mutinying, demanding higher pay. Mul Raj's followers attacked the mutineers and totally dispersed them. This victory so baffled the *darbar* and strengthened Mul Raj's position that the new *nazim* was actually able to negotiate the payment of a much smaller *nazrana*; after a period of intense bargaining the *darbar* accepted Mul Raj's offer of Rs.18 *lakh*, less than one-fifth of its original demand.[117]

Conclusion

The rise of the Sikh Empire was so quick and dramatic that historians often likened Ranjit Singh to Napoleon due to his extraordinary military astuteness and enigmatic leadership. However, this comparison does not fully portray his personality. Maharaja Ranjit Singh was a vigilant warrior with a deep insight into martial matters. He would never antagonize an enemy whom he thought would be difficult to defeat.[118] He built a great army out of a crowd of undisciplined and unruly Sikh groups. Although he was brutal in battle, he was very peaceful and fair in dealing with and governing his heterogeneous and multi-religious subjects. His successors lacked his prudence and foresight and hence lost everything.[119] They ruined the *Khalsa* state, which Ranjit Singh had built with great care and hard work. After his death, Sikh rulers were more occupied in conspiring and killing each other than strengthening or consolidating the Sikh Empire. Their energies were drained by their internal disputes and fighting for the throne. Consequently the Sikh state came to an unfortunate and abrupt end at the hands of the British.

Nevertheless, Maharaja Ranjit Singh can also be held responsible for this downfall, in not leaving a succession plan and not training potential successors in the art of running the state and army. His failure to do so resulted in incapable rulers and hence the end of *Khalsa* rule in the Punjab. However, despite all the chaos and anarchy, his successors did maintain the path of fair and benevolent treatment of the non-Sikh communities, including Muslims. Religion and ethnic origin had never set the course of state policies during the days of Ranjit Singh and this continued after his death, throughout the period 1839–49. All the Muslim nobles continued to enjoy their positions and privileges in the Lahore *Darbar* during this time, and even the unruly army had great regard for most of the Muslim notables, especially the Fakir brothers.

CONCLUSION

This study was undertaken with a new paradigm to understand the condition of the Muslims under Sikh rule in the Punjab. It challenges the stereotypical approaches, which highlight contradictions between Muslims and Sikhs. Some historians have pointed out that the Sikh rulers mistreated the Muslims, harmed their religion and damaged their religious places. In support of this, they claim that not only did the Muslims of India show resentment, but also that some of them started *Tehrik-e-Mujahidin* against Ranjit Singh's state. The author, with new evidence from the Fakir Khana archives in Pakistan and England, has developed the hypothesis that the Sikhs under Ranjit Singh and his successors adopted a secular approach towards minorities, including the Muslims – that is, there was not a single movement within the Punjab started by Muslims against the Sikh rulers. Instead, the *Tehrik-e-Mujahidin* that was launched against the alleged maltreatment of the Muslims was actually the result of a misperception of the Muslims' condition in the Punjab, and a number of studies have already shown that *Tehrik-e-Mujahidin* had many other motives as well.

A summary of the findings of the research follows.

Maharaja Ranjit Singh was a gifted and fortunate Sikh leader who out of nothing carved a great state for the Sikhs. His secularism has always been a subject of discussion and disagreement among historians, his policies and stance towards the Muslims and other religions being frequently questioned. Some historians emphasize that his secularism served a political purpose, earning him the support of all the religious minorities in order to extend his rule, and claiming that he did not treat the fallen Muslim rulers well. However, ample evidence exists that supports the Maharaja's secular and unbiased administrative and military affairs of state. Osborne comments: 'although Ranjit Singh is a Sikh but he is careless in his religion and it's very difficult to say that this secularism is false'.[1] The famous traveller Baron Charles Hügel remarked:

> The state established by the Maharaja Ranjit Singh was the most wonderful object in the whole world, like a skillful architect the Maharaja raised a majestic fabric, with the help of rather insignificant, or uncompromising fragments, and evolved a structure of power by which he could reconcile all important sections of his subjects to his support.[2]

The Maharaja might not have been secular in the strictest sense of the concept, yet he was liberal and fair enough to maintain a fine balance among different communities and their interests. He patiently and cleverly kept the atrocities of extremist *Akalis* away from the non-Sikh segments of society. He also assigned some very important state portfolios to Muslims. Therefore, the argument over whether his secularism was real or a farce becomes irrelevant, as he actually acted like a secular ruler. He maintained this posture and policy throughout his rule, aware that such a heterogeneous society as the Punjabis needed to be treated and run impartially. In fact, the Maharaja's catholicity and liberality in these matters was similar to the policies of the Emperor Akbar.

Indeed, political pragmatism always demands fair and impartial administration of state affairs. Ranjit Singh, therefore, could not afford to be biased or unfair, and the allegation of bias and partiality has no solid ground. His shrewd mind could well understand that the Sikhs were a small minority in the Punjab. Therefore, it was imperative for him to have the support of other communities, especially the landed and religious aristocracy. Indeed, the policy that required fair and just conduct of state affairs helped strengthen social harmony and wellbeing in the Punjab. It is worth mentioning here that despite slaughtering thousands on the battlefield, he hardly ever took the life of anyone, whether innocent or an offender, off the battleground. In the early nineteenth century he prohibited capital punishment and, despite strong pressure from different groups, he never resorted to cold-blooded killing of his personal or political opponents. Instead he provided even his defeated enemies with respectful living.

Ranjit Singh ruled the Punjab with common sense and principles of nature. He protected his people from outside invasion and from internal disorder. Hence he created a social and political environment for his people to realize their potential. Religion was never a criterion or consideration in his dispensation of state affairs. He often preferred to stand with his people rather than with his officers, as illustrated by his frequent change of governors in Peshawar and Kashmir. He knew the art of reading people and their talents, gathering around him an extraordinary pool of people of high calibre and ability. His court and camps comprised people from a wide range of nationalities, religions and professions. His *darbar* also had nobles and officials from all religions and communities: Sikhs, Hindus, Christians and Muslims. The Muslim nobles of Lahore welcomed the Sikh ruler, and he had the support of the Gilani and Bokhari Syeds in Multan,[3] as he offered the Muslim population a safe abode.[4] He employed Hindus and Muslims in his *darbar*, and kept up the Muslim *qazis*, which continued to perform nearly all the old duties.

When Ranjit Singh came to power, he wanted all his subjects, including Hindus and Muslims, to feel themselves as part of the Sikh state. Hence, he created an environment in which his people had equal rights, no matter what religion or community they belonged to. Among the talented people from all religions and communities who composed the *darbar*, the most famous Muslim courtiers were the three Fakir brothers, Elahi Bukhsh, Ghause Khan and Qazi Nizam-ud-din. A number of Europeans, such as Ventura and Allard, were also members of the Lahore *Darbar*. Therefore, personal ability, competence and hard work, not religion, were the essence of state service and the main criteria for appointment and rise in status and position.

Besides his courage and acumen, Ranjit Singh's most outstanding feature was this ability to select his team. He kept near him those persons whom he could trust for their wisdom and loyalty, and therefore Hindus, Muslims and Europeans served the *Khalsa* state during his lifetime and afterwards. They proved themselves to be truly trustworthy professionals who delivered according to the desires of the Maharaja and his successors until 1849.

In short, the Maharaja never ignored the Muslims, offering them their due share in all walks of life. This is evident from the important positions they held during his reign. Ranjit Singh appointed Muslim judges to manage Muslim matters. Under his rule, individuals and especially religious and educational institutions of different communities continued to receive grants in the form of tax-free lands or cash. The *qazis* enjoyed the old grants and privileges as well as new grants. He created a department of *dharmarth* that looked after the affairs of all the religious communities, including granting charity and assistance. He mostly assigned revenue matters to the holders of religious posts such as *imams*, *khadims* (servants), *mujawers* and *fakirs*, or the administrators of mosques and *khanqahs*. The department of *dharmarth* maintained a long list of beneficiaries of state grants, including Muslims – both Sunni and Shia – and Hindus.[5]

The Maharaja's greatest achievement was the unstinted and uncommon loyalty he commanded from all sections of his men, whether Muslim, Hindu, Sikh or Rajput, or even European. This sense of comradeship was achieved within four decades. Although he spent most of his time in fighting far from his capital, not a single man rose up against his authority.

European writers of the time were not trained historians. Most of them were travellers and some were in the service of their government, so the historical perspective varies from person to person. Despite all the criticism, Prinsep ranks Ranjit Singh among those whose career was not stained with brutal killings and crimes. Steinbach portrays him as an ambitious yet very superstitious person, although he reports that he was always considerate to all religions. M'Gregor, who served the Maharaja as his surgeon, insists: 'many erroneous reports are in circulation regarding Ranjit Singh, and it is but just, on the part of the one who had experienced some degree of kindness and attention from him to place his character in its true light'.[6] The Maharaja was known for his love of wealth,[7] but he was no miser: his annual charity stood at Rs.12 *lakh*.[8]

Ranjit Singh ruled the Punjab from 1799 to 1839, as an intelligent and resourceful head with an ambitious political agenda. With his gift for leadership and his military genius, he turned a crowd of *Khalsa* fighters into a formidable army that, out of nowhere, built a huge kingdom. This study concludes that while annexing territory to his kingdom, Ranjit Singh did not view any state or ruler from the viewpoint of a Sikh leader, but rather like any expansionist of his time. Given that he wished to become ruler of the Punjab, he waged wars, irrespective of religion, against all those rivals who stood in his way. Not only Muslim rulers were subdued; Hindus and Sikhs were not spared in his effort to expand his territory.

The present study reports that he treated his fallen enemies and the common population benevolently during his conquest of the Punjab. He granted *jagirs* and positions to his defeated enemies. The common people were allowed religious freedom, economic opportunities and access to education.

Muslims were appointed to high posts during the rule of Ranjit Singh, even in the conquered areas. He held the *qazis* in high esteem and in villages and towns, Muslim or non-Muslim, he allowed them to continue. There are a number of instances where deeds between Muslim and Muslim, Muslim and non-Muslim, and even non-Muslim and non-Muslim were executed by the *qazis*. Ranjit Singh continued the state grants to Muslim scholars started during the Mughal Empire.

Ranjit Singh used the state's resources well to help bring together various communities under his empire and exploit their potential.[9] His political, social, religious and administrative policies were free of bias and favouritism. Muslims had full access to education, employment and economic opportunities. The policies and programmes initiated and subsequently pursued by the Maharaja profited all segments of society. The state strategy was to incentivize farmers to bring more and more land under cultivation with the aim of increasing agricultural produce and subsequently revenue. The lower class of Punjabis was a great deal more comfortable than at any other time in recent memory. Similarly, there was significant increase and improvement in exchange and business during this period, as a result of which an increase in urban development was seen in the Punjab.

The downfall of the Sikh Empire under the successors of Ranjit Singh was as rapid and dramatic as had been its rise under him. His successors lacked his qualities of leadership and farsightedness and hence failed to preserve their *Khalsa* state. With their parochial policies and pursuit of personal interests, they hastened its decline betweecn 1839 and 1849, more occupied in conspiring and slaying each other than strengthening or consolidating the Sikh Empire Ranjit Singh had built through hard work. Internal fights for the throne drained their energies and the Sikh state came to a sad and abrupt end at the hands of the British.

Nevertheless, despite chaos and anarchy, and contrary to existing anecdotal evidence, his successors maintained the path of fair and benevolent treatment of the non-Sikh communities, including Muslims. Like Ranjit Singh, they never considered religion while formulating state policy. Thus, all the Muslim nobles continued to enjoy their positions and privileges in the Lahore *Darbar*, even maintaining the respect of the unruly army. History fails to narrate any significant incident upsetting the life of common Muslim citizens, who continued to have socio-economic and religious freedom.

The annals of history provide adequate evidence of how Hindu shrewdness and Muslim orthodoxy brought about the Gurus' fall. Muslim rulers played into the hands of Hindu *pandits* and willingly helped their designs come true. However, history must not forget that even under the worst circumstances, the common Muslims always helped the Gurus. They stood by them, fought for them, and many died for them. Many Muslim saints remained associated with Gurus. The murders of Guru Arjun, Guru Tegh Bahadur and finally Guru Gobind Singh still remain obscure and disputed under the intricate layers of the subcontinent's history.

However, one thing becomes clearer after each review of the subject: it was not religion or faith that were responsible for the unfortunate events,[10] rather the political ambitions and designs of Hindus, Muslims and later Sikhs themselves.

At the time of separation in 1947, we witnessed the horrifying results of this estrangement. While the Muslims were struggling against the Hindu majority and the British, the Sikh community decided to ally themselves with the Hindus. Whether or not this was a diplomatic failure of Muslims in their struggle for freedom, or political expediency on the part of Sikh leaders, it was largely the result of successful manoeuvring by the Hindu political leadership and intelligentsia. The Brahminic mind painted an unpleasant picture of the relationship between Muslims and Sikhs, creating a gulf of differences and misconceptions between the two natural allies.

In the light of the above facts and analyses, it is imperative to revisit the history of Sikh–Muslim relationships. The Sikh Gurus were never against Islam itself, but the biased policies and treatment of the Mughal nobility and *darbar* that did them many injustices. Moreover, let us not forget the similar biases, discriminatory policies and staunch opposition that the Hindu elite meted out to Sikhs. Historians should bring this aspect of the story to light to enable the Sikh community to decide for themselves. It is highly lamentable to see that numerous books on Sikh history do no more than demonstrate the sufferings of the Gurus at the hands of Muslim rulers, ignoring all the evils and injustices done to Sikhs by the Hindu vested groups.

In short, this book has shed new light on the history of Sikh–Muslim relations. Although these relations passed through a number of phases, yet they were not as bleak as the picture painted by some historians, which widens the gulf between Muslims and Sikhs. Rather, this study has proved that Muslims under the Sikh rule occupied key positions in the echelons of civil and military administration and played an important role in the formation and execution of state policies. There is ample room for further research to draw an even clearer picture of Sikh–Muslim relations. It is needless to stress that it is high time for both communities to revisit their relationship, seeing it from a true historical perspective and joining hands to usher in a new culture of dialogue, tolerance and mutual respect for each other's faith. This study may be considered as an attempt to achieve this end, building a better future for coming generations.

GLOSSARY

Aazan Muslim call to prayer
Akali Order of the Sikhs, literally meaning an immortal
Amir Title denoting a Muslim of high rank
Amir-ul-Momneen Leader of the Muslims
Bahadur Brave, a title of merit
Basanti Orange (colour)
Bhai Literally a 'brother'; a title of respect among the Sikhs and also the Muslims
Bhangi The name of a Sikh *misl*
Bigha Measure of land equal to half an acre or 4 *kanals*
Bowli Well
Chabook swar Officer in the *Khalsa* army
Chaudhari The chief person of the village, usually rich and distinguished
Darbar A court; an audience hall presided over by the king
Darbar Sahib The Golden Temple
Dargah Mausoleum
Dar-ul-Aman Abode of peace
Daswandh Tithe
Daswanth Charity (Sikh)
Dervish Sufi saint, *fakir*
Dharmarth Charity or for charitable purposes; department of religious affairs
Dharmshala Orphanage, poorhouse
Dhimmi Non-Muslim living in a Muslim state, under state protection
Din-i-Ilahi Religion propounded by Akbar the Great
Diwan The head of the finance department; also a minister, a steward
Doab Territory lying between two rivers; in the Punjab particularly that between the Sutlej and Beas
Dogra Inhabitant of Duggar Desh situated in the lower hills in Jammu, generally of Rajput origin
Doshala Double shawl
Durood Prayer
Fakir Mendicant; religious-minded person devoted to meditation
Farman Royal command
Fauj-i-khas Special royal corps. Here it refers to the French Brigade
Fiqh Islamic knowledge of laws
Gur Hard brown sugar
Gurdwara Gateway to the Guru, place of worship of Sikhs
Guru Granth Sahib The Sikh scripture
Gurumar Murderer of the Gurus
Gurumukhi New script established by Guru Angad
Hajj Pilgrimage (to Mecca)
Hakim Medical professional, scholar
Haramzadaz Bastard

Harhi (rabi) Summer harvest
Harmandir Sahib The Golden Temple
Haveli Villa, bungalow
Howdah Seat on an elephant
Hukka An Indian pipe and its apparatus by which tobacco is smoked through water
Imam Leader of prayer
Inam Gift
Jagir Feudal land given by government as a reward for services or as a fee
Jagirdar The holder of a *jagir*
Jihad Holy war
Jizya Tax on non-Muslims for their protection
Jubbah Cloak
Kafir Person who does not believe in God
Kanwar Prince; generally denoting princes other than the heir-apparent
Kardar Officer in charge of the revenue and local administration of a *pargana* or *taluqah*
Kaur Female form of respect
Khadim Servant
Khalsa The brotherhood of the Sikhs, particularly those conforming to the instructions of Guru Gobind Singh
Khalsa Sarkar Sikh government
Khanqah Monastery
Khatri Member of the fighting caste of the Hindu community according to the traditional duties enjoined upon the four castes
Khilat Robe of honour generally conferred by the king
Khizri Darwaza One of the gates of the fort
Khoja Muslim merchant community
Khoji Experts in tracing footprints of criminals
Khwaja Men of wealth and decency (Persian)
Kiladar Master of the fort or garrison
Koel Songbird
Kotwal Police officer
Kumedan Commandant (from French)
Kunwar Prince
Lakh One hundred thousand
Langar Free kitchen, food
Lungi Sarong
Madrassa Traditional religious school
Mafidar Holder of revenue-free land
Maharaja The great king
Mai Mother; a respectable form of address to a woman
Maktab Informal school
Maro, waddo, lutto Cry of guerilla warriors
Messiah Redeemer
Mina Protector of the *Granth Sahib*
Misldar Belonging to a Sikh; holder of a portion or all of the *misl*
Misl Sikh confederacy
Misr Name or a title given to Brahmins
Moharana Fee charged for affixing the government seal
Moulvi Muslim religious persons

Mufti Religious scholar
Muhallah Locality
Mujawar Custodian of mausoleum or shrine
Mullah Muslim priest
Munshi Writer, scribe, secretary
Mutsaddi Accountant, clerk
Naib Deputy in charge
Namaz Prayer
Nanakshahi Sikh rupee coin, current in Sikh times to the value of sixteen annas
Nazar Offering to a superior or a holy person
Nazim Governor of a province or an area
Nazrana Tribute on a regular basis or on special occasions
Nihang An order of Sikhs
Nizamat Kingship
Nuskha Copy of the Holy Quran
Palki Carrier, litter
Panchayat Village court of arbitration consisting of five or more members. It was the lowest rung in the hierarchy of judicial administration, here used for the executive council of a Sikh regiment elected by troops
Pandit Learned Brahmin; literally a wise or learned man
Panj Kakar The Five Ks or Sikh articles of faith: *kais* (uncut hair), *kanga* (comb), *kara* (iron bangles), *karpan* (sword), and *kacha* (undergarment)
Panj Piare The five loved ones, the first individuals of the *Kahlsa* fraternity
Para Holy Quran is divided into 30 parts each one is called 'para'.
Paracha Muslim merchant community
Parcha Cloth
Pargana Tract of country consisting of 50–100 villages
Pashmina Kind of fine wool; woollen goods
Pathshala Hindu religious school
Patwari Village accountant, revenue official
Pir Spiritual guide among the Muslims
Pruhat Hindu priest
Qari Reciter of the Holy Quran
Qazi Justice
Qissa Fictional story
Rabi Spring crop generally sown in October/November and harvested in April/May
Rai Title of respect bestowed by Sikh rulers on many of their dignitaries; Hindu chief
Raja King, prince; title of high rank
Rauza Shrine
Sahukar Banker, money-lender
Sajda-e-ta'zeem The prostration of respect
Sajjada nashin Successor of the shrine
Sarayi Resting place for travellers
Sardar Chief, commander; a form of address for all respectable Sikhs and Afghan chiefs
Sarkar Government, king's court; a title by which Maharaja Ranjit Singh was popularly addressed by his people
Shahi farman Imperial order
Shakar Soft brown sugar
Shalouk A form of Punjabi poetry; also *shabat, dhora, kaafi, alania*

Shariah Islamic code
Shastar Divine order of Hindus, code
Shehr-e-sabz Green city
Sheikh The head of a Muslim religious brotherhood or fraternity
Sulh-i-kul Absolute peace and tolerance
Suttee Ritual whereby a widow burns herself on the funeral pyre of her dead husband
Swar Horseman
Syed Descendants of Holy Prophet Muhammad (PBUH)
Takht Throne, platform
Takiaha Platform or place of shelter
Taluqa Revenue administrative area
Taqiyya Disguise
Tehrik-e-Mujahidin Armed movement against the Sikhs started by Syed Ahmed
Tiwana A caste in Punjab
Topchi Cannon operator
Topkhana Arsenal or magazine; artillery
Toshakhana Storeroom, wardrobe; chamber in which objects of value or rare articles are kept
Ulema Religious scholars in Islam
Wakil Ambassador, agent, representative
Waliullah Friend of God
Waqf Donation
Wazir Lieutenant of a king, counsellor of state, minister
Zafar Jang Winner of battles
Zakat Charity (Muslim)
Zamindar Landlord, proprietor or occupant of land
Zamzama Famous cannon, known as the *toap Bhangian*
Zeafat Lavish food

NOTES

Introduction

1. J. D. Cunningham, *History of the Sikhs* (New Delhi: n.p, 1966), 120.
2. Sita Ram Kohli, 'The Organization of Ranjit Singh's Army', in Teja Singh and Ganda Singh (eds), *Maharaja Ranjit Singh* (Reprint) (Patiala: n.p, 1970), 60–1.
3. H. T. Prinsep, *Sikh Power in the Punjab and Political Life of the Maharajaranjit Singh, with an Account of the Present Condition, Religion, Laws, and Customs of the Sikhs* (Calcutta: Military Orphan Press, 1834), 142–3.
4. N. K. Sinha, *Ranjit Singh* (Calcutta: n.p, 1960), 189–92.
5. Gurdashan Singh Dhillon, *The Sikh Rule and Ranjit Singh* (Patiala: Bharat Sarkar, Punjab Publishing House, 1992), 26.
6. Eric Bentley, *Century of Hero-Worship* (Boston: n.p, 1957), 3–8.
7. J. B. Macaulay, *Lord Macaulay's Legislative Minutes* (London: n.p, 1946), 2–3.
8. Jean-Marie Lafont, *Maharaja Ranjit Singh, Lord of the Five Rivers* (New Delhi: Oxford University Press, 2002).
9. H. S. Bhatia and S. R. Bakhshi, *Maharaja Ranjit Singh* (New Delhi: Elegant Printers, 2000), 23.
10. Ibid.
11. Lafont, *Maharaja Ranjit Singh, Lord of the Five Rivers.*
12. Lepel Henry Griffin, *Ranjit Singh* (Oxford: Clarendon Press, 1892), 45.
13. Ibid.
14. W. G. Osborne, *The Court and Camp of Ranjit Singh; with an Introductory Sketch of the Origin and Rise of the Sikh State* (Lahore: Mahbub Alam, 1895 [1840]).
15. Lafont, *Maharaja Ranjit Singh.*
16. G. S. Dhillon, *The Sikh Rule and Ranjit Singh: Studies in Sikhism and Comparative Religion,* Vol. 10 (New Delhi: Guru Nanak Foundation, 1991).
17. Ibid.
18. Griffin, *Ranjit Singh*, 46.
19. Osborne, *The Court and Camp of Ranjit Singh.*
20. Sohan Lal Suri, *Umdat-ut-Tawarikh*, trans. V. S. Suri. Vols 1–5 (Amritsar: Guru Nanak Dev University, 2002).
21. Griffin, *Ranjit Singh.*
22. Syed Muhammed Latif, *History of the Punjab* (Lahore: People's Publishing House, 1889).
23. Kanaya Lal, *Tarekh-e-Punjab* (Lahore: Sang-e-Meel, 1891).
24. Surjit Hans, 'The Gurbilas in the Early Nineteenth Century', *Journal of Regional History,* Vol. II. (Amritsar: Guru Nanak Dev University, 1981).
25. W. L. M'Gregor, *The History of the Sikhs; the Lives of the Gurus; the History of the Independent Sirdars, or Missuls, and the Life of the Great Founder of the Sikh Monarchy, Maharaja Ranjit Singh.* 2 vols (London: James Madden, 1846).

26 A. F. M. Abdul Ali, 'Notes on the Life and Times of Ranjit Singh', *Proceedings of the Indian Historical Records Commission* (1925).
27 H. S. Bhatia and S. R. Bakshi, *Encyclopaedic History of the Sikhs and Sikhism*, vol. 6 (New Delhi: Deep&Deep Publications, 1999).
28 Ikram Ali Malik, *A Book of Reading on the History of the Punjab, 1799–1947* (Lahore: Ilmi Printing Press, 1970).
29 Fakir Syed Waheeduddin, *The Real Ranjit Singh* (Karachi: Lion Art Press, 1965).
30 A. Nadeem, 'Need a History Lesson', http://blogs.tribune.com.pk/story/2313/need-a-history-lesson-babar-awan/: retrieved 10/04/2013.
31 Dhillon, *The Sikh Rule and Ranjit Singh*.
32 Lafont, *Maharaja Ranjit Singh, Lord of the Five Rivers*.
33 Fauja Singh and A.C. Arora (eds), *Maharaja Ranjit Singh: Politics, Society, and Economy* (Patiala: Publication Bureau, Punjabi University, 1984).
34 G. S. Chhabra, *Advanced History of the Punjab*. 2 vols. (Jullundher: New Academic Publishing Co, 1969).
35 Fauja Singh Bajwa, *Military System of the Sikhs During the Period 1799–1849* (Delhi: Shri Jainendra Press, 1964).
36 Khushwant Singh, *Ranjit Singh (1780–1839)* (n.p: Allen & Unwin, 1962).
37 J. S. Grewal, *The Sikhs of the Punjab: The New Cambridge History of India* (Cambridge: Cambridge University Press, 1990).
38 Fakir Syed Aijazuddin, *The Resourceful Fakirs: Three Muslim Brothers at the Sikh Court of Lahore* (Delhi: Three Rivers Publishers, 2014).
39 K. S. Duggal, *Ranjit Singh: A Secular Sikh Sovereign* (Delhi: Abhinav Publications, 1989).
40 Rajinder Singh, *The Secular Maharaja: Maharaja Ranjit Singh* (Delhi: Dynamic Publications, 2008).
41 J. S. Grewal and Indu Banga (eds), *Maharaja Ranjit Singh and His Times* (Amritsar: Department of History, Guru Nanak Dev University, 1980).
42 Patwant Singh and M Rai Jyoti, *Empire of the Sikhs: The Life and Times of Maharaja Ranjit Singh* (New Delhi: Hay House India, 2008).
43 J. S. Grewal, *Sikh Ideology Polity and Social Order* (Delhi: Man Mohan Publishers, 1996).
44 Indu Banga, *Agrarian System of the Sikhs: Late Eighteenth and Early Nineteenth Century* (Amritsar: Manohar Publisher, 1978).
45 Amarinder Singh, *The Last Sunset: The Rise and Fall of the Lahore Durbar* (New Delhi: Lotus Collection Roli Books, 2010).
46 J. S. Grewal, *The Reign of Maharaja Ranjit Singh: Structure of Power, Economy and Society* (Patiala: Punjabi University, 1981).
47 Purnima Dhavan, *When Sparrows Became Hawks: The Making of the Sikh Warrior Tradition, 1699–1799* (Oxford: Oxford University Press, 2011).
48 Jaspal Kaur Singh, *Violance and Resistance in Sikh Gendered Identity* (USA: Taylor & Francis Group, 2020).
49 Dalvir Singh Pannu, *The Sikh Heritage: Beyond Borders* (Lahore: Fiction House, 2019).
50 Mohammad Sheikh, *Emperor of the Five Rivers: The Life and Times of Maharaja Ranjit Sing,* (London: I.B. Tauris, 2017).
51 Sarbpreet Singh, *The Camel Merchant of Philadelphia* (Chennai: Westland Publications, 2019).

Chapter 1

1. Khwaja Hasan Nizami, *Dai-i-Islam* (Amritsar: n.p, 1923).
2. J. S. Grewal, *Essays in the Sikh History, from Guru Nanak to the Maharaja Ranjit Singh* (Amritsar: Gru Nanak Dev University, 1972), 17.
3. W. H. McLeod, *Textual Sources for the Study of Sikhism*, trans. W. H. McLeod (Manchester: Manchester University Press, 1984), 57.
4. Ibid.
5. http://sikhspectrum.com/2002/10/interview-makhdoom-syed-chan-pir-qadri-on-sikh-muslim-relations/#sthash.JO6VW4Iy.dpuf: retrieved 20/09/2014.
6. R. C. Dogra, *The Sikh World: An Encyclopedic Survey of Sikh Religion and Culture* (New Delhi: UBSPD, 2003), 34.
7. http://sikhspectrum.com/2002/10/interview-makhdoom-syed-chan-pir-qadri-on-sikh-muslim-relations/#sthash.JO6VW4Iy.dpuf: retrieved 21/09/2014.
8. Henry Francis B. Espiritu, 'Dilip Singh on Muslim–Sikh Relations in Mogul India: A Pluralist Appraisal', *Understanding Sikhism – The Research Journal* 12, no. 1 (2010): 42–8.
9. Ibid.
10. Davinder Singh Chahal, *Nankian Philosophy: Basics for Humanity* (Quebec: Institute for Understanding Sikhism, 2008), 43–54.
11. Ibid.
12. The *Akal Takht*, meaning 'throne of the timeless one', is one of five takhts of the Sikh religion. It is located in the *Harmandir Sahib* complex in Amritsar, Punjab, about 250 miles northwest of New Delhi.
13. Dogra, *The Sikh World*, 38.
14. http://www.amritsar.com/The%20Five%20K.shtml: retrieved 13/08/2021.
15. Yoginder Sikand, 'Building Bridges between Sikhs and Muslims', *Studies in Interreligious Dialogue*, 9, no. 2 (1999): 178–88.
16. Nizami, *Dai-i-Islam*.
17. Fredrick Pincott, *Sufi Influence on the Formation of Sikhism in the World of the Sufis* (London: Octagon Press, 1979), 121–45.
18. Thomas Patrick Hughes, *Dictionary of Islam* (London: W. H. Allen, 1885), 23.
19. Davinder, *Nankian Philosophy*, 43–54.
20. 'Guru Nanak's Understanding of God by Bipin Kujur', http://snphilosophers2005.tripod.com/bipin.pdf: retrieved 27/07/2015.
21. Habil James Massey, 'Guru Nanak Dev Ji's Teachings in the Context of Inter-Faith Dialogue', *Sikh Review* 51, no. 5 (2013): 19–23. See also James Massey, 'A Fresh Look at Sikh Religion', *Studies in Sikhism and Comparative Religion* 6, no. 1 (1985): 69–79.
22. Christopher Columbus (1450–1506) was an Italian explorer, navigator, colonizer and citizen of the Republic of Genoa. Under the auspices of the Catholic Monarchs of Spain, he completed four voyages across the Atlantic Ocean.
23. Vasco da Gama (d. 1524) was the first European to reach India by sea, linking Europe and Asia for the first time by ocean route, as well as the Atlantic and the Indian oceans entirely and definitively, and in this way, the West and the Orient. This was accomplished on his first voyage to India (1497–9).
24. Michelangelo di Lodovico Buonarroti Simoni (1475–1564) was an Italian sculptor, painter, architect, poet and engineer of the High Renaissance, who exerted an unparalleled influence on the development of Western art. 'Michelangelo biography', *Encyclopædia Britannica*.

25 Raffaello Sanzio da Urbino (Raphael) (1483–1520), was an Italian painter and architect of the High Renaissance. His work is admired for its clarity of form, ease of composition, and visual achievement of the Neoplatonic ideal of human grandeur. Hugh Honour and John Fleming, *A World History of Art* (London: Macmillan Reference Books, 1982), 357.
26 Leonardo da Vinci (1452–1519) was a painter, sculptor, architect, scientist, musician, mathematician, engineer, inventor, anatomist, geologist, astronomer, cartographer, botanist, historian and writer. He is widely considered to be one of the greatest painters of all time and perhaps the most diversely talented person ever to have lived in the Western world. Helen Gardner, *Art Through the Ages* (London: Bell and Sons, 1959), 450–6.
27 Martin Luther (1483–1546) was a German friar, priest and professor of theology who was a seminal figure in the Protestant Reformation. Luther came to reject several teachings and practices of the Roman Catholic Church.
28 Huldreich Zwingli (1484–1531) was a leader of the Reformation in Switzerland.
29 John Calvin (1509–64) was an influential French theologian and pastor during the Protestant Reformation.
30 Massey, 'A Fresh Look at Sikh Religion'.
31 Grewal, *Sikh Ideology, Polity and Social Order* (Delhi: Manmohan Publishers, 1996), 12.
32 Ibid.; see also Syed Muhammed Latif, *History of the Punjab* (Lahore: People's Publishing House, 1889), 241–5.
33 Grewal, *Sikh Ideology, Polity and Social Order*, 12.
34 Bhai Das was one of the earliest devotees of the Guru Nanak.
35 Namadeva (traditionally, *c.* 1270–*c.* 1350) was a poet-saint from the Maharashtra state of India who is significant to the Varkari sect of Hinduism. He is also venerated in Sikhism.
36 Ramananda was a fouirteenth-century Vaishnava devotional poet saint in the Ganges river region of Northern India. The Hindu tradition recognizes him as the founder of the Ramanandi Sampradaya, the largest monastic Hindu renunciant community in modern times. William Pinch, *Peasants and Monks in British India* (University of California Press, 1996), 53–89.
37 Surdas was a fifteenth-century blind saint, poet and musician, known for his devotional songs dedicated to Lord Krishna Surdas. He is said to have written and composed a hundred thousand songs in his magnum opus the 'Sur Sagar' (Ocean of Melody), out of which only about 8,000 are extant. He is considered a saguna bhakti poet and so also known as Sant Surdas, a name which literally means 'servant of melody'.
38 Kabir was a fifteenth-century mystic poet and saint of India, whose writings influenced Hinduism's Bhakti movement and Sikhism's founder Nanak. His early life was in a Muslim family, but he was strongly influenced by his teacher, the Hindu bhakti leader Ramananda.
39 Khwaja Fariduddin Ganj Shakar (1173–1266) was a Sufi saint and Muslim missionary in the Punjab region of South Asia, belonging to the Chishti Order. Baba Farid, as he is commonly known, has his poetry included in the *Guru Granth Sahib*, the most sacred scripture of Sikhism, which includes 123 (or 134) hymns composed by Farid. Guru Arjun, the 5th Guru of Sikhism, included these hymns himself in the *Adi Granth*, the predecessor of the *Guru Granth Sahib*.
40 Mian Mir was a famous Sufi Muslim saint who resided in Lahore. Mian Mir holds a pivotal legendary place in Sikhism. Sikh people around the world learn about him, his spiritual contribution and his place in Sikh history.

41 G. M. D. Sufi, *Kashīr - Being a History of Kashmīr from the Earliest Times to Our Own*, 2nd ed. (Lahore: University of the Punjab, 1949), 707-8.
42 Sikand, 'Sikh-Muslim Harmony, Contribution of Khawaja Hassan Nizami', *Economic and Political Weekly* 31 (2004): 1113-16.
43 Sikand, 'Building Bridges between Sikhs and Muslims', *Studies in Interreligious Dialogue*, 9, no. 2 (1999): 178-88.
44 Dominique-Sila Khan received her doctorate from the Sorbonne University, Paris. She has worked as an independent researcher, associated with the Institute of Rajasthan Studies. She has specialized in the study of Hindu-Muslim interactions in South Asia, particularly the study of obscure branches of Nizaria Ismailis in India. Ibid.; Sikand, 'Sikh-Muslim Harmony', 1113-16.
45 Sila Khan, 'Nizaria Ismailis in India', PhD thesis. https://www.iis.ac.uk/people/dominique-sila-khan.
46 K. S. Duggal, *The Sikh People Yesterday and Today* (New Delhi: UBS, 1994), 12.
47 Ibid.
48 G. S. Chhabra, *Advanced History of the Punjab*, vol. 1 (Jullundher: New Academic Publishing Co, 1969), 77-8.
49 Kirpal Singh, *The Partition of the Punjab, Revised by Sri Ram Sharma* (Patiala: Punjabi University, 1972), 16; Harish K. Puri, 'The Scheduled Castes in the Sikh Community - A Historical Perspective', *Economic and Political Weekly* (June 2003): 2-3; A. L. Basham, *The Wonder That Was India* (Fontana: Sedgwick & Jackson, 1971), 148-52.
50 Aziz Ahmad, *Studies in Islamic Culture in the Indian Environment* (London: Oxford University Press, 1964), 152.
51 Tara Chand, *Influence of Islam on Indian Culture*, 2nd ed. (Lahore: Book Traders, 1979), 169.
52 Ibid.
53 Ethne K. Marenco, *The Transformation of Sikh Society* (New Delhi: Heritage Publishers, 1976), 24.
54 C. H. Loehlin, *The Granth of Guru Gobind Singh and the Khalsa Brotherhood* (Lucknow: Lucknow Publishing House, 1971), 1.
55 R. M. Chopra, 'Guru Nanak's Teachings', *The Sikh Review* 44, no. 515 (11-1996): 19-22.
56 'Iqbal's Estimate of Guru Nanak M. Abadulla Farooqi', http://www.allamaiqbal.com/publications/journals/review/oct62/8.htm: retrieved 16/03/2015.
57 'Guru Nanak's Understanding of God by Bipin Kujur', http://snphilosophers2005.tripod.com/bipin.pdf: retrieved 23/07/2015.
58 Chhabra, 54.
59 Ibid., 55.
60 Ibid., 56.
61 Iqbal Qaiser, *Historical Sikh Shrines in Pakistan* (Lahore: Punjab History Board, 1998), 12.
62 Ibid.
63 Chhabra, 55.
64 These are all types of Punjabi poetry.
65 Chhabra, 59.
66 Manmohan Singh, trans., *Siri Guru Granth Sahib*, 4th ed. (Amritsar: Shiromani Gurdawara Parbandhak Committee, Golden Offset Press, 1993), 210.
67 W. L. M'Gregor, *The History of the Sikhs; the Lives of the Gurus; the History of the Independent Sirdars, or Missuls, and the Life of the Great Founder of the Sikh Monarchy, Maharaja Ranjit Singh*, vol. 1 (London: James Madden, 1846), 32.

68 H. S. Bhatia and S. R. Bakshi, *Encyclopaedic History of the Sikhs and Sikhism*, vol. 1, 12.
69 Massey, 'A Fresh Look at Sikh Religion'.
70 'Guru Nanak's Understanding of God by Bipin Kujur', http://snphilosophers2005.tripod.com/bipin.pdf: retrieved 24/07/2015.
71 Khushwant Singh, *The Sikhs* (Calcutta: Orient Longmans, 1959), 5.
72 For the Sikhs, *Japji Sahib* begins with the definitions of God, known as the 'Mool Mantra' – the basic statement of Sikh belief.
73 'Medieval Indian History and Culture Through the Ages', http://www.nios.ac.in/media/documents/SecICHCour/English/CH.04.pdf: retrieved 22/02/2015.
74 'Great Seer and Philosopher Part II', http://www.dawn.com/news/794292/Guru-Nanak-a-Great-Seer-and-a-True-Son-of-Soil-part-ii: retrieved 11/10/2014.
75 Massey, 'A Fresh Look At Sikh Religion'.
76 Ibid.; see also Dogra, *The Sikh World*.
77 Bhatia and Bakshi, *Encyclopedic History of the Sikhs and Sikhism*, vol. 2, 118; see also M'Gregor, *The History of the Sikhs*, 48.
78 Bhatia and Bakshi, 11.
79 Ibid.; see also Chhabra, *Advanced History of the Punjab*, vol. 1, 118.
80 Ibid., 119; see also Bhatia and Bakshi, 12.
81 Chhabra, *Advanced History of the Punjab*, vol. 1, 120.
82 Bhatia and Bakshi, 13.
83 Guru Angad died in March 1552. Bhatia and Bakshi, 13.
84 Ibid., 34; Dogra, *The Sikh World*, 32.
85 Chhabra, *Advanced History of the Punjab*, vol. 1, 129.
86 M'Gregor, *The History of the Sikhs*, 50.
87 Tarn Taran Sahib is a city in the state of Punjab, Northern India. It was founded by Guru Arjun Dev, the fifth Guru of the Sikhs.
88 The Udasis were founded by Baba Sri Chand (1494–1629), the eldest son of Guru Nanak. Udasi, from the root 'udas', means detachment, withdrawal from worldly life, solitary, sadness and grief, and so refers to one who renounces. Traditionally Baba Sri Chand is said to have opposed his father's appointment of Guru Angad as the second Guru, and so he started his own order.
89 M'Gregor, *The History of the Sikhs*, 51.
90 *Baisakhi* refers to the harvest festival of the Punjab region, the Punjabi New Year falling on the same day. The day represents Spring, which occurs around 21 March, but the festival is marked on 13 or 14 April due to changes in the calendar
91 Bhatia and Bakshi, 14.
92 Dogra, *The Sikh World*, 34.
93 M'Gregor, *The History of the Sikhs*, 52, 54.
94 Bhatia and Bakshi, 15.
95 Chhabra, *Advanced History of the Punjab*, vol. 1, 143.
96 Guru Ramdas was impressed by the teachings of Guru Angad and embraced Sikhism. He was a young man with a beautiful physique and internal beauty of mind. He won the heart of Guru Amar Das, who married his daughter Bibi Bhani to him. Bhatia and Bakshi, 16.
97 Chhabra, 144.
98 Ibid., 52, 54.
99 Bhatia and Bakshi, 17.
100 Ibid.

101 The *Harmandir Sahib*, also *Darbar Sahib* and informally referred to as the 'Golden Temple', is the holiest Sikh *Gurdwara* located in the city of Amritsar, Punjab, India.
102 Ibid.; Dogra, *The Sikh World*, 33.
103 Martin Latham, *The Sikhs* (n.p: n.p, 1985), 21–9.
104 Ibid., 21.
105 Ibid., 21; Chhabra, *Advanced History of the Punjab*, vol. 1, 199.
106 Bhatia and Bakshi, 22.
107 M'Gregor, *The History of the Sikhs*, 61.
108 Bhatia and Bakshi, 25.
109 Ibid.
110 M'Gregor, *The History of the Sikhs*, 63.
111 Chhabra, *Advanced History of the Punjab*, vol. 1, 236.
112 Baba Bakala is a historical town and Tehsil in the Amritsar district in Punjab, India. Baba Bakala is closely associated with the ninth Guru of Sikhs, Guru Tegh Bahadur Sahib. The Guru meditated here for twenty years.
113 Chhabra, *Advanced History of the Punjab*, vol. 1, 236; see also Bhatia and Bakshi, 27.
114 Bhatia and Bakshi, 27.
115 Ibid., 28.
116 Ibid.
117 Anandpur Sahib is a city in Rupnagar district in the state of Punjab, India. It is one of the Sikhs' most important sacred places, closely linked with their religious traditions and history.
118 Mir Farina, *The Social Space of Language: Vernacular Culture in British Colonial Punjab* (Berkeley: University of California Press, 2010), 207–37.
119 M'Gregor, *The History of the Sikhs*, 66–7.
120 Bhatia and Bakshi, 51.
121 H. R. Gupta, *History of the Sikhs: The Sikh Gurus, 1469–1708*, vol. 1, (Delhi: New Gion Offset Press, 1991), 188.
122 Cynthia Keppley Mahmood, *Fighting for Faith and Nation Dialogues with Sikh Militants* (Philadelphia: University of Pennsylvania Press, 1996), 43–5.
123 Gurbakhsh Singh, *Sikhs Under Brahmanical Siege* (n.p: Canadian Sikh Study and Teaching Society, 2014), 44.
124 Indubhusan Banerjee, *Evolution of the Khalsa* (Calcutta: A. Mukerjee, 1963), 25.
125 Wazir Khan was Governor of Sirhind, administering a territory of the Mughal Empire between the Sutlej and Yamuna rivers. Harjinder Singh, *Sikh History*, vol. 2 (Belgium: Sikh University Press, 2010), 31.
126 Chitra Soundar, *Gateway to Indian Culture* (n.p: Asiapac Books, n.d), 59; see also Dilip Singh, *Guru Gobind Singh and Khalsa Discipline* (Amritsar: Singh Bros, 1992), 256.
127 Prithi Pal Singh, *The History of Sikh Gurus* (n.p: Educa Books, 2007), 158.
128 Chhabra, *Advanced History of the Punjab*, vol. 1; see also Bhatia and Bakshi, 309.
129 Ibid., 59; Soundar, *Gateway to Indian Culture*.
130 While he appointed *Sri Guru Granth Sahib* as his spiritual successor, he also declared the *Khalsa* as his physical successor. Guru Gobind Singh felt that all the wisdom needed by Sikhs for spiritual guidance in their daily lives could be found in *Sri Guru Granth Sahib*, the eternal Guru of the Sikhs. *Sri Guru Granth Sahib* is unique in the world of religious scriptures not only because of its status of being the spiritual head of the Sikh religion, but also because of the poetry of the Gurus and the writings of saints of other faiths whose thoughts were consistent with those of the Sikh Gurus. Dogra, *The Sikh World*, 34.

131 Kanaya Lal, *Tareekh-e-Punjab* (Lahore: Majlis-e-Tarakiay Adab, 1981), 34.
132 M'Gregor, *The History of the Sikhs*, 103–4,
133 Henry Francis B. Espiritu, 'Dalip Singh On Muslim-Sikh Relations in Mogul India: A Pluralist Appraisal' *Understanding Sikhism – The Research Journal* 12, no. 1 (2010): 42–66.
134 Sardar Shiakh Muhammad Yousuf, 'Sikh Muslim Relation', *Noor* (1948), 10.
135 One bigha is equal to half an acre of land.
136 Yousuf, 'Sikh Muslim Relation'.
137 Ibid.
138 Sufi, 701.
139 Nooruddin Mohammad Jahrangir, *Tuzkiajahangiri*, ed. Henry Beveridge, trans. Alexander Rogers (London: Royal Asiatic Society, 1909), vol, 1: 72–3; J. S. Grewal and Irfan Habib, *Sikh History from Persian Sources: Translations of Major Texts* (Lahore: Fiction House, 2004), 3–4.
140 Chhabra, *Advanced History of the Punjab*, vol. 1, 169.
141 Ibid., 170.
142 Ibid.; Nooruddin Mohammad Jahrangir, *Tuzkiajahangiri*, 72.
143 Mohammad Jahangir Tamimi, *Sikh–Muslim Taluqaatek: Tehkeeki Jayaiza* (Lahore: South Asian Study Center Punjab University, 2007), 30; Grewal and Irfan Habib, 4.
144 Chhabra, *Advanced History of the Punjab*, vol. 1, 169.
145 Shaikh Ahmad Sirhindi (1564–24) was an Islamic scholar in India and a member of the Naqshbandi Sufi order. He has been described by some followers as a Mujaddid, meaning a 'reviver', for his work in rejuvenating Islam and opposing the newly made religion of Din-i-Ilahi and other dissident opinions of Mughal Emperor Akbar.
146 Annemarie Schimmel, *Islam in the Indian Subcontinent* (Leiden: Brill, 1980), 90.
147 Ibid., 92.
148 Khwaja Baqi Billah (1564–1603) was a Sufi saint from Kabul and the originator and pioneer of the Naqshbandi Order in the subcontinent.
149 Teja Singh and Ganda Singh, *A Short History of the Sikhs* (Bombay: Orient Longmans, 1950), 32; see also Grewal, *The New Cambridge History of India: The Sikhs of the Punjab*, 55.
150 Sirdar Kapoor Singh, 'Guru Arjun's Martyrdom: Contemporary Perceptions', in Prithipal Singh Kapoor et al. (eds), *Guru Arjun Dev: Life, Martyrdom and Legacy* (New Delhi: Gurdawara Management Committee, 2006), 102–3.
151 Pashaura Singh, *Life and Work of Guru Arjan: History, Memory, and Biography in the Sikh Tradition* (New Delhi: Oxford University Press, 2006), 231.
152 *Jizya* is a tax taken from non-Muslims in an Islamic state for their protection.
153 *Maktoobat-e-Imam Rabbani*, 193.
154 Chhabra, *Advanced History of the Punjab*, vol. 1, 174.
155 Prithipal Singh and Mohinder Singh, *Guru Arjun's Contribution, Martyrdom, and Legacy* (Amritsar: Singh Brothers, 2009), 163; see also Louis E. Fenech, *Martyrdom in the Sikh Traditions: Playing the 'Game of Love'* (New Delhi: Oxford University Press, 2002), 117–18; Yohanan Friedmann, *Shaykh Ahmad Sirhindi: An Outline of his Thoughts and a Study of his Image in the Eyes of Posterity* (Montreal: McGill University, n.p, 1966), 73.
156 A religion propounded by the Mughal Emperor Akbar the Great in 1582 AD, intending to merge the best elements of the religions of his empire, and thereby reconcile the differences that divided his subjects.
157 Nooruddin Mohammad Jahrangir, *Tuzkiajahangiri*, 73.

158 Syed Athar Abbas Rizvi, *Muslim Revivalist Movements in Northern India in the Sixteenth and Seventeenth Centuries* (New Delhi: Munshiram Manoharlal, 1995), 287.
159 Ibid., 287.
160 Chhabra, *Advanced History of the Punjab*, vol. 1, 175.
161 Grewal and Irfan Habib, 4.
162 Chhabra, *Advanced History of the Punjab*, vol. 1, 170, 171.
163 Ibid., 174; Nooruddin Mohammad Jahangir, *Tuzkiajahangiri*, vol. 1.
164 Ibid., 14; Tamimi.
165 Chhabra, *Advanced History of the Punjab*, vol. 1, 172–3.
166 Sardar Kapoor Singh, 'Martyred by Shamanistic Laws', in Prithipal Singh Kapoor et al. (eds), *Guru Arjun Dev: Life, Martyrdom and Legacy* (New Delhi: Gurdawara Management Committee, 2006), 76.
167 Ibid., 76; Grewal and Irfan Habib, 4.
168 Prithipal Singh and Mohinder Singh, *Guru Arjun's Contribution, Martyrdom, and Legacy*, 21; see also Fenech, 117–18; Grewal and Irfan Habib, 57.
169 Prithipal Singh and Mohinder Singh, 21; see also Grewal and Irfan Habib, 56.
170 Fenech, 117–18.
171 Sardar Kapoor, 78.
172 Prithipal Singh and Mohinder Singh, 44.
173 Sufi, vol. 2, 703.
174 Grewal and Irfan Habib, 4; see also Hardip Singh Syan, *Sikh Militancy in the Seventeenth Century: Religous Violence in Mughal and Early Modern India* (New York: I.B. Tauris, 2013), 21.
175 J.S. Grewal, *The Sikhs of the Punjab: The New Cambridge History of India* (Cambridge: Cambridge University Press, 1990), 64.
176 Ibid.
177 Prithipal Singh and Mohinder Singh, 145; Grewal, *The Sikhs of the Punjab*, 72.
178 Ranbir Singh, *Glimpses of the Divine Masters, Guru Nank – Guru Gobind Singh, 1469-1707* (New Delhi: International Traders Corporation, 1965), 212; see also Grewal, *The Sikhs of the Punjab*, 72.
179 Ibid., 213; see also Grewal, *The Sikhs of the Punjab*, 72.
180 Sardar Ratnal Singh, *The Khalsa* (Amritsar: Gurdawara Parbandhak Committee, 1979), 5; see also Grewal, *The Sikhs of the Punjab*, 72.
181 Jaswinder Singh Kang, 'Shahada Deh Sartaj Guru Arjun Dev', *Monthly Z-Premier UK* (2000), 50.
182 M'Gregor, *The History of the Sikhs*, 66–7, 95–6.
183 Tegh Bahadur, the eighth successor of (Guru) Nanak, became a man of authority with a large number of followers. In fact several thousand persons used to accompany him as he moved from place to place. His contemporary Hafiz Adam, a fakir belonging to the group of Shaikh Ahmad Sirhindi's followers, had also come to have a large number of murids and followers. Both these men (Guru Tegh Bahadur and Hafiz Adam) used to move about in the Punjab, adopting a habit of coercion and extortion. Tegh Bahadur used to collect money from Hindus and Hafiz Adam from Muslims. The royal *waqia navis* (news reporter and intelligence agent) wrote to the Emperor Aurangzeb of their manner of activity, adding that if their authority increased they could become even refractory. Mir Farina, *The Social Space of Language: Vernacular Culture in British Colonial Punjab*, 207–37.
184 Latif, *Tarikh e Punjab*, 520.

185 Bute Shah, *Gulam Muhayy-ud-Din: Tawarikh-i-Punjab* (Patiala: Punjabi University, n.d), 34.
186 Ibid.; Latif, *Tarikh e Punjab*, 522.
187 Sufi, vol. 2, 703.
188 Ernest Trumpp, *The Adhi Granth* (London: n.p, 1871), 14.
189 Major Henry Court, *History of the Sikhs* (Lahore: Civil and Military Gazette Press, 1888), 35.
190 Tamimi, 63.
191 Chhabra, 21.
192 William Owen Cole and Piara Singh Sambhi, *The Sikhs: Their Religious Beliefs and Practice* (n.p: Sussex Academic Press, 1995), 36.
193 *Gazetteer of the Sirmur State* (New Delhi: Indus Publishing, 1996), 9.
194 Harjinder Singh Dilgeer, *Sikh History,* vol. 1 (n.p: Sikh University Press, 2010), 11.
195 Ajay Singh Rawat, *Garhwal Himalaya: A Study in Historical Perspective* (n.p: Indus Publishing, 2002), 50–4.
196 Gopal Singh, *A History of the Sikh People, 146–1978* (Delhi: World Sikh University Press, 1979), 289–90.
197 Hardip Singh Syan, *Sikh Militancy in the Seventeenth Century: Religious Violence in Mughal and Early Modern India*, (New York: I.B. Tauris, 2013), 219.
198 Indubhusan Banerjee, *Evolution of the Khalsa* (Calcutta: A. Mukerjee, 1963), 25.
199 Prithi Pal Singh, 128–47.
200 Dilip Singh, *Life of Sri Gobind Singh Ji*, 290.
201 Ibid., 294.
202 Sufi, vol. 2, 704.
203 M'Gregor, 91–99.
204 Sufi, vol. 2, 704.
205 Ibid., 704.
206 Prithi Pal Singh, *The History of Sikh Gurus*, 158.
207 Dilip Singh, *Life of Sri Gobind Singh Ji*, 296.
208 Ibid., 300.
209 Ibid., 328, 331.
210 Ibid., 330, 329.
211 Latif, *Tarikh e Punjab*, 547.
212 Aziz Ahmad Chaudhary, *Punjab Mughloon Kay Ahd e Zawal main* (Lahore: Punjab Research Foundation, 1980), 20.
213 Sonipat is a town in Haryana Punjab.
214 O. P. Ralhan, *The Great Gurus of the Sikhs: Banda Bahadur* (n.p: Anmol Publications Pvt Ltd, 1997), 38.
215 Samana is a city and a municipal council in Patiala district in the Indian state of Punjab.
216 Teja Singh, *A Short History of the Sikhs: 1469–1765* (Patiala: Punjabi University, 1999), 79.
217 Gurbaksh Singh, *The Khalsa Generals* (n.p: Canadian Sikh Study and Teaching Society, 1927), 8.
218 H. S. Singha, *Sikh Studies,* vol. 6 (n.p: Hemkunt Press, 2005), 14.
219 Harbans Singh, *The Encyclopaedia of Sikhism: A–D* (Patiala: Punjabi University, 1995), 27.
220 Tony Jaques, *Dictionary of Battles and Sieges* (London: Greenwood Publishing Group, 2007), 595; see also H. R. Gupta, *History of the Sikhs: Evolution of Sikh*

      Confederacies, 1708–1769 (3rd rev. ed.) (The University of Virginia: Munshiram Manoharlal, 1978), 19.
221 Gurbaksh Singh, *The Khalsa Generals*, 10.
222 Teja Singh, *A Short History of the Sikhs: 1469–1765*, 93.
223 Ibid., 94.
224 Nahar Awandha, *Glimpses of Sikhism* (New Delhi: Sanbun Publishers, 2010), 82.
225 Dale Hoiberg, *Students' Britannica India*, vol. 1 (New Delhi: Popular Prakashan, 2000), 157.
226 Gurbaksh Singh, *The Khalsa Generals*, 12; see also Surinder Johar, *Guru Gobind Singh* (University of Michigan: Enkay Publishers, 1987), 208.
227 Ganda Singh, *Life of Banda Singh Bahadur: Based on Contemporary and Original Records* (Amritsar: Sikh History Research Department, 1935), 229.
228 Hari Ram Gupta, *Later Mughal History of the Punjab, 1707–1793* (Lahore: Sang-e-Meel Publications, 1976), 46–7.
229 Hari Ram Gupta, *A History of the Sikhs from Nadir Shah's Invasion to the Rise of Ranjit Singh (1739–1799)*, vol. I: *Evolution of the Sikh Confederacies (1739–1768)* (Simla: Minerva Book House, 1952), 68–9. Translation: Mannu is like a sickle for us but despite his killing, we grow more and more in number. Bhagat Singh, 'Mu'in ul-Mulk', *The Encyclopedia of Sikhism* (Patiala: Punjabi University, 1997), 3.131.
230 According to the *Punjabi-English Dictionary*, the definitions of 'Ghalughara' are as follows: 'holocaust, massacre, great destruction, deluge, genocide, slaughter, (historically) the great loss of life suffered by Sikhs at the hands of their rulers, particularly on 1 May 1746 and 5 February 1762.' S. S. Joshi and Mukhtiar Singh Gill (eds), *Punjabi-English Dictionary* (Patiala, India: Punjabi University Publication Bureau, 1994), 293.
231 Sardar Singh Bhatia, 'Vadda Ghallughara', *The Encyclopedia of Sikhism*, vol. 4 (Patiala: Punjabi University, 1998), 396; Syad Muhammad Latif, *The History of Punjab from the Remotest Antiquity to the Present Time* (New Delhi: Eurasia Publishing House Pvt, Ltd, 1964), 283.
232 Khushwant Singh, *A History of the Sikhs, 1469–1839*, vol. 1 (Delhi: Oxford University Press, 1978), 154–5.
233 Sangat Singh, *The Sikhs in History*, 2nd ed. (New Delhi: Uncommon Books, 1996), 106.
234 Ganda Singh, *Ahmad Shah Abdali* (Lahore: Takhliqat, 1993), 285.
235 Bijla Singh, *Abdali and the Sikhs*, http://gurmatbibek.com/forum/read.php?3,11139,11139;quote=1#REPLY: retrieved 14/01/2015.
236 Chhabra, *Advanced History of the Punjab*, vol. 1, 119.
237 Sufi, vol. 2, 727.
238 Sufi, vol. 2, 704.
239 Dilip Singh and Espiritu, *Sikh Muslim Relations*, 66.

Chapter 2

1 Preminder Singh Sandhawalia, *Noblemen and Kinsmen: History of a Sikh Family* (New Delhi: Munshiram Manoharlal, 1999), 11.
2 Khushwant Singh, *Ranjit Singh (1799–1839)*, 3.
3 Grewal, *The Sikhs of the Punjab*, *The New Cambridge History of India*, 100.
4 Ibid.

5 Ibid.
6 Khushwant Singh, *Ranjit Singh*, 3.
7 *Sarbat Khalsa*, a Punjabi phrase, was a biannual deliberative assembly (on the same lines as a Parliament in a direct democracy) of the entire *Khalsa* held at Amritsar in Punjab during the eighteenth century.
8 *Misl* generally refers to the sovereign states of the Sikh Confederacy that rose during the eighteenth century in the Punjab region. Although the *misls* were unequal in strength and each *misl* attempted to expand its territory and resources at the expense of others, they acted in unison in relation to other states. The *misls* held biannual meetings of their legislature, the *Sarbat Khalsa* in Amritsar.
9 Grewal, *Maharaja Ranjit Singh and His Times*, 249.
10 Alexander Haughton Campbell Gardner, *Soldier and Traveller: Memoirs of Alexander Gardner* (Edinburgh and London: William Blackwood and Sons, 1898), 298.
11 Khushwant Singh, *Ranjit Singh*, 1; see also Harbans Singh (ed.), *Encyclopedia of Sikhism* (Patiala: Punjabi University, 1992), s.v.
12 Ikram Ali Malik, *A Book of Reading on the History of the Punjab, 1799–1947* (Lahore: Ilmi Printing Press, 1970), 2.
13 Grewal, *The Sikhs of the Punjab*, 103.
14 Ibid., 101.
15 Latif, *History of the Punjab*, 349; see also Chhabra, *Advanced History of the Punjab*, vol. 1, 33.
16 Jasbir Singh Ahluwalia and Param Bakhshish Singh, *An Overview of Maharaja Ranjit Singh and His Times* (Delhi: Anand Sons, 2001), 117.
17 Santokh Singh Ji, 'Rise of Sikh Power (1784–1839)', http://www.panthkhalsa.org/raj/raj_puratan2.php: retrieved 23/07/2015.
18 *Umdatu-ut-Tawarikh*, vol. 4, 53; see also Latif, *History of the Punjab*, 355.
19 Ibid., 68; Latif, *History of the Punjab*, 355.
20 *Umdat-ut-Tawarikh*, vol. 2, 52; see also Latif, *History of the Punjab*, 678.
21 Punjab Government, *Gazetteer Ferozepure District 1883–4* (Lahore: Civil and Military Gazette Press, n.d), 25.
22 J. D. Cunnigham, *History of the Sikhs* (New Delhi: n.p, 1966), 120, 116.
23 Giani Gian Singh, *Tawarikh e Guru Khalsa* (Urdu) *Hissa Dom* (n.p: Guru Gobind Singh Press, 1892), 90, 108.
24 Punjab Government, *Gazetteer Ferozepure District 1883–4*, 25.
25 Ibid., 40; see also Chhabra, *The Advanced History of the Punjab*, 37; Grewal, *The Sikhs of the Punjab*, 101.
26 Chhabra, *The Advanced History of the Punjab*, 43.
27 Punjab Government, *Gazetteer Ferozepure District 1883–4*, 25.
28 Griffin, *Punjab Chiefs*, 343.
29 Punjab Government, *Gazetteer Ferozepure District 1883–4*, 25; see also Chhabra, *The Advanced History of the Punjab*, 41.
30 Hugh Chisholm (ed.), *Encyclopedia Britannica*, 11th ed. (Cambridge: Cambridge University Press, 1910–11), 892.
31 Ibid., 50; also see also Khushwant Singh, *A History of the Sikhs 146–1839*, vol. 1, 249.
32 Ibid., 51; Chhabra, *The Advanced History of the Punjab*.
33 *Encyclopedia Britannica*, 893.
34 It is said that Ranjit Singh, after capturing the city of Lahore, received the authority letter from the Afghan ruler as the governor of Punjab from the king of Kabul, Tamur Shah.

35 *Encyclopedia Britannica,* 893; Chhabra, *The Advanced History of the Punjab;* see also Khushwant Singh, *A History of the Sikhs,* vol. 1, 249.
36 Ibid.; Chhabra.
37 S. M. Latif, *Tarikh i Punjab,* 689.
38 *Umda -tu-Tawarikh,* vol. 4, 55; Latif, 689; Griffin, *Ruler of India, Ranjit Singh,* 182.
39 Kanhaiya Lal, *Tareekh e Punjab,* 162.
40 Ibid.
41 Ibid.
42 Grewal, *The Sikhs of the Punjab,* 103.
43 Ibid.; see also Griffin, *Ranjit Singh,* 183.
44 Kanhaiya Lal, 169.
45 Khuswant Singh, *Ranjit Singh,* 126; see also Ikram Ali Malik, 115, 116.
46 Ibid.; see also Ikram Ali Malik, 116.
47 Lepel Henery Griffin, *Chiefs and Families of Note in the Punjab,* (Lahore: Government Printing Press Punjab, 1940), 477–88.
48 Ibid., 567.
49 Ganda Singh, *The Punjab in 1839-40, Selection from the Punjab Akhbars, Punjabi Intelligence etc.* (Amritsar: Sikh History Society, 1952), 6.
50 Ibid., 127; Khushwant Singh, *A History of the Sikhs,* vol. 1, 251.
51 Latif, *History of the Punjab,* 689; Kanhaiya Lal, 167.
52 Kanhaiya Lal, 167, 168.
53 Ibid.
54 Ahmad Khan had two cannons but the soldier in charge of them was not expert.
55 Kanhaiya Lal, 169.
56 Ibid.
57 Ibid.
58 Ibid.
59 Mufti Ghulam Server, *Tarikh e Makhzan e Punjab* (n.p: Mnshi Nok Shor Man, 1859), 247; Ikram Ali Malik, 117; see also Griffin, *Punjab Chiefs,* 273.
60 Ikram Ali Malik, 117.
61 Griffin, *Punjab Chiefs,* 545, 550.
62 Ikram Ali Malik, 115, 128, 129.
63 Griffin, *Tazkara e Raosay Punjab, Hissa Dom,* trans. Syed Nawazish Ali, vol. 1 (Lahore: Sang e Meel Publications, 1993), 208–52.
64 Ikram Ali Malik, 130.
65 Hari Ram Gupta, *History of the Sikhs: The Sikh Lion of Lahore, Maharaja Ranjit Singh 1799-1839,* vol. 5 (Delhi: New Gion Offset Press, 1991), 169.
66 Ibid.
67 Grewal, *The Sikhs of the Punjab,* 105.
68 Chhabra, 61.
69 Khushwant Singh, *Ranjit Singh,* 21.
70 Chhabra, 62; also see Khushwant Singh, *A History of the Sikhs,* vol. 1, *1469-1839,* 254.
71 Chhabra, 63; Khushwant Singh, *A History of the Sikhs,* vol.1, *1469-1839,* 254.
72 Chhabra; Khushwant Singh, *A History of the Sikhs,* vol. 1, 254.
73 Chhabra; Khushwant Singh, *A History of the Sikhs,* vol. 1, 263.
74 Alexander Burnes, *Travels into Bokhara: Containing the Narrative of a Voyage on the Indus from the Sea to Lahore and an Account of a Journey from India to Cabool, Tartary and Persia in the Years 1831, 1832, and 1833,* Kathleen Hopkirk (ed.) (London: Eland, 2012), 95.

75 Chhabra, 64.
76 Latif, 532.
77 Ibid., 533.
78 Rajinder Singh, *The Secular Maharaja, Maharaja Ranjit Singh* (Delhi: Dynamic Publications, 2008), 157.
79 Alexander Burnes, 98.
80 Sufi, 733.
81 Mian Muhammed Saeed, *Ulema e Hind Ka Shandar Mazi, Hissa Dom* (Delhi: n.p, 1957), 143.
82 Ibid., 143.
83 Ganda Singh (ed.), *Private Correspondence Relating to the Anglo-Sikh Wars. Being Private Letters of Lords Ellenborough, Hardinge, Dalhousie and Gough and of Political Assistants Addressed to Sir Frederick Currie as British Resident at Lahore, etc.* (Amritsar: Sikh History Society, 1955), 30; see also Khushwant Singh, *A History of the Sikhs,* vol. 1, 271.
84 Lafont, *Essays in Indo-French Relations, 1630–1976* (New Delhi: Manohar Publishers, 2000), 204.
85 Sufi, 734.
86 Olivier Roy, *Islam and Resistance in Afghanistan* (Cambridge: Cambridge University Press, 1985), 57–8.
87 Chhabra, 65.
88 Rajinder Singh, *The Secular Maharaja, Maharaja Ranjit Singh*, 159.
89 Henry Thoby Prinsep, *History of the Punjab, and of the Rise, Progress, and Present Condition of the Sect and Nation of the Sikhs. Based in Part on the 'Origin of the Sikh Power in the Punjab and Political Life of Muha-Raja Runjeet Singh'* (London: W. H. Allen & Co, 1846), 150.
90 Khushwant Singh, *Ranjit Singh*, 164, 165.
91 A place in Saudi Arabia where Wahhabism was started.
92 S. M. Latif, *Maharaja Ranjit Singh, Builder of a Common Wealth* (Delhi: National Book Shop, 2002), 120; see also Chhabra, 41.
93 Rajinder Singh, *The Secular Maharaja, Maharaja Ranjit Singh,* 160.
94 Khushwant Singh, *Ranjit Singh,*165; see also Khushwant Singh, *A History of the Sikhs,* 274.
95 Chhabra; see also Khushwant Singh, *A History of the Sikhs,* 274.
96 Kanhaiya Lal, 187; Latif, *Tarikh e Punjab,* 530.
97 K. S. Duggal, *Ranjit Singh – a Secular Sikh Sovereign* (Delhi: Abhinav Publications, 1989), 103.
98 Chhabra, 66.
99 A story told by a member of the Fakir Khana family and published in *The Express Tribune*, 15 October 2011.
100 Iqbal Salahuddin, *Tareekh e Punjab* (Lahore: Aziz Publishers, 1974), 520.
101 Ibid., 521.
102 Ibid.
103 Sinha, 149.
104 Diaries of Ranjit Singh Darbar from 1822 to 1826 in Fakir Khana family.
105 Sindh is one of the four provinces of Pakistan, located in the southeast of the country.
106 Salahuddin, 494.
107 Ibid.
108 Ibid.

109 Ibid.
110 Duggal, 112; see also Salahuddin, *Tareekh-e-Punjab*, 494.
111 Griffin, *Chiefs and Families of Note in the Punjab*, 55.
112 Latif, *Tarikh e Punjab*, 534.
113 Khushwant Singh, *Ranjit Singh, Maharaja of the Punjab*, 45; see also Sharma, *Maharaja Ranjit Singh, Ruler and Warrior* (Chandi Garh: Punjab University, 2005), 67.
114 Punjab Government, *Gazetteer Dera Ghazi Khan District 1883–4* (Calcutta: Calcutta Centeral Press, n.d), 20.
115 Punjab Government, *Gazetteer Dera Ismail Khan District 1883–4* (Lahore: Arya Press, 1884), 37; see also Khushwant Singh, *A History of the Sikhs*, vol. 1, 257.
116 Khushwant Singh, *A History of the Sikhs*, vol. 1, 256, 257.
117 Punjab Government, *Gazetteer Dera Ismail Khan District 1883–4*, 37–38; see also Khushwant Singh, *A History of the Sikhs*, vol. 1, 257.
118 Punjab Government, *Gazetteer Bannu District 1883–4* (Calcutta: Calcutta Central Press, n.d), 36.
119 Khushwant Singh, *A History of the Sikhs*, vol. 1, 237.
120 Ibid., 254.
121 Ibid., 255.
122 Sohan Lal Suri, *Umdat-ut-Tawarikh*, 84.
123 Ibid., Iqbal Salahuddin, 500.
124 Khushwant Singh, *A History of the Sikhs*, vol. 1, 255.
125 Ibid., 255.
126 A magnificent and famous touring place in northern part of Pakistan endowed with mountains, rocks, pine trees, valleys and fountains.
127 Sufi, 721.
128 Ibid., 504.
129 Ibid.
130 *The Lahore Darbar: In the Light of the Correspondence of Sir C. M. Wade (1823–49)* (Lahore: Punjab Government Records Office, 1930).
131 Duggal, *Ranjit Singh – a Secular Sikh Sovereign*, 112.
132 Harbans Singh and Bilbir Singh, *Maharaja Ranjit Singh: Being Tribute to the Memory of the Great Monarch, Published on the Occasion of the First Death Century* (Lahore: University Sikh Association, 1939), 27.
133 Bikrama Jit Hasrat, *Life and Times of Ranjit Singh, a Saga of Benevolent Despotism* (Hoshiarpur: V.V Research Institute Book Agency, 1977), 41–2.
134 T. R. Sharma, 148.
135 Hasrat, 45.
136 Sharma, *Maharaja Ranjit Singh, Ruler and Warrior*, 148.
137 Hasrat, 51.
138 Ibid., 50.
139 Ibid., 49.
140 Khushwant Singh, *Ranjit Singh, Maharaja of the Punjab*, 26.
141 Ibid.
142 Osborne, 36.
143 Gulam Muhaiy-ud-Din Bute Shah, *Tawarikh-i-Punjab* (Patiala: Punjabi University, n.d), 53–4.
144 Hasrat, 50.
145 Hasrat, 50; see also Sharma, *Maharaja Ranjit Singh*, 150.

146 Hasrat, 53.
147 William Moorcroft and George Trebeck, *Travels in the Himalayan Provinces of Hindustan and the Panjab: In Ladakh and Kashmir; In Peshawar, Kabul, Kunduz, and Bokhara from 1819–1825* (Patiala: Languages Dept, 1970), 75, 76.
148 Khushwant Singh, *A History of the Sikhs*, 232.
149 Prinsep. *History of the Punjab, and of the Rise, Progress, and Present Condition of the Sect and Nation of the Sikh*s, 111, 112; see also Khushwant Singh, *A History of the Sikhs*, 232.
150 Hasrat, 54.
151 N. B. Sen, *Maharaja Ranjit Singh and Koh-i-Noor Diamond* (New Delhi: New Book Society India, 2001), 75.
152 Sen, 75; Stephen Howarth, *The Koh-i-Noor Diamond, the History and the Legend* (London: Quartet Books, 1980), 65.
153 Narendernath Ganguli, 'The Koh-i-Noor', *Past and Present* 73, 137 (July–December 1954): 91–103; see also Howarth, *The Koh-i-Noor Diamond*, 87.
154 Ghulam Ghaus, *The Koh-i-noor Diamond* (Peshawar: Taj Mahal Company, 1993), 61.
155 Narendernath Ganguli, 'The Koh-i-Noor', 91–103.
156 Ibid.
157 Khushwant Singh, *Ranjit Singh, Maharaja of the Punjab,* 105.
158 Suri, vol. 3, 129; see also Sen, *Maharaja Ranjit Singh and Koh-i-Noor Diamond*, 72, 73.
159 Khushwant Singh, *Ranjit Singh,* 107.
160 Ibid., 108.
161 Diaries of the Fakir Khana Collection.
162 Sen, 76, 77.
163 Iradj Amini, *Koh-i-Noor* (New Delhi: The Lotus Collection, 1994), 194.
164 Narendra Krishna Sinha and Arun Kumar Dasgupta (eds), *Selections from Ochterlony Papers, 1818–1825, in the National Archives of India* (Calcutta: University of Calcutta, 1964), 88; see also Latif, *Tarikh i Punjab,* 339.
165 H. T. Prinsep, *Sikh Power in the Punjab and Political Life of the Maharaja Ranjit Singh, with an Account of the Present Condition, Religion, Laws, and Customs of the Sikhs* (Calcutta: Military Orphan Press, 1834), 98.
166 Lieut Barnett, 'Autobiographical Sketch by Shah Shuja', *Monthly Journal*, 1826–7. Quoted in J. M. Lafont, *Maharaja Ranjit Singh, the French Connections* (Amritsar: Guru Nanak Dev University, 2001), 15.
167 H. M. L Lawrence, *Adventures of an Officer in Punjab*, vol. 1(London: Oxford University Press, 1975), 30–1.
168 Griffin, *Ranjit Singh*, 54.
169 Griffin, *Punjab Chiefs*, 343.
170 Ibid., 207.
171 Ibid., 208.
172 Ibid., 240.
173 Ibid., 273.
174 Major G. Carmichael Smyth, *A History of the Reigning Family of the Lahore, with Some Accounts of the Jumoo Rajhas, the Seik Soldiers and Their Sardars* (Calcutta: W. Thaker & Co, 1847), 213–14.
175 Ibid.
176 Griffin, *Punjab Chiefs*, 304, 305.
177 Ibid., 486.

178 Waheeduddin, 21.
179 Radha Sharma, *The Lahore Darbar* (Amritsar: Guru Nanak Dev University, 2001), 15; B. J. Hasrat, *Life and Times of Maharaja Ranjit Singh*, 263, 265; see also Grewal and Indu Banga (eds), *Maharaja Ranjit Singh and His Times* (Amritsar: Department of History, Guru Nanak Dev University, 1980), 27–8.
180 H. Lawrence, *Adventures of an Officer in Punjab*, vol. 1 (London: Oxford University Press, 1975), 57.
181 Ibid., 58.
182 Alexander Burnes, *Travels into Bokhara*, vol. I (London: n.p, 1834), 285.
183 Griffin. *Ranjit Singh*, 190.
184 Ibid.,191.
185 Grewal, *The Sikhs of the Punjab*, 101, 106.

Chapter 3

1 Waheeduddin, *The Real Ranjit Singh*, 21; see also Lafont, *Maharaja Ranjit Singh, Lord of the Five Rivers*, 81.
2 Griffin reports that obliteration of Islam was the main objective of Sikhism, reperted in Muhammad Bashir Dar, 'Sikhoon Kay Ahad Main Muslimanoon Ki Saqafti Halat, 1954' (MA diss., Punjab University, 1954), 65.
3 *Report on the Census, Taken on the 1st January 1855, of the Population of the Punjab Territories.* (Calcutta: Calcutta Gazette Office, 1856), IOR/V/23/2, no. 11, 20.
4 *Punjab, Political Settlement, Grants of lands or money and tenure by religious institutions to be dealt with and annual report to be made by Commissioner as in India Office Records and Private Papers (1854–1855)*, IOR/Z/E/4/25/P1051.
5 *Report on the Revenue Settlements of the Lahore District 1865*, 27, 36.
6 *Census Report, 1855*, 21.
7 Ibid., 22.
8 H. Lawrence, *The Adventures of an Officer*, 2nd ed, vol. 1, 84.
9 Punjab Government, *Gazetteer Bannu District 1883–4*, 54; see also Punjab Government, *Gazetteer Gujrat District 1883-4* (Lahore: Arya Press, 1884), 34; see also Fauja Singh and A. C. Arora (eds), *Maharaja Ranjit Singh: Politics, Society, and Economy*, 276.
10 Server, 152.
11 The Jats' sub-castes included Sidhu, Sansi, Sandhu, Randhawa, Shergill, Mann, Gill, Dhillon, Kahlon, Chahal, Bains, Bhinder, Virk, Sohal, Warraich and Bajwa.
12 The Khatries comprised 17 per cent of the population, and their sub-castes included Chopra, Duggal, Badhera, Bhandari, Khanna, Puri, Sahni, Behl, Anand, Kochhar, Sethi, Mehra, Maini, Uppal and Kapur. The tribes of Chopra, Duggal, Badhera, Bhandari, Nanda and Kapur were greater in numbers.
13 Griffin, *The Panjab Chiefs*, 523–72; Radha Sharma, *The Lahore Darbar* (Amritsar: Guru Nanak Dev University, 2001), 109–19; Inderyas Bhatti, 'Nobility Under Lahore Darbar' (MPhil diss.), (Guru Nanak Dev University, 1981), 4.
14 The exact number of these European officers who took service under Ranjit Singh cannot be determined, though Carmichael Smyth enumerates them as thirty-nine in total: Italian, French, English. Major G. Carmichael Smyth, *A History of the Reigning Family of the Lahore, with some Accounts of the Jumoo Rajhas, the Seik Soldiers and Their Sardars* (Calcutta: W. Thaker & Co, 1847), 1; see also Hasrat, *Life and Times of Maharaja Ranjit Singh*, 271.

15 Muhammad Bashir Dar, 65.
16 Ibid.
17 H. T. Prinsep, *Origin of the Sikh Power in the Punjab and Political Life of the Maharaja Ranjit Singh, with an Account of the Present Conditions, Religion, Laws and Customs of the Sikhs* (Calcutta: Military Orphan Press, 1834), 210, 211.
18 Muslims' call for prayer.
19 Khan Muhammed, 109.
20 Most evidence on the subject comes from the travelogues of the famous travellers who wrote their diaries, accounts and biographies. However, most of these travellers were British and French who had overt or covert political ambitions in the subcontinent. Later some historians and researchers worked in these areas; nevertheless, they were predominantly the Hindus or the British with clear sociopolitical and economic interests in the subcontinent, especially the Punjab, which was mainly Muslim and also under the control of Sikhs.
21 Victor Jacquemont was a French traveller who visited India in 1828–32.
22 Victor Jacquemont, *Letters from India: Describing a Journey in the British Dominions of India, Tibet, Lahore and Cashmere during the Years 1828, 1829, 1830, 1831*, vol. 1 (Karachi; Oxford: Oxford University Press, 1979), 399.
23 *Punjab, Political Settlement, Grants of lands or money and tenure of by religious institutions to be dealt with and annual report to be made by Commissioner as in India Office Records and Private Papers (1854–1855)*, 48. IOR/Z/E/4/25/P1051.
24 Waheeduddin, 21.
25 Khushwant Singh, *Ranjit Singh*, 1.
26 Kanaya Lal, *Tareekh-e-Punjab*, 144.
27 Garrett and Chopra, 30.
28 A detailed list to this effect is attached as an annexure to this book.
29 A long list of the donations is available in the family archives of Fakir Khana family, including the names of the recipients, mosques, the people who were serving the mosques and the Muslim shrines, and is attached as an annexure to this book.
30 Noor Ahmad Chishti, *Tahqiqat e Chishti* (Lahore: Nashran wa Tajran Jutab, 1867), 169.
31 Ibid., 815.
32 Suri, *Umdat-ut-Tawarikh*, vol. 3, 184.
33 Noor Ahmad Chishti, 817.
34 Ibid., 186.
35 Ibid., 193.
36 Indu Banga, *Agrarian System of the Sikhs, Late Eighteenth and Early Nineteenth Century* (Amritsar: Manohar Publisher, 1978), 164.
37 Jasbir Singh Ahluwalia and Param Bakhshish Singh, *Ranjit Singh and His Times* (Patiala: Punjabi University, 2001), 138.
38 Chishti, 207.
39 Ibid., 163.
40 Ibid., 223.
41 Ibid., 257.
42 Ibid.
43 Ibid., 354–60.
44 Ibid., 891.
45 P. N. Chopra, *Society and Culture During Mughal Age* (Agra: Shiva Lal Agarwal and Co, 1963), 84; H. R. Gupta, *History of the Sikhs*, vol. 4, 469.

46 K. M. Ashraf, *Life and Condition of the People of Hindustan* (New Delhi: Munshiram Manoharlal, 1970), 241; B. S. Nijjar, *Punjab Under the Later Mughals (1526–1707)* (Bombay: Thacker and Co, 1968), 276.
47 Chopra, 84; Gupta, *History of the Sikhs*, vol. 4, 469.
48 Chishti, 466, 467.
49 Fauja Singh and A. C. Arora (eds), *Maharaja Ranjit Singh: Politics, Society, and Economy*, 280; *Heer Waris*, Shamsher Singh Ashok (ed.) (Patiala: Punjab Languages Department, 1976), 12.
50 Fauja Singh and A. C. Arora, 280; Waris Shah, 12.
51 William Moorcroft and George Trebeck, *Travels in the Himalayan Provinces of Hindustan and the Panjab; in Ladakh and Kashmir; in Peshawar, Kabul, Kunduz and Bokhara . . . from 1819 to 1825* (London: 1841), 120.
52 Chishti, 774.
53 Server, 213.
54 Ibid., 221.
55 Chishti, 897.
56 Lafont, *Maharaja Ranjit Singh, Lord of the Five Rivers*, 74, 75; this story was also described in the Diaries of the Fakir Khana family's private collections.
57 Lafont, *Maharaja Ranjit Singh, Lord of the Five Rivers*, 75.
58 Lieutenant William Barr, *Journal of a March from Delhi to Peshawur, and from Thence to Cabul, with the Mission to Lieut-Col. Sir C. M. Wade, etc. with Plates* (London: J. Madden & Co, 1844), 71.
59 Khushwant Singh, *Ranjit Singh*, 127.
60 Patwant Singh and Jyoti M. Rai, 207.
61 Khushwant Singh, *A History of the Sikhs*, vol. 1, 295.
62 Patwant Singh and Jyoti M. Rai, 208.
63 Ganda Singh, *The Punjab in 1839–40: Selection from the Punjab Akhbars, Punjabi Intelligence etc.* (Amritsar: Sikh History Society, 1952), 6.
64 Server, 530, 531.
65 Ibid., 243.
66 Ganda Singh, *The Punjab in 1839–40*, 6.
67 Griffin, *Tazkara i Raoosa e Punjab*, vol. 2, 497.
68 Indu Banga, *Agrarian System of the Sikhs*, 164.
69 Mir Ahmad, *Dastur al amal-i-Kashmir*, 184, 206, 208, 209.
70 Baron Charles Hügel, *Travels in Kashmir and the Punjab: Containing a Particular Account of the Government and Character of the Sikhs / from the German* (London: J. Petheram, 1845), 354.
71 Punjab Government, *Gazetteer Peshawar District 1883–4*, 207–8.
72 Jasbir Singh and Param Bakhshish Singh, 123.
73 Punjab Government, *Gazetteer Bannu District 1883–4*, 194–6.
74 Punjab Government, *Gazetteer Dera Ghazi Khan District 1883–4*, 120. Jasbir Singh and Param Bakhshish Singh, 123.
75 Indu Banga, *Agrarian System of the Sikhs*, 165.
76 Henry Thoby Prinsep, *History of the Punjab, and of the Rise, Progress, and Present Condition of the Sect and Nation of the Sikhs. Based in part on the "Origin of the Sikh Power in the Punjab and Political Life of Muha-Raja Runjeet Singh"* (London: W. H. Allen & Co, 1846), 167.
77 Server, 194.
78 Ibid., 192–5.

79 Holder of *muafi,* which means a specific portion of land, held revenue-free.
80 B. H. Baden-Powell, *The Land-Systems of British India with Maps,* vol. 2 (Oxford: Clarendon Press, 1892), 698–9.
81 Irfan Habib, *The Agrarian System of Mughal India 1556–1707* (Bombay: n.p, 1963), 298–316.
82 Indu Banga, *Agrarian System of the Sikhs,* 166.
83 *Report on the Administration of the Punjab for the Years 1849–50 and 1850–51* (Calcutta: Calcutta Gazette Office, 1853), IOR/V/23/1, no. 2.
84 *Muharram* is a religious occasion that the Muslims observe in commemoration of the sacrifice offered by the grandson (Imam Hussain SA) of the Holy Prophet Muhammad.
85 Sinha, *Ranjit Singh,* 143, 152.
86 *Tazia* represents the image of the grave/shrine of the Imam Hussain (AS), third Imam of Shias, who was martyred in Karbala (Iraq).
87 N. K. Sinha, *Ranjit Singh,* 171.
88 Garrett and Chopra, *Events at the Court of Ranjit Singh, 1810–1817,* 30.
89 Chishti, 1083.
90 Khushwant Singh, *Ranjit Singh,* 127; see also Arminder Singh, *The Last Sunset – The Rise and Fall of the Lahore Durbar* (New Delhi: Roli Books, 2010), 21.
91 *Umdat-ut-Tawarikh,* 624; Fakir Syed Aijazuddin, *The Resourceful Fakirs, Three Muslim Brothers at the Sikh Court of Lahore* (Delhi: Three Rivers Publishers, 2014), 244.
92 *Eid-ul-Fitar* is a religious festival that Muslims celebrate after fasting in the month of Ramazan.
93 Waheeduddin, 20, 21.
94 Chishti, 1083.
95 Jasbir Singh Ahluwalia and Param Bakhshish Singh, 111.
96 Khan Muhammed, 109.
97 Waheeduddin, 22, 23.
98 Prithipal Kapur and Dharam Singh, *Maharaja Ranjit Singh: Commemoration Volume on the Bicentenary of His Coronation, 1801–2001,* Prithipal Singh Kapur (ed.) (Patiala: Publication Bureau, Punjabi University, 2001), 146–7.
99 Chishti, 692, 701.
100 Prithipal Singh Kapur and Dharam Singh, 146, 147.
101 W. G. Osborne, *The Court and Camp of Maharaja Ranjit Singh,* 44.
102 Chishti, 734.
103 Prithipal Singh Kapur and Dharam Singh, 145.
104 William Barr, 65.
105 Azizuddin Ahmad, 42.
106 Chishti, 927
107 Azizuddin Ahmad, 47.
108 Ibid., 42.
109 Server, 213.
110 Gregor, *The History of the Sikhs; the Lives of the Gurus; the History of the Independent Sirdars, or Missuls, and the Life of the Great Founder of the Sikh Monarchy, Maharaja Ranjit Singh,* vol. 2, 239.
111 http://www.newsplus24.com/2011/10/28/ranjit-singh-as-observed-by-an-english-lady/: retrieved 15/07/2014.
112 Suri, *Umdat–ut-Tawarikh,* (1974), 526; see also Aijazuddin, 215.

113 Victor Jacquemont, *Letters from India: Describing a Journey in the British Dominions of India,* vol. 1, 399.
114 Denzil Ibbetson, *Punjab Castes* (Delhi: B.R. Publishing Corporation, 1974), 228–9; B. J. Hasrat, *Life and Times of Maharaja Ranjit Singh,* 406; H. R. Gupta, *History of the Sikhs: The Sikh Lion of Lahore, Maharaja Ranjit Singh, 1799–1839,* vol. 4 (Delhi: New Gion Offset Press, 1991), 434.
115 M'Gregor, *The History of the Sikhs,* vol. 2, 237–9.
116 Lieut Alexander Burnes, *Travels into Bokhara: Containing the Narrative of a Voyage on the Indus from the Sea to Lahore and an Account of a Journey from India to Cabool, Tartary and Persia in the Years 1831, 1832, and 1833,* ed. Kathleen Hopkirk (London: Eland, 2012), 72.
117 Emily Eden, *Up the Country: Letters Written to her Sister from the Upper Provinces of India,* introduction by Elizabeth Claridge; notes by Edward Thompson (London: Virago, 1997), 209.
118 Ibid.; *Umdatut–ut-Tawarikh,* 593; see also Aijazudin, 233.
119 Carmichael Smyth, 185, 186.
120 Ibid., 187.
121 Khushwant Singh, *Ranjit Singh,* 92.
122 Ibid.
123 Ibid.
124 Khushwant Singh, *A History of the Sikhs,* vol. 1, 203.
125 Osborne, 93.
126 F. S. Bajwa, *Military System of the Sikhs,1799–1849* (Delhi: n.p, 1964), 32.
127 Prinsep, *History of the Punjab,* 45.
128 Shahamet Ali, *In ihe Sikhs and Afghans, in Connexion with India and Persia, Immediately Before and After the Death of Ranjeet Singh: From the Journal of an Expedition to Kabul through the Punjab and the Khaibar Pass* (London: n.p, 1847), 23.
129 Waheeduddin, 23.
130 Ibid., 21.
131 Ibid., 23.
132 Ibid., 24.
133 http://searchsikhism.com/maharaja-ranjit-singh/financial-civil-and-military-administration-of-the-maharaja#sthash.kL4XknoA.dpuf: retrieved 23/08/2015.
134 Sufi, 722.
135 Ibid., 634.
136 Fauja Singh and A. C. Chopra, 149.
137 Sufi, 723.
138 William Moorcroft, *Travels 1819–25,* vol. 2, 123, 124.
139 Tahir Asghar, *From Star to Galaxy: A Biography of Haji Bashir Ahmed and Abdul Ghafoor* (Faisalabad, Nisar Art Press, 2003), 30.
140 Muhammad Aslam, *1947 Mein Ludhiana K Musalmano Per Kia Guzri* (Lahore: Darul Kitab Publishers, 2014), 100.
141 Datta, Vishwa N., 'Panjabi Refugees and the Urban Development of Greater Delhi', *Delhi Through the Ages. Essays in Urban History, Culture and Society* (Delhi: Oxford University Press, 1986), 442–60.
142 Lafont, *Maharaja Ranjit Singh, Lord of the Five Rivers,* 88, 89.
143 Server, 576.
144 Lafont, *Maharaja Ranjit Singh, Lord of the Five Rivers,* 88.

145 Sir C. M. Wade, *The Lahore Darbar: In the Light of the Correspondence of Sir C. M. Wade (1823–49). Notes on the State of our Relations with the Punjab, and the Best Mode of their Settlement* (Lahore: Punjab Government Records Office, 1930); see also Lafont, *Maharaja Ranjit Singh, Lord of the Five Rivers*, 88–90.
146 Fauja Singh and A. C. Chopra, 149.
147 William Moorcroft, *Travels*, vol. 2, 293–4.
148 Ibid., 123–4.
149 G. T. Vigne, *A Personal Narrative of a Visit to Ghazni, Cabul and Afghanistan and of a Residence at the Court of Dost Mohammad*, vol. 1 (London: Whittaker & Co., 1840), 308.
150 Sufi, 722.
151 Ibid.
152 Fauja Singh and A. C. Chopra, 149.
153 Sufi, 739.
154 Fauja Singh and A. C. Chopra, 150.
155 Ibid., 151.
156 Lafont, *Maharaja Ranjit Singh, Lord of the Five Rivers*, 97.
157 Punjab Government, *Gazetteer Mooltan District 1883–4* (Lahore: Arya Press, 1884), 43, 44, 45; see also Server, 240.
158 A dress for the lower part of the body mostly worn by men, very popular in the southern Punjab.
159 Waheeduddin, 120.
160 Fauja Singh, *Some Aspects of State and Society Under Ranjit Singh* (New Delhi: Master Publishers, 1982), 237.
161 Alexender Burnes, 239.
162 Server, 579.
163 Ibid., 581.
164 S. P. Singh and J. S. Saber, *Rule of Maharaja Ranjit Singh, Nature and Relevance* (Amritsar: Guru Nanak Dev University, 2001), 197.
165 Walter Hamilton, *Geographical Statistical and Historical Developments of Hindustan*, vol. 2 (London: John Murray, 1820), 21.
166 Singh and Saber, *Rule of Maharaja Ranjit Singh, Nature and Relevance*, 197.
167 Ibid.
168 Mohan Lal, *Journal of Travel through the Punjab, Afghanistan and Turkistan etc.* (London: Longman Green, 1834), 397.
169 Ibid., 243.
170 Rakesh Sharma, *Socio-Economic Status of Business Communities in the Kingdom of Lahore: 1799–1839* (New Delhi: Writers Choice, 2015), 21.
171 Denzil Ibbetson, *Punjab Castes*, 253; Grewal, *The Reign of Maharaja Ranjit Singh*, 25.
172 Grewal, *The Reign of Maharaja Ranjit Singh*, 25.
173 H. A. Rose, *A Glossary of the Tribes and Castes of the Punjab and North West Frontier Provinces of India*, vol. 2 (Patiala: Punjab Languages Department, 1970), 537.
174 Baron Charles Hügel, *Travels in Kashmir and the Panjab*, 19.
175 Sita Ram Kohli, 'Land Revenue Administration Under Maharaja Ranjit Singh', *Journal of the Punjab Historical Society*, 7, no. 1 (1918): 85.
176 Indu Banga, *The Agrarian System of the Sikhs*, 76, 77.
177 Ibid., 111.
178 Suri, *Umdat-tu-Twarikh*, vol. 3, 102.
179 *Punjab Settlement Record Manual*, 20.

180 Indu Banga, *The Agrarian System of the Sikhs,* 111.
181 Punjab Government, *Gazetteer Montgomery District 1883-4* (Lahore: Arya Press, 1884), 22.
182 Punjab Government, *Gazetteer Peshawar District 1883-4* (Calcutta: Calcutta Central Press, n.p), 41.
183 *Land Settlement Record of British 1865,* IOR/L/PJ/5/477.
184 Ganda Singh, *The Punjab in 1839-40: Selection from the Punjab Akhbars, Punjabi Intelligence Etc.* (Amritsar: Sikh History Society, 1952), 6.
185 Singh and Saber, *Rule of Maharaja Ranjit Singh, Nature and Relevance,* 199.
186 *Umdat-ut-Tawarikh,* vol. 2, 173, 188, 447.
187 Ibid.
188 Sita Ram Kohli, *Land Revenue Administration under Maharaja Ranjit Singh, Punjab Past and Present,* vol. 2, 440, 441.
189 Ganda Singh, *The Punjab in 1839-40,* 6.
190 *Report on the Census of the Punjab 1855* (IOR), 22, 23.
191 Punjab Government, *Gazetteer Amritser District 1883-4,* 43, 60.
192 Punjab Government, *Gazetteer Gurdaspur District 1883-4,* 59, 88.
193 Mohan Lal, *Travels in the Punjab,* 239.
194 Prinsep, *Origin of the Sikh Power in the Punjab and Political Life of the Maharaja Ranjit Singh,* 178.
195 Waheeduddin, 31.
196 Fauja Singh and A. C. Arora, 302.
197 *Gurmukhi* is Punjabi writing script. It was developed and standardized during the sixteenth century by Guru Angad, the second Guru of Sikhism. The Old Punjabi word *Gurmukhi* means 'from the mouth of the Guru'. The whole of the *Guru Granth Sahib* is written in this script, and it is the script most commonly used by Sikhs and Hindus for writing the Punjabi language.
198 Fauja Singh and A. C. Arora, 303.
199 Ibid., 305.
200 H. R. Goulding, *Old Lahore: Reminiscences of a Resident* (Lahore: Sang e Meel Publications, 1924), 106, 107.
201 G. W. Leitner, *History of Indigenous Education in the Punjab, Since Annexation and in 1882* (Lahore: Sang e Mil Publications, 2002), 53.
202 Ibid., 56.
203 Ibid.
204 Lafont, *Maharaja Ranjit Singh, Lord of the Five Rivers,* 76.
205 Moulana Iltaf Hussain Hali, *Hayat e Javaid* (n.p: National Book House, 1986), 38.
206 Fauja Singh and A. C. Arora, 307.
207 Ibid., 308.
208 'The emergence of triumph of Punjabi as a literary language was the result of the recognition which the creative writers of the Punjab gave to the people of the Punjab.' Grewal, 'Historical Geography of Punjab', *Journal of Regional History,* vol. 1 (1980): 11.
209 Ajmer Singh, *Maharaja Ranjit Singh Ate Punjabi Sahit* (Punjabi) (Patiala: Publication Bureau, Punjabi University, 1982), 18–19.
210 Server, 216.
211 Rattan Singh Jaggi, *Punjabi Sahit Da Srot-Mulak Itihas,* vol. 3 (Patiala: Publication Bureau, Punjabi University, 1999), 296.
212 Fauja Singh and A. C. Arora, 306.

213 Ibid., 309.
214 Ibid.
215 W. G. Leitner, 152.
216 H. R. Mehta, *History of the Growth of Western Education in the Punjab* (n.p: Vintage Books, 1996), 6.
217 Server, 218.
218 The phenomenon of state-in-person carries the contradiction of the Sikh society and the Punjabi culture – some aspects of Maharaja Ranjit Singh's approach towards the languages or texts.
219 Lafont, *Maharaja Ranjit Singh, Lord of the Five Rivers*, 76.
220 Fauja Singh, *Some Aspects of State and Society under Ranjit Singh*, 139–41.
221 Chopra, 90.
222 Khushwant Singh, *Ranjit Singh*, 161.
223 John Martin Honigberge, *Thirty-Five Years in the East: Adventures, Discoveries, Experiments, and Historical Sketches, Relating to the Punjab and Cashmere* (London: 1852), 1.
224 Khushwant Singh, *Ranjit Singh*, 161.
225 Grewal, *The Shari'at at and the Non-Muslims of Batala,* Proceedings Punjab History Conference (sixth Session) (Patiala: n.p, 1972), 154.
226 Ibid., 155.
227 Ibid.
228 Grewal, *In the By-lanes of History: Some Persian Documents from a Punjab Town* (Simla: Iindian Institute of Advanced Study, 1975), 32.
229 Diaries of the Fakir family.
230 Khushwant Singh, *Ranjit Singh*, 161.
231 Ibid.
232 Chopra, 137.
233 Osborne, 29.
234 Waheeduddin, *The Real Ranjit*, 31.
235 Ibid., 32.
236 An extract from the letter is reproduced here *'Ujjal Didar Nirmal Budh Sardar Amir Singh Ji and our sincere well-wisher, Fakir Nuruddin Ji, may you live long by the grace of Sri Akal Purakh and enjoy the protection of Sri Akal Budh. By the grace of Sri Sar Guruji, the exalted command is issued to you that, deeming yourselves to be responsible for the security of Lahore, you should take care of the duties pertaining thereto. Sri Sat Guruji forbid, if His Highness, his beloved son Kharak Singh Ji, Kunwar Sher Singh Ji, the Raja Kalan Bahadur, Raja Suchet Singh Ji, or Jamadar Ji should commit any inappropriate act, you should bring it to the notice of His Highness. Secondly, you should send your trusted representative to the Sardars with instructions to refrain from committing inappropriate acts. If the Sardars act according to your instructions, well and good; otherwise you should send word to them that you will bring the matter to the notice of His Highness. Moreover, you should not permit forcible possession to be taken of any person's land or any person's house to be demolished. Nor should you allow any high-handedness to be practiced upon woodcutters, fodder vendors, oil-vendors, horse-shores, factory-owners etc. In such cases also you should prevent the oppressor from oppression you should administer matters in the same way as Sardar Desh Singh ji. Should prevent the oppressor from oppression. You should forward to His Highness any petition intended for him Furthermore, you should daily send for Chand Mall, Kotwal of the Royal Court, and Babu Panda, and obtain from them news of all*

happenings so that every person's rights are secured and no person is oppressed. The frames of the city gates should be caused to be repaired from the revenue of the Court. Hazara Sawars should be appointed to watch the roads and, considering the security of the whole of Lahore city as your responsibility, you should act in accordance with this decree. Dated Lahore 19 Pos, 1888 Sambat' Ibid., 34.

237 *Punjab Akhbar*, 10 March, 1839.
238 Suri, *Umdat-tu-Tawarikh*, vol. 3, 292, 293.
239 Osborne, 129.
240 Lafont, *Maharaja Ranjit Singh, Lord of the Five Rivers*, 81.
241 Ibid., 33.
242 William Murray, *History of the Punjab*, vol. 1 (London: William Allen, 1846; Languages Department Punjab, Patiala, 1970) (reprint), 174.
243 Baron Charles Hügel, *Travels in Kashmir and Punjab*, 239.
244 Gurdashan Singh Dhillon, *The Sikh Rule and Ranjit Singh*, https://www.allaboutsikhs.com/sikhism-articles/the-sikh-rule-and-ranjit-singh: retrieved 23/05/2014.
245 http://searchsikhism.com/maharaja-ranjit-singh/financial-civil-and-military-administration-of-the-maharaja#sthash.kL4XknoA.dpuf: retrieved 14/05/2014.

Chapter 4

1 Waheeduddin, 25.
2 Waheeduddin, 26.
3 Hira Singh (b. 1816) was the son of Raja Dhian Singh. Dhian Singh, an influential courtier, introduced his son to Maharaja Ranjit Singh, who adored the young boy. From the very beginning the Maharaja treated him with great generosity, bestowing upon him the title of Raja in 1828, then proclaiming him *Farzand-e-Khas* (a favoured son). He granted him numerous *Jagirs* amounting in total to nearly Rs.5 *lakh* annually.
4 Waheedudin, 28.
5 Ibid., 29.
6 The exact number of these European officers who served under Ranjit Singh cannot be determined, although Carmichael Smyth enumerates them as 39 in all: Italian, French, English. Carmichael Smyth, *A History of the Reigning Family of Lahore*, 1; see also B. J. Hasrat, *Life and Times of Maharaja Ranjit Singh* (Hoshiarpur: V.V.R.I, 1968), 271.
7 G. L. Chopra, *The Punjab as a Sovereign State*, 118.
8 Radha Sharma, *The Lahore Darbar*, 15; see also Bikrama Jit Hasrat, *Life and Times of Ranjit Singh: A Saga of Benevolent Despots*, 263, 265.
9 Guru Gobind Singh constructed a war drum named *Ranjit Nagra* to motivate his army, Harjinder Singh Dilgeer, *Sikh History*, vol. 1 (in English) (n.p: Sikh University Press, 2010), 11.
10 Jasbir Singh Ahluwalia and Parm Bakhshish Singh (eds), *An Overview of Maharaja Ranjit Singh and His Times* (Patiala: Publication Bureau, Punjabi University, 2001), 111.
11 Patwant Singh and M. Rai Jyoti, 242.
12 Grewal, *The Reign of the Maharaja Ranjit Singh: Structure of Power, Economy and Society*, 23.
13 Ibid., 112.
14 Ibid., 120.
15 Ibid., 121.
16 Ibid.

17 Daljit Singh, *Punjab Social and Economic Condition 1501–1700* (New Delhi: Commonwealth Publishers, 2004), 87.
18 Griffin, *Ranjit Singh*, 98–99.
19 S. N. Qanungo, 'Decline and Fall of the Maratha Power', in Majumdar, R. C. (ed.), *The History and Culture of the Indian People: The Maratha Supremacy* (Bombay: n.p, 1971), 515–16.
20 G. L. Chopra, *The Punjab as a Sovereign State*, 136.
21 Shahamet Ali, 17.
22 Ibid., 16–17.
23 Ibid.
24 Jasbir Singh Ahluwalia and Param Bakhshish, 121.
25 Grewal, *In the By-Lanes of History: Some Persian Documents from a Punjab Town*, 12; see also Grewal, *Polity and Society of Sikh Rule*, 59.
26 Waheeduddin, 34.
27 Grewal and Indu Banga (ed. and trans.), *Early Nineteenth Century Punjab from Ganesh Das's Char Bagh-i-panjab* (Amritsar: Dept. of History, Guru Nanak University, 1975), 71.
28 Grewal and Indu Banga, *Early Nineteenth Century Punjab*, 71.
29 Suri, *Umdat -ut -Tawarikh*, vol. 3, 5.
30 Ali-ud-Din Mufti, *Ibratnama*, vol. 2 (Lahore: n.p, 1961), 470.
31 W. L. M'Gregor, *The History of the Sikhs*, vol. 2, 154; see also S. M. Latif, *History of the Punjab*, 364.
32 Ali-ud-Din Mufti, *Ibratnama*, vol. 2, 470.
33 Sohan Lal Suri, *Umdat-ut-Tawarikh*, vol. 2, 58.
34 Latif, *History of the Punjab*, 364.
35 G. L. Chopra, *The Punjab as a Sovereign State*, 104; Waheeduddin, 96.
36 Suri, *Umdat-ut-Tawarikh*, vol.2, 76; and Bute Shah, *Tawarikh-i-Punjab*,52. ; Giani Gian Singh, *Tawarikh Guru Khalsa* vol. 2(Patiala: n.p,2003),313.
37 Suri, *Umdat-ut-Tawarikh*, vol. 2, 66; see also Bute Shah, *Tawarikh-i-Punjab*, 51–2.
38 Bute Shah, *Tawarikh i Punjab*, 53–4.
39 Amarnath, *Zafarnama-i-Ranjit Singh* (Persian), Sita Ram Kohli (ed.) (Lahore: University of the Punjab, 1928), 85; see also Suri, *Umdat-ut-Tawarikh*, 172.
40 G. S. Chhabra, *Advanced History of the Punjab*, vol. 2 (Jullundher: New Academic Publishing Co., 1969), 199.
41 Suri, *Umdat-ut-Tawarikh*, vol. 3, 67.
42 Ibid., 171.
43 William Murray, *History of the Punjab (*London: William Allen, 1846; Languages Department Punjab, Patiala, 1970), 23; see also Griffin, *The Punjab Chiefs*, 556, who notes that as a general he had been almost always successful, his administrative talents were as great as his military ones, and in his death the Maharaja lost his most loyal and devoted servant. According to M'Gregor, *History of the Sikhs*, vol. I, 174, the Diwan was a man of the greatest military tact and had always been successful in various important commands bestowed on him by the Maharaja.
44 W. E. Purser, *Final Report of the Revised Settlement of the Jalandhar District in the Punjab* (Lahore: Central Jail Press, 1892), 41.
45 *Doab* is the region lying between and reaching to the confluence of two rivers.
46 Amarnath, *Zafarnama-i-Ranjit Singh*, 85.
47 Amarnath, *Zafarnama-i-Ranjit Singh*, 100; see also Bute Shah, *Tawarikh-i-Punjab*, 168.
48 Ibid., 132; see also Suri, *Umdat-ut-Tawarikh*, vol. 2, 355; see also Ali-ud-Din Mufti, *Ibratnama*, vol. 2, 519.

49 Ali-ud-Din Mufti, *Ibratnama*, vol. 2, 35.
50 Murray, *History of the Punjab*, vol. 2, 79–80.
51 Suri, *Umdat-ut-Tawarikh*, vol. 2, 111–12.
52 Ibid., 327.
53 Ibid., 67.
54 Baron Schonberg, *Travels in India and Kashmir*, vol. 2 (London, 1853), 96–7, cited in Sufi, 731.
55 Bute Shah, *Tawarikh i Punjab*, 207.
56 *Ibid.*, 220.
57 *Final Report of the Revised Settlement of the Jalandhar District in the Punjab*, 41.
58 Punjab Government, *Gazetteer Gujrat District 1883–84* (Lahore: Arya Press, 1884), 120; Grewal and Indu Banga, *Early Nineteenth Century Punjab*, 71.
59 Suri, *Umdat-ut-Tawarikh*, vol. 3, 216, 223.
60 Grewal and Indu Banga, *Early Nineteenth Century Punjab*, 101.
61 Sinha, *Ranjit Singh*, 175.
62 G. L. Chopra, *The Punjab as a Sovereign State 1799–1839*, 109; Gulcharan Singh, *Ranjit Singh and His Generals* (Jalandhar: 1949), 14, 49.
63 Gupta, *History of the Sikhs*, vol. 5, 332.
64 Suri, *Umdat-ut-Tawarikh*, vol. 2, 164; see also Ali-ud-Din Mufti, *Ibratnama*, vol. 2, 81; Bute Shah, *Tawarikh i Punjab*, 124.
65 Ali-ud-Din Mufti, *Ibratnama*, vol. 2, 558.
66 Suri, *Umdat-ut-Tawarikh*, vol. 2, 395; Raja Ram Tota, *Gulgashta-i-Punjab* (Patiala: Punjab State Archives, n.d), 298. Diwan Chand died at Lahore of a stroke of paralysis.
67 Amarnath, *Zafarnama-i-Ranjit Singh*, 115.
68 Suri, *Umdat-ut-Tawarikh*, vol. 2, 394.
69 Gulcharan Singh, *Ranjit Singh and His Generals*, 63.
70 Shahamat Ali, 19.
71 Ibid., 20.
72 Hasrat, *Life and Times of Maharaja Ranjit Singh*, 256; according to Harbans Singh, Dina Nath was born in 1795: Harbans Singh (ed.), *Encyclopedia of Sikhism* (Patiala: Punjabi University, 1995), s.v. 585.
73 Amarnath, *Zafarnama-i-Ranjit Singh*, 80.
74 Griffin, *The Punjab Chiefs*, 137.
75 Giani Gian Singh, *Tawarikh Guru Khalsa*, vol. 2, 380.
76 Shahamat Ali, 20.
77 Griffin, *The Punjab Chiefs*, 137.
78 B. R. Chopra, *Kingdom of the Punjab 1839–45* (Hoshiarpur: Vishveshvaranand Institute, 1969), 104.
79 Ibid., 104.
80 Suri, *Umdat-ut-Tawarikh*, vol. 4, 275.
81 Similar to the moderate old guard of Ranjit Singh's time.
82 Major H. Pearse (ed.), *Soldier and Traveller: Memoirs (Chiefly in His Own Words) of Alexander Gardner, Colonel of Artillery in the Service of Maharaja Ranjit Singh* (Edinburgh: W. Blackwood & Sons, 1898), 263.
83 Ali-ud-Din Mufti, *Ibratnama*, vol. 2, 629.
84 Griffin, *The Punjab Chiefs*, 135.
85 Ibid., 135.
86 Ibid., 136.
87 Ibid., 135.

88 Shahamat Ali, 19; Grewal and Indu Banga, *Early Nineteenth Century Punjab,* 47; see also Griffin, *Chiefs and Families of Note in the Punjab,* vol. I, 361.
89 Debi Prashad, *Tarikh-i-Gulshan-i-Punjab* (Lucknow, 1872), trans. Harminder Singh Kohli (Patiala: 2003), 94.
90 Ali-ud-Din Mufti, *Ibratnama,* vol. 2, 93–4.
91 Suri, *Umdat-ut-Tawarikh,* vol. 3, 351.
92 Hasrat, *Life and Times of Maharaja Ranjit Singh,* 267.
93 Jean-Marie Lafont, *Maharaja Ranjit Singh, the French Connections* (Amritsar: Guru Nanak Dev University, 2001), 15.
94 This is the information provided by Allard to Guizot in 1835–6 for Ventura's nomination as Chevalier; see also Lafont, *Maharaja Ranjit Singh, the French Connections,* 23.
95 Harbans Singh and Bilbir Singh, *Maharaja Ranjit Singh, Being Tribute to the Memory of the Great Monarch, Published on the Occasion of the First Death Century* (Lahore: University Sikh Association, 1939), 98–9.
96 Lafont, *Maharaja Ranjit Singh, the French Connections,* 23.
97 Harbans and Bilbir, 92.
98 Fakir Syed Aijazuddin, *The Resourceful Fakirs: Three Muslim Brothers at the Sikh Court of Lahore* (Delhi: Three Rivers Publishers, 2014), 31.
99 Harbans and Bilbir, 101.
100 A British army officer during the period of Ranjit Singh.
101 Harbans and Bilbir, 92.
102 Lafont, *Maharaja Ranjit Singh, the French Connections,* 25.
103 Ibid., 26.
104 G. L. Chopra, *The Punjab as a Sovereign State,* 244, 281.
105 A treaty was signed between the British, the Sikhs and Shah Shuja to help Shah Shuja in getting the throne of Kabul. Fauja Singh Bajwa, *Military System of the Sikhs during the Period 1799–1849* (Delhi: Motilal Banarsidass, 1964), 123.
106 *The Lahore Darbar: In the Light of the Correspondence of Sir C. M. Wade (1823–49)* (Lahore: Punjab Government Records Office, 1930).
107 Harbans and Bilbir, 115.
108 *Runjit Singh, Maharajah of Lahore, Request for Attendance of Dr. Murray.* IOR/Z/E/4/14/R721.
109 Ibid.
110 Lafont, *Maharaja Ranjit Singh, the French Connections,* 31.
111 Victor Jacquemont, *Letters from India: Describing a Journey in the British Dominions of India,* vol. 2, 1.
112 Almost all the travellers who visited the court of Maharaja Ranjit Singh had discussed it.
113 Fauja Singh, *The Military System of the Sikhs,* 71.
114 Ibid.
115 A Chagtai, 'Lessons from the Zam Zamma Gun', *Journal of the Research Society of Pakistan,* 12 (1975): 17–44.
116 G. L. Chopra, *Punjab as a Sovereign State,* 326.
117 Fauja Singh, *The Military System of the Sikhs,* 79.
118 Lafont, *Maharaja Ranjit Singh, the French Connections,* 37.
119 *The Lahore Darbar: In the Light of the Correspondence of Sir C. M. Wade (1823–49);* see also Lafont, *Maharaja Ranjit Singh, the French Connections,* 37.
120 Lafont, *Essays in Indo-French Relations, 1630–1976,* 206.

121 Lafont, *Maharaja Ranjit Singh, the French Connections*, 37.
122 Lafont, *Essays in Indo-French Relations, 1630–1976*, 207.
123 The Sikhs mostly made noise during the war period, shouting words meaning to kill, cut or loot their rivals.
124 Harbans and Bilbir, *Maharaja Ranjit Singh*, 96, 97.
125 G. L. Chopra, *Punjab as a Sovereign State*, 326.
126 Harbans and Bilbir, 98.
127 Ibid., 103.
128 Fauja Singh, *The Military System of the Sikhs*, 122.
129 Jasbir Singh Ahluwalia and Param Bakhshish Singh, *Ranjit Singh and His Times*, 126.
130 Ibid., 126.
131 Fauja Singh, *The Military System of the Sikhs*, 122.
132 Harbans and Bilbir, *Maharaja Ranjit Singh*, 110.
133 Ibid., 96.
134 Khushwant Singh, *A History of the Sikhs*, vol. 2, 95.
135 Hennery Lawrence, *Adventures of an Officer in the Service of Ranjit Singh*, vol. I (London: Colburn, 1846), 1.
136 Khushwant Singh, *A History of the Sikhs*, vol. 2, 97.
137 Harbans and Bilbir, 111.
138 Ibid., 111.
139 Fauja Singh, *The Military System of the Sikhs*, 126.
140 Suri, *Umdat-ut-Tawarikh*, vol. 3, 409.
141 Hasrat, *Life and Times of Ranjit Singh*, 77.
142 Lafont, *Maharaja Ranjit Singh, the French Connections*, 72.
143 Ibid., 77.
144 Suri, *Umdat-ut-Tawarikh*, vol. 3, 196, 263, 193, 182.
145 Ibid., 184.
146 Ibid., 193.
147 Ibid., 465.
148 Ibid., 512.
149 Baron Charles Hügel, *Travels in Kashmir and the Panjab*, 317.
150 Suri, *Umdat-ut-Tawarikh*, vol. 3, 161, 196, 533.
151 H. G. Rawlinson, *Buddha, Ashoka, Akbar, Shivaji and Ranjit Singh: A Study in Indian History* (New Delhi: Ess Ess Publications, 1913), 182–3.
152 Grewal, *In the By-Lanes of History: Some Persian Documents from a Punjab Town*, 11.
153 Ibid.; Grewal, *Polity and Society of Sikh Rule*, 59.
154 Narender Krishan Sinha, *Ranjit Singh* (Lahore: Nafees Printers, 1992), 164.
155 H. M. L. Lawrence, *Adventures of an Officer in Punjab*, vol. I, 30–1.
156 K. K. Khullar, *Maharaja Ranjit Singh* (New Delhi: n.p, 1980), 183.
157 Waheeduddin, 34.
158 Victor Jacquemont, *Letters from India: Describing a Journey in the British Dominions of India*, vol. 1, 31.
159 Diaries of the Fakir Khana Family; Waheeduddin, 39.
160 Diaries of the Fakir Khana Family; Waheeduddin, 40, 41.
161 *Encyclopedia of Sikhism*, 21.
162 Diaries of the Fakir Khana Family; Waheeduddin, 40, 41; see also Griffin, *Ranjit Singh*, 23.

163 Diaries of the Fakir Khana Family.
164 He had lost the sight of one eye from smallpox in childhood. In an age when being blind precluded one from ruling, having only one eye was never an issue for Ranjit Singh, who regularly commented that it enabled him to see things all the more intensely. Griffin, *Ranjit Singh*, 34.
165 Waheeduddin, 41.
166 Ibid., 42.
167 Ikram Ali Malik, *A Book of Reading on the History of the Punjab* (Lahore: Ilmi Printing Press, 1970), 102.
168 Ibid., 103.
169 Aijazuddin, *The Resourceful Fakirs*, 37.
170 A seat for riding on the back of an elephant or camel, typically with a canopy and accommodating two or more people.
171 Aijazuddin, 45.
172 Griffin, *Ranjit Singh*, 23.
173 Garrett and Chopra, *Events at the Court of Ranjit Singh, 1810–1817*, 250; see also Fakir Aijazuddin, 22.
174 Griffin, *Ranjit Singh*, 21.
175 Harbans and Bilbir, 28, 29.
176 Garrett and Chopra, 254; see also Aijazuddin, 22.
177 Aijazuddin, 31, 32, 33; Garrett and Chopra, 167.
178 Aijazuddin, 214.
179 Emily Eden, *Up the Country: Letters Written to her Sister from the Upper Provinces of India; Introduction by Elizabeth Claridge; notes by Edward Thompson* (London: Virago, 1997), 207.
180 Madanjit Kaur, *The Regime of Maharaja Ranjit Singh: Historians' Observations* (Chandigarh: Unistar Books Ltd, 2007), 123.
181 Gregor, *History of the Sikhs*, vol.1, 19.
182 Madanjit Kaur, 123; see also Waheeduddin, 32.
183 Waheeduddin, 32.
184 Chopra, 178, 179.
185 Ikram Ali Malik, *A Book of Reading on the History of the Punjab*, 105.
186 Aijazuddin, 35.
187 Prithipal Singh Kapur and Dharam Singh, *Maharaja Ranjit Singh: Commemoration Volume on Bicentenary of his Coronation, 1801, 2001* (Patiala: Punjabi University, 2001), 129.
188 Waheeduddin, 44.
189 Ibid., 45.
190 Ikram Ali Malik, *A Book of Reading on the History of the Punjab*, 105.
191 Lieutenant William Barr, *Journal of a March from Delhi to Peshâwur, and from thence to Câbul, with the Mission to Lieut-Col. Sir C. M. Wade, etc.* (London: J. Madden & Co., 1844), 74, 75.
192 Moorcroft and Trebeck, *Travels in the Himalayan Provinces of Hindustan and the Panjab: In Ladakh and Kashmir; In Peshawar, Kabul, Kunduz, and Bokhara from 1819–1825* (Patiala: Languages Dept, 1970), 94, 95.
193 Niccolo Machiavelli, *The Prince. Translated and with an Introduction by George Bull, etc. 1469–1527* (London: Folio Society, 1970), 124.
194 K. K. Khullar, 183.

Chapter 5

1. *Encyclopedia Britannica Eleventh Edition*, vol. 22 (1910–1911), 892.
2. Grewal, *The Sikhs of the Punjab*, 107; see also K. S. Duggal, *Ranjit Singh: A Secular Sikh Sovereign* (Delhi: Abhinav Publications, 1989), 27.
3. Khushwant Singh, *A History of the Sikhs*, vol. 2, 1.
4. Griffin, *Ranjit Singh*, 32.
5. Ganda Singh (ed.), *Private Correspondence Relating to the Anglo–Sikh Wars. Being Private Letters of Lords Ellenborough, Hardinge, Dalhousie and Gough and of Political Assistants Addressed to Sir Frederick Currie as British Resident at Lahore, etc.* (Amritsar: Sikh History Society, 1955), 49–50.
6. Bawa Satinder Singh, *The Jammu Fox – A Biography of Maharaja Gulab Singh of Kashmir* (Carbondale, IL: Southern Illinois University Press, 1974), 40.
7. Khushwant Singh, *A History of the Sikhs*, vol. 2, 1.
8. J. M. Honigberger, *Thirty-Five Years in the East: Adventures, Discoveries, Experiments, and Historical Sketches, Relating to the Punjab and Cashmere* (London: 1852), 101.
9. *Punjab Akhbar*, 27/28 June 1839.
10. Khushwant Singh, *The Sikhs*, 2.
11. Ganda Singh, 68–70.
12. Ibid., 79.
13. *Punjab Akhbar*, 26 June 1839.
14. Bawa Satinder Singh, 41.
15. M. L. Ahluwalia, 'Kharak Singh, Maharaja (1801–1840)', *Encyclopedia of Sikhism* (Patiala: Punjab University). https://www.abebooks.com/Encyclopaedia-Sikhism-4-Vols-Harbans-Singh/2960257543/bd: retrieved 15/08/2021.
16. Bawa Satinder Singh, 40.
17. Chet Singh was married to the niece of Mangal Singh Sindhu, brother-in-law of Kharak Singh. Since 1834 Chet Singh had displaced Mangal Singh as manager of Kharak Singh's civil and financial affairs. Griffin, *Chiefs and Families*, vol. 2, 56.
18. Ganda Singh, 123.
19. Two companies of troops carried Wazir Singh and his brothers through the bazaar, 'beating them with shoes and with every other degradation': *Punjab Akhbar*, 7 October 1839.
20. Ganda Singh, 124.
21. Khushwant Singh, *A History of the Sikhs*, vol. 2, 5.
22. Major Hugh Pearse (ed.), *Soldier and Traveller – Memoirs of Alexander Gardner* (Edinburgh: William Blackwood and Sons, 1898), 222.
23. Harbans Singh Noor, *Connecting the Dots in Sikh History* (Chandigarh: Institute of Sikh Studies, 2004), 45.
24. *Punjab Akhbar*, 8 October 1839.
25. Pearse, 222.
26. Khushwant Singh, *A History of the Sikhs*, vol. 2, 5.
27. Sardar Singh Bhatia. 'Nau Nihal Singh Kanvar (1821–1840)', *Encyclopedia of Sikhism* (Patiala: Punjab University). https://archive.org/stream/TheEncyclopediaOfSikhism-VolumeIiiM-r/TheEncyclopediaOfSikhism-VolumeIiiM-r_djvu.txt: retrieved 23/05/2015.
28. Griffin, *Chiefs and Families*, vol. 2, 195.
29. Chopra, *Kingdom of the Punjab*, 63–4.
30. Ganda Singh (ed.), *The Panjab in 1839–40*, 216.

31 Ibid., 259.
32 Chopra, *Kingdom of the Punjab*, 49, 63–4.
33 Pearse, 224, 226.
34 Ibid.
35 Ibid., 227.
36 Honigberger, *Thirty-Five Years in the East*, 103.
37 Chand Kaur was from the Sandhanwalia clan, fierce rivals of the Dogras. They controlled the army and could remove Dogra influence at court if they wished.
38 Khushwant Singh, *A History of the Sikhs*, vol. 2, 7.
39 Ibid., 8.
40 Suri, *Umdat-ut-Tawarik*, vol. 5, 111, 133.
41 It is estimated that Sher Singh gave away Rs.5 *lakhs* during the twenty-four hours before the assault on the Lahore fort began; Chand Kaur gave away Rs.3 *lakhs*. Sita Ram Kohli, *Sunset of the Sikh Empire*, Khushwant Singh (ed.) (Bombay: Orient Longmans, 1967), 34.
42 Smyth, *Reigning Family of Lahore*, 43–61.
43 Latif, 634.
44 Griffin, *Chiefs and Families*, vol. 2, 26–30.
45 Suri, *Umdat-ut-Tawavikh*, vol. 5, 168–70.
46 Amarinder Singh, *The Last Sunset – The Rise and Fall of the Lahore Durbar* (New Delhi: Roli Books, 2010), 55.
47 'Women in Power (1840–1870)', *Worldwide Guide to Women in Leadership*. http://www.guide2womenleaders.com/womeninpower/Womeninpower1840.htm: retrieved 06/02/2015.
48 Khushwant Singh, *A History of the Sikhs*, vol. 2, 7.
49 Amarinder Singh, 56.
50 Hasrat, 'Sher Singh, Maharaja', *Encyclopedia of Sikhism* (Patiala: Punjab University). https://archive.org/stream/TheEncyclopediaOfSikhism-VolumeIvS-z/TheEncyclopediaOfSikhism-VolumeIvS-z_djvu.txt: retrieved 14/05/2015.
51 Griffin, *Chiefs and Families*, vol. 1, 363.
52 Kohli, *Sunset of the Sikh Empire*, 41.
53 Griffin, *Chiefs and Families*, vol. 2, 195.
54 Ibid., 129.
55 Amarinder Singh, 56.
56 Suri, *Umdat-ut-Tawarikh*, vol. 5, 247.
57 Amarinder Singh, 57.
58 B. J. Hasrat, 'Sher Singh, Maharaja', *Encyclopedia of Sikhism* (Patiala: Punjab University).
59 Bhagat Singh, 'Chand Kaur', *Encyclopedia of Sikhism* (Patiala: Punjab University). http://www.guide2womenleaders.com/womeninpower/Womeninpower1840.htm: retrieved 05/09/2015.
60 Hira Singh bestowed gifts worth about Rs.54,300 on various influential people in order to secure their support at the installation of Dilip Singh. Sita Ram Kohli, *Catalogue of Records*, vol. 2, 250.
61 Hugh Cook, *The Sikh Wars – The British Army in the Punjab 1845–1849* (London: Leo Cooper, 1975), 21.
62 Griffin, *Chiefs and Families*, vol. 1, 363, 407–8, 508; vol. 2, 136.
63 Hasrat, *Anglo–Sikh Relations*, 229.; Bajwa, *Military System*, 83,
64 Bajwa, *Military System*, 97, 102–3.

65 Latif, 966.
66 Ibid.
67 Ibid.
68 Ibid., 967.
69 Suri, *Umdat-ut-Tawarikh*, vol. 5, 310–12.
70 Cook, *The Sikh Wars*, 22.
71 Suri, *Umdat-ut-Tawavikh*, vol. 5, 313–14.
72 Griffin, *Chiefs and Families*, vol.1, 482.
73 Hasrat, *Anglo–Sikh Relations*, 256–7.
74 Bawa Satinder Singh, *The Jammu Fox – A Biography of Maharaja Gulab Singh of Kashmir*, 107.
75 Colonel Alexander Gardner (1785–1877) was an American soldier-of-fortune who found his way to the Lahore *Darbar* and entered into the service of Ranjit Singh as an artillery commander. He wrote his memoirs, detailing the fall of the Sikh kingdom and discussed the various persons concerned. After the first Anglo–Sikh War he served Gulab Singh in Kashmir until his death.
76 Pearse, 261–2.
77 Cook, *The Sikh Wars*, 23.
78 Griffin, *Tazkara e Raosay Punjab*, vol. 1, 487.
79 Ibid., 489.
80 Ibid., 490.
81 Ibid., 496.
82 Ibid., 497.
83 Ibid., 498–9.
84 Ibid., 532.
85 Khushwant Singh, *A History of the Sikhs*, 6.
86 Ibid., 6.
87 Ganda Singh (ed.), *The Panjab in 1839–40*, 102, 106.
88 The village *panchayat* was a small council made up of the representatives of the different sections of the village, which met to regulate social behaviour and settle small disputes.
89 Fauja Singh Bajwa, *Military System of the Sikhs*, 102.
90 Suri, *Umdat-ut-Tawarikh*, vol. 5, 239.
91 Hasrat, *Anglo–Sikh Relations*, 229; Bajwa, *Military System*, 83, 96–7. The regular, trained army accounted for about one-third of the total strength, the remaining two-thirds representing the *jagirdari* levies.
92 Amarinder Singh, *The Last Sunset*, 55–7.
93 Pearse, *Soldier and Traveller*, 230. They did this to exploit the increased pay, but were nothing more than brigands, according to Gardner.
94 Khushwant Singh, *A History of the Sikhs*, 7.
95 Hasrat (ed.), *The Punjab Papers*, 67, 69, 78.
96 British efforts to support Shah Shuja as ruler in Afghanistan against his rival, Dost Mohammad Khan, were partly due to Dost Mohammad's unwillingness to commit fully to the British and his continued dabbling with the Russians. Ellenborough thus sanctioned an invasion of Afghanistan. Although Shah Shuja was reinstalled, opposition to the British presence saw the expulsion and massacre of the British troops and their families. Shah Shuja was overthrown and killed in 1842, and Dost Mohammad, who had been exiled to India, was permitted to return. Cook, *The Sikh Wars*, 23.

97 Patwant Singh and Jyoti M. Rai, *Empire of the Sikhs* (n.c: Peter Owen Publishers, 2013), 228.
98 Lawrence James, *Raj – The Making and Unmaking of British India* (New York: St Martin's Griffin, 1997), 103.
99 Penderel Moon, *The British Conquest and Dominion of India*, 2nd ed. (London: Duckworth Press, 1990), 576–9.
100 Ibid., 594.
101 Ibid., 595.
102 Pearse, *Soldier and Traveller,* 268–9.
103 K. M. Panikkar, *The Founding of the Kashmir State – A Biography of Maharaja Gulab Singh (1792–1958)*, 2nd ed. (London: George Allen & Unwin Ltd, 1953), 76–7.
104 Ibid.
105 Amarpal S. Sidhu, *The First Anglo–Sikh War* (London: Amberley, 2010), 82–4.
106 Ibid., 125.
107 Ibid., 162.
108 Ganda Singh (ed.), *The Panjab in 1839–40*, 97–8, 100–4, 125.
109 Griffin, *Chiefs and Families*, vol.2, 97, 338.
110 Punjab Government, *Gazetteer Montgomery District 1883–4* (Lahore: Arya Press, 1884), 38.
111 Griffin, *Chiefs and Families*, vol. 1, 367; vol. 2, 338.
112 Chopra, *Kingdom of the Punjab*, 160–7, 317–19.
113 Ibid.
114 *Political Diaries of Lieutenant Reynall G. Taylor, P. Sandys Melvill, Pandit Kunahya Lai, Mr P. A. Vans Agnew, Lieutenant J. Nicholson, L. Bowring and A. H. Cocks 1847–1849* (1849), 368. IOR/V/27/47/6.
115 Ibid., 431.
116 Ibid., 394.
117 Griffin, *Chiefs and Families*, vol. 2, 97–100.
118 S. P. Singh and J. S. Sabar (eds), *Rule of Maharaja Ranjit Singh: Nature and Relevance*, 75–6.
119 Patwant Singh and Jyoti M. Rai, *Empire of the Sikhs,* 225.

Conclusion

1 Osborne, 63.
2 Baron Charles Hügel, *Travels in the Kashmir and the Punjab*, 293.
3 H. S. Bhatia (ed.), *Rare Documents on the Sikhs and Their Rule in Punjab* (Delhi: n.p, 1981), 86.
4 C. A. Bayly, 'The Pre-History of "Communalism"? Religious Conflict in India, 1700–1860', *Modern Asian Studies*, vol. 19, no. 2 (1985): 177–203. http://www.jstor.org/stable/312153: retrieved 23/05/2015.
5 B. R. Grover, *Political and Social Situations of Punjab after Ranjit Era* (Delhi: Punjabi Academy, 1992), 5; see also Irfan Habib, *The Agrarian System of Mughal India 1556–1707* (Bombay: n.p, 1963), 298, 316.
6 M'Gregor, *History of the Sikhs,* 262.
7 *Punjab Government Records, 1847*, 372.
8 Sufi, 711, 712.
9 Grewal, *Maharaja Ranjit Singh and His Times*, 249.
10 Dilip Singh and Espirito, *Sikh Muslim Relations*, 66.

BIBLIOGRAPHY

Primary Sources

India Office Record

Collection of Itineraries in the North-Western Provinces including diary of Lord Auckland's journey to meet Ranjit Singh 1838–39, probably compiled by Sir Frederick Currie, 1st Bart (1799–1875), Bengal Civil Service 1820–53, Foreign Secretary, Government of India 1842–49. Mss Eur D158.

Kohli, Sita Ram. Catalogue of Khalsa Darbar Lahore. IOR/V/27/37/32.

Notes on the state of our relations with the Punjab, and the best mode of their settlement / by Sir C. M. Wade.

Land Settlement Record of British 1865. IOR/L/PJ/5/477.

Ochterlony, Sir David, Unspecified, 1st Baronet, Major-General. Contents: Declaration of trust, dated 24 June 1816, made between Maj-Gen Sir David Ochterlony, 1st Bart (1758–1825), and Messrs George Fraser and John Maurice, in respect of £4027 17s in 3% consolidated bank annuities for Ochterlony's daughters remaining unmarried at his death. Mss Eur E298.

Political Diaries of Lieutenant Reynall G. Taylor, Mr P. Sandys Melvill, Pandit Kanaya Lai, Mr P. A. Vans Agnew, Lieutenant J. Nicholson, Mr L. Bowring and Mr A. H. Cocks 1847–1849. IOR/V/27/47/6.

Punjab, Political Settlement, Grants of lands or money and tenure of by religious institutions to be dealt with and annual report to be made by Commissioner. IOR/Z/E/4/25/P1051.

Purser, W. E. *Final Report of the Revised Settlement of the Jalandhar District in the Punjab.* Lahore: Central Jail Press, 1892.

Report by Captain C. M. Wade on Amherst's meeting with Maharaja Ranjit. Mss Eur F140/155.

Report on the Administration of the Punjab for the years 1849–50 and 1850–51. Calcutta: Calcutta Gazette Office, 1853. IOR/V/23/1, no. 2: 1853.

Report on the Census, taken on the 1st January 1855, of the Population of the Punjab Territories. Calcutta: Calcutta Gazette Office, 1856. IOR/V/23/2, no. 11: 20.

Report on the Revenue Settlements of the Lahore District 1865, 27, 36.

Report on the Census of the Punjab 1855, 22, 23. IOR.

Runjeet Singh, Maharajah of Lahore, Request for attendance of Dr. Murray complied with. IOR/Z/E/4/14/R721: 1834–1837.

Wade, Captain C. M., Political Agent, Commended for Conduct of Negotiations with Runjeet Singh. IOR/Z/E/4/15/W5: 1837–1839.

Punjab Government Gazetteer

Punjab Government, *Gazetteer Bannu District 1883–4*. Calcutta: Calcutta Central Press, n.d.
Punjab Government, *Gazetteer Dera Ghazi Khan District 1883–4*. Calcutta: Calcutta Central Press, n.d.
Punjab Government, *Gazetteer Dera Ismail Khan District 1883–4*. Lahore: Arya Press, 1884.
Punjab Government, *Gazetteer Ferozepure District 1883–4*. Lahore: Civil and Military Gazette Press, n.d.
Punjab Government, *Gazetteer Gujrat District 1883–4*. Lahore: Arya Press, 1884.
Punjab Government, *Gazetteer Jhelum District 1883–4*. Calcutta: Calcutta Central Press, n.d.
Punjab Government, *Gazetteer Montgomery District 1883–4*. Lahore: Arya Press, 1884.
Punjab Government, *Gazetteer Mooltan District 1883–4*. Lahore: Arya Press, 1884.
Punjab Government, *Gazetteer Peshawar District 1883–4*. Calcutta: Calcutta Central Press, n.d.
Punjab Government, *Gazetteer Rawalpindi District 1883–4*. Lahore: Civil and Military Gazette Press, n.d.
Punjab Government, *Gazetteer Sialkot District 1883–4*. Lahore: Civil and Military Gazette Press, n.d.
The Lahore Darbar: In the Light of the Correspondence of Sir C. M. Wade (1823–49). Lahore: Punjab Government Records Office, 1930.

Books

Ahluwalia, M. L. (ed.). *Select Documents Relating to Maharaja Ranjit Singh's Negotiations with British Envoy Charles Theophilus Metcalf 1808–1809*. New Delhi: Ashoka International Publishers, 1982.
Aitcheson, Sir Charles. *A Collection of Treaties Engagements and Sannads Relating to India and Neighbouring Countries*. Calcutta: The Punjab Government, 1892.
Ajudhia Parshad Diwan. *Waqai-i-Jang-i-Sikhan* (Pherosheher and Sobaon 1846). Rendered into English by V. S. Suri. Chandigarh: Punjab Itihas Prakashan, 1975.
Ali, Shahamat. *In The Sikhs and Afghans, in Connexion with India and Persia, Immediately Before and After the Death of Ranjeet Singh: From the Journal of an Expedition to Kabul through the Panjab and the Khaibar Pass*. London: 1847.
Barnett, Lieut. Autobiographical Sketch by Shah Shuja Written by Himself in Ludhiana. *Monthly Journal*, 1826–27.
Barr, Lieut. William. *Journal of a March from Delhi to Peshâwur, and from Thence to Câbul, with the Mission to Lieut-Col. Sir C. M. Wade, etc. with Plates*. London: J Madden & Co., 1844.
Burnes, Sir Alexander. *Travels Into Bokhara: Containing the Narrative of a Voyage on the Indus from the Sea to Lahore and an Account of a Journey from India to Cabool, Tartary and Persia in the Years 1831, 1832, and 1833*. Ed. Kathleen Hopkirk. London: Eland, 2012.
Carmichael Smyth, G. *A History of the Reigning Family of Lahore with Some Account of Jammoo Rajahs, the Sikh Soldiers and Their Sirdars*. Calcutta: W. Thacker & Co., 1887.
Carmichael Smyth, G. *Lahore and Its Rulers: A History of Reigning Families of Lahore and the Rajas of Jammu*. Delhi: Ishubhi Publications, 1998.

Chopra, G. L and Garrett, H. L. O. (eds). *Events at the Court of Ranjit Singh 1810–1817* (translation), Monograph no. 17. Patiala: Languages Department Punjab, 1988 (reprint).
Conolly, Arthur, *Journey to the North of India,* 2 vols. London: Richard Bentley, 1838.
Court, Major Henry. *History of the Sikhs.* Lahore: Civil and Military Gazette Press, 1888.
Cunnigham, J. D. *History of the Sikhs.* New Delhi: n.p, 1966.
Eden, Emily. *Up the Country: Letters Written to her Sister from the Upper Provinces of India.* Introduction by Elizabeth Claridge; notes by Edward Thompson. London: Virago, 1997.
Edwardes, H. *Political Diary of Lieutenant H. B. Edwardes, Assistant to the Resident at Lahore, On Deputation to Bannu from the 22nd to the 24th February, 1847.*
Edwardes, H. *A Year on the Punjab Frontier 1848–49,* London: 1851. Lahore: 1963. (Reprint).
Fane, Sir Henry. *Five Years in India, 1835–39,* 2 vols. London: Henry Colburn, 1842.
Fraser, J. B. *Military Memories of Lt. Col. James Skinner,* 2 vols. London: Smith Elder & Co., 1851.
Gardner, Alexander Haughton Campbell. *Soldier and Traveller: Memoirs of Alexander Gardner,* H. Pearse (ed.). Edinburgh and London: William Blackwood and Sons, 1898; Patiala: Language Department Punjab, 1970.
Grewal, J. S. *In the By-line of History: Some Persian Documents from a Punjab Town.* Simla: Indian Institute of Advanced Study, 1975.
Grewal, J. S. and Indu Banga (eds). *Civil and Military Affairs of Maharaja Ranjit Singh.* Amritsar: Guru Nanak Dev University, 1987.
Hamilton, Walter. *Geographical Statistical and Historical Developments of Hindustan,* vol. 2. London: 1820.
Honigberge, John Martin. *Thirty-Five Years in the East: Adventures, Discoveries, Experiments, and Historical Sketches, Relating to the Punjab and Cashmere.* London: 1852.
Hügel, Baron Charles. *Travels in Kashmir and the Panjab: Containing a Particular Account of the Government and Character of the Sikhs / from the German.* London: J. Petheram, 1845.
Jacquemont, Victor. *Letters from India: Describing a journey in the British dominions of India, Tibet, Lahore and Cashmere during the years 1828, 1829, 1830, 1831. Victor Jacquemont, 1801–1832.* 2 vols. Ed. Catherine Alison Phillips, s.l, s.n, 1936; Karachi, Oxford: Oxford University Press, 1979.
Jahrangir, Noor-ud-din Mohammad. *Tuzkiajahangiri,* vol. 1. Ed. Henry Beveridge, trans. Alexander Rogers. London: Royal Asiatic Society, 1909.
Lal, Mohan. *Travel in the Punjab, Afganistan and Turkistan to Balk, Bokhara and Herat, and a Visit to Great Britain and Germany.* London: W. H. Allen, 1846.
Lawrence, H. M. L. *Adventures of an Officer in Punjab.* London: Oxford University Press, 1975.
Masson, Charles. *Narrative of Various Journeys in Baluchistan, Afghanistan and the Punjab,* vols 1–4. London: Richard Bentley, 1842.
M'Gregor, W. L. *The History of the Sikhs; the Lives of the Gurus; the History of the Independent Sirdars, or Missuls, and the Life of the Great Founder of the Sikh Monarchy, Maharaja Ranjit Singh.* 2 vols. London: James Madden, 1846.
Moorcroft, William, and George Trebeck. *Travels in the Himalayan Provinces of Hindustan and the Panjab: In Ladakh and Kashmir; In Peshawar, Kabul, Kunduz, and Bokhara from 1819–1825.* Patiala: Languages Dept, 1970.

Murray, William. *History of the Punjab.* London: William Allen, 1846; Patiala: Languages Dept Punjab, 1970.
Orlich, Captian Leopold von. *Travels in India Including Sind and the Punjab,* vols I, II. London: Green and Longmans, 1845.
Osborne, W. G. *The Court Camp of Ranjit Singh . . . with an Introductory Sketch of the Origin and Rise of the Sikh State, 1840.* Lahore: Mahbub Alam, 1895.
Pearse, Major H. (ed.). *Soldier and Traveller. Memoirs [chiefly in His Own Words] of Alexander Gardner, Colonel of Artillery in the Service of Maharaja Ranjit Singh.* Edinburgh: W. Blackwood & Sons, 1898.
Prinsep, Henry T. *Sikh Power in the Punjab and Political Life of the Maharaja Ranjit Singh, with an Account of the Present Condition, Religion, Laws, and Customs of the Sikhs.* Calcutta: Military Orphan Press, 1834.
Prinsep, Henry T. *History of the Punjab, and of the Rise, Progress, and Present Condition of the Sect and Nation of the Sikhs. Based in part on the 'Origin of the Sikh Power in the Punjab and political life of Muha-Raja Runjeet Singh'.* London: W. H. Allen & Co., 1846.
Punjab Akhbar, June, 1839, 1840.
Schonberg, Erich von. *Travels in India and Kashmir,* 2 vols. London: Hurst and Blackett Publishers, 1853.
Singh, Ganda (ed.). *The Punjab in 1839–40: Selection from the Punjab Akhbars, Punjabi Intelligence Etc.* Amritsar: Sikh History Society, 1952.
Singh, Ganda (ed.). *Private Correspondence Relating to the Anglo-Sikh Wars. Being Private Letters of Lords Ellenborough, Hardinge, Dalhousie and Gough and of Political Assistants Addressed to Sir Frederick Currie as British Resident at Lahore, etc.* Amritsar: Sikh History Society, 1955.
Singh, Giani Gian. *Twarikh Guru Khalsa,* vol. II. Patiala: 2003.
Sinha, Narendra Krishna, and Arun Kumar Dasgupta (eds). *Selections from Ochterlony Papers, 1818–1825, in the National Archives of India.* Calcutta: University of Calcutta, 1964.
Suri, Sohan Lal. *Umdat-ut-Tawarikh,* vols 1–5. Trans. V. S. Suri. Amritsar: Guru Nanak Dev University, 2002.
Trumpp, Dr Ernest. *The Adhi Granth.* London: n.p., 1871.
Vigne, G. T. *A Personal Narrative of a Visit to Ghazni, Cabul and Afghanistan and of a residence at the Court of Dost Mohammad.* London: Whittaker & Co., 1840.
Wolff, Rev. Joseph. *Travels and Adventures of the Rev. Joseph Wolff.* London: Saunders, Otley & Co., 1861.

Unpublished Urdu Primary Sources

Decision of the Board of Revenue, VT 498.
Diaries of Ranjit Singh Darbar from 1822 to 1826 in Fakir Khana family archive.
Judicial Commission Circular Orders, VT 700.
Punjab or audh la ilhaq, papers of Lord Dalhousie, 306, 22, A, 29.
Revenue Cases from 1866 to 1876 of Punjab, VT 835.
Scroll in Persian in the archives of Fakir Khana family (details of monthly payments and donations given to the custodians of the mosques, tombs and other religious places).
Secular Order of the Board of the Revenue of NWFP, 306, 23, F, 9.
Treaties and Sanads, 306, 24, F, 10.

Secondary Sources

Ahluwalia, Jasbir Singh, and Param Bakhshish Singh. *An Overview of Maharaja Ranjit Singh and His Times*. Delhi: Anand Sons, 2001.
Ahluwalia, Jasbir Singh, and Param Bakhshish Singh. *Ranjit Singh and His Times*. Patiala: Punjabi University, 2001.
Ahmad, Aziz. *Studies in Islamic Culture in the Indian Environment*. London: Oxford University Press, 1964.
Aijazuddin Syed Fakir. *The Resourceful Fakirs: Three Muslim Brothers at the Sikh Court of Lahore*. Delhi: Three Rivers Publishers, 2014.
Al Basham. *The Wonder that was India*. London: Sidgwick & Jackson, 1971.
Ali, Imran. *The Punjab under Imperialism, 1885–1947*. New Jersey: Princeton University Press, 1988.
Amarnath, *Zafarnama-i-Ranjit Singh* (Persian). Ed. Sita Ram Kohli. Lahore: University of the Punjab, 1928.
Amini, Iradj. *Koh-i-noor*. New Delhi: The Lotus Collection, 1994.
Awandha, Nahar. *Glimpses of Sikhism*. New Delhi: Sanbun Publishers, 2010.
Baden-Powell, B. H. *The Land-Systems of British India, with Maps*. 3 vols. Oxford: Clarendon Press, 1892.
Bajwa, Fauja Singh. *Military System of the Sikhs, During the Period 1799–1849*. Delhi: Shri Jainendra Press, 1964.
Bakshi, S. R. *Ranjit Singh and Metcalf*. n.p: Vishwavidya Publishers, 1980.
Bakshi, S. R. *Early Aryans to Swaraj*. n.p: Sarup & Sons, 2005.
Banerjee, Indubhusan. *Evolution of the Khalsa*. Calcutta: A Mukerjee, 1963.
Banerjee, S. N. *Ranjit Singh*. Lahore: Atma Ram & Sons, 1933.
Banga, Indu. *Agrarian System of the Sikhs, Late Eighteenth and Early Nineteenth Century*. Amritsar: Manohar Publishers, 1978.
Banga, Indu. *Five Punjabi Centuries, Polity, Economy, Society, and Culture, 1500–1990: Essays for J. S. Grewal*. New Delhi: Manohar Publishers, 1997.
Bentley, Eric. *Century of Hero-Worship*. Boston: 1957.
Chahal, Davinder Singh. *Nankian Philosophy – Basics for Humanity*. Quebec: Institute for Understanding Sikhism, 2008.
Chand, Tara. *Influence of Islam on Indian Culture*. 2nd ed. Lahore: Book Traders, 1979.
Chopra, B. R. *Kingdom of the Punjab 1839–45*. Hoshiarpur: Vishveshvaranand Institute, 1969.
Chopra, G. L. *The Punjab as a Sovereign State*. Lahore: Uttar Chand Kapur & Sons, 1928.
Chopra, G. L. *Advanced History of the Punjab*, vols 1, 2. Jullundher: New Academic Publishing Co., 1969.
Chopra, G. L. *The Punjab as a Sovereign State*. Hoshiar Pur: Vishveshver Anand Vedic Institute, 1969.
Cole, William Owen, and Piara Singh Sambhi. *The Sikhs: Their Religious Beliefs and Practice*. n.p: Sussex Academic Press, 1995.
Cook, Hugh, *The Sikh Wars – The British Army in the Punjab 1845-1849*. London: Leo Cooper, 1975.
Cunningham, Joseph Davey. *A History of the Sikhs: From the Origin of the Nation to the Battles of the Sutlej*. London, New York: Oxford University Press, 1918.
Das, Ganesh (ed.). *Early Nineteenth Century Punjab from Ganesh Das's Char Bagh-i-Panjab*. Ed. and trans. J. S. Grewal and Indu Banga. Amritsar: Dept. of History, Guru Nanak Dev University, 1975.

Dhavan, Purnima. *When Sparrows Became Hawks: The Making of the Sikh Warrior Tradition, 1699–1799.* Oxford: Oxford University Press, 2011.

Dilgeer, Harjinder Singh. *Sikh History.* 10 vols (English). n.p: Sikh University Press, 2010.

Duggal, K. S. *Ranjit Singh: A Secular Sikh Sovereign.* Delhi: Abhinav Publications, 1989.

Duggal, K. S. *The Sikh People: Yesterday and Today.* New Delhi: UBS, 1994.

Fakir Syed Waheeduddin. *The Real Ranjit Singh.* Karachi: Lion Art Press, 1965.

Fenech, Louis E. *Martyrdom in the Sikh Traditions: Playing the 'Game of Love'.* New Delhi: Oxford University Press, 2002.

Garrett, H. L. O., and G. L. Chopra. *Events at the Court of Ranjit Singh, 1810–1817 translated from the original papers.* New Delhi: Amar Prakashan, 1979.

Ghaus, Ghulam. *The Koh-i-noor Diamond.* Peshawer: Taj Mahal Company, 1993.

Goulding, Colonel H. R. *Old Lahore: Reminiscences of a Resident.* Lahore: Sang e Meel Publications, 1924.

Grewal, J. S. *Essays in the Sikh History, from Guru Nanak to the Maharaja Ranjit Singh.* Amritsar: Guru Nanak Dev University, 1972.

Grewal, J. S. *The Shari'at and the Non-Muslims of Batala, Proceedings Punjab History Conference (6th session).* Patiala: 1972.

Grewal, J. S. *Miscellaneous Articles.* Amritsar: Guru Nanak Dev University, 1974.

Grewal, J. S. *The Reign of Maharaja Ranjit Singh, Structure of Power, Economy and Society.* Patiala: Punjabi University, 1981.

Grewal, J. S. *The Sikhs of the Punjab: The New Cambridge History of India.* Cambridge: Cambridge University Press, 1990.

Grewal, J. S. *Sikh Ideology, Polity and Social Order, from Guru Nanak to Maharaja Ranjit Singh.* Delhi: Manohar Publishers, 2007.

Grewal, J. S., and Indu Banga (eds). *Maharaja Ranjit Singh and His Times.* Amritsar: Department of History, Guru Nanak Dev University, 1980.

Grewal, J. S., and Irfan Habib. *Sikh History from Persian Sources Translations of Major Texts.* Lahore: Fiction House, 2004.

Griffin, Lepel Henry. *The Panjab Chiefs: Historical and Biographical Notices of the Principal Families in the Territories under the Panjab Government.* Lahore: 1865.

Griffin, Lepel Henry. *Ranjit Singh.* Oxford: Clarendon Press, 1892.

Griffin, Lepel Henry. *Chiefs and Families of Note in the Punjab.* Lahore: Government Printing Punjab, 1940.

Grover, B. R. *Political and Social Situations of Punjab after Ranjit Era.* Delhi: Punjabi Academy, 1992.

Gupta, Hari Ram. *A History of the Sikhs from Nadir Shah's Invasion to the Rise of Ranjit Singh (1739–1799); Vol. I: Evolution of the Sikh Confederacies (1739–1768).* Simla: Minerva Book House, 1952.

Gupta, Hari Ram. *Later Mughal History of the Punjab, 1707–1793.* Lahore: Sang-e-Meel Publications, 1976.

Gupta, Hari Ram. *History of the Sikhs: The Sikh Lion of Lahore, Maharaja Ranjit Singh, 1799–1839,* vol. 5. Delhi: New Gion Offset Press, 1991.

Gupta, Hari Ram. *History of the Sikhs: Evolution of Sikh Confederacies, 1708–1769* (3rd rev. ed.). The University of Virginia; New Delhi: Munshiram Manoharlal, 1978.

Hamilton, Walter. *Geographical Statistical and Historical Developments of Hindustan.* London: n.p, 1820.

Hasrat, B. J. *Anglo-Sikh Relations During the First Anglo-Afgan War*. Hoshiarpur: University of the Punjab, 1959.
Hasrat, B. J. *British Policy Towards the State of Lahore, 1842-1849*. Chandigarh: University of the Punjab, 1962.
Hasrat, B. J. *Life and Times of Ranjit Singh – a Saga of Benevolent Despotism*. Hoshiarpur: V,V Research Institute Book Agency, 1977.
Hoiberg, Dale. *Students' Britannica India*, vols 1-5. New Delhi: Popular Prakashan, 2000.
Howarth, Stephen. *The Koh-i-noor Diamond – the History and the Legend*. London: Quartet Books, 1980.
Ibbetson, Denzil. *Panjab Castes*. Delhi: B. R. Publishing Corporation, 1974.
Johar, Surinder. *The Secular Maharaja: A Biography of Maharaja Ranjit Singh*. Delhi: Manas Publications, 1985.
Johar, Surinder. *Guru Gobind Singh*. The University of Michigan: Enkay Publishers, 1987.
Kaur, Madanjit. *The Regime of Maharaja Ranjit Singh: Historians' Observations*. Chandigarh: Unistar Books Ltd, 2007.
Khullar, K. K. *Maharaja Ranjit Singh*. New Delhi: n.p, 1980.
Kohli, Sita Ram. *Sunset of the Sikh Empire*. Ed. Khushwant Singh. Bombay: Orient Longmans, 1967.
Kohli, Sita Ram. 'The Organization of Ranjit Singh's Army', in Teja Singh and Ganda Singh (eds), *Maharaja Ranjit Singh*. Patiala: n.p, 1970.
Lafont, Jean-Marie. *Essays in Indo-French Relations, 1630-1976*. New Delhi: Manohar Publishers, 2000.
Lafont, Jean-Marie. *Maharaja Ranjit Singh, the French Connections*. Amritsar: Guru Nanak Dev University, 2001.
Lafont, Jean-Marie. *Maharaja Ranjit Singh, Lord of the Five Rivers*. New Delhi: Oxford University Press, 2002.
Latham, Martin. *The Sikhs*. n.p: n.p, 1985.
Latif, S. M. *History of the Punjab*. New Delhi: Eurasia Publishing House Pvt. Ltd, 1964.
Latif, S. M. *History of the Punjab*. Lahore: People's Publishing House, 1989.
Latif, S. M. *Maharaja Ranjit Singh, Builder of a Common Wealth*. Delhi: National Book House, 2002.
Lawrence, James. *Raj – The Making and Unmaking of British India*. New York: St Martin's Griffin, 1997.
Leitner, G. W. *History of Indigenous Education in the Punjab, Since Annexation and in 1882*. Lahore: Sang e Mil Publications, 2002.
Loehlin, C. H. *The Granth of Guru Gobind Singh and the Khalsa Brotherhood*. Lucknow: Lucknow Publishing House, 1971.
Macaulay, J. B. *Lord Macaulay's Legislative Minutes*. London: 1946.
Machiavelli, Niccolò. *The Prince. Translated and with an introduction by George Bull, etc. 1469-1527*. London: Folio Society, 1970.
Mahmood, Cynthia Keppley. *Fighting for Faith and Nation Dialogues with Sikh Militants*. Philadelphia: University of Pennsylvania Press, 1996.
Malik, Ikram Ali. *A Book of Reading on the History of the Punjab, 1799-1947*. Lahore: Ilmi Printing Press, 1970.
Marenco, Ethne K. *The Transformation of Sikh Society*. New Delhi: Heritage Publishers, 1976.
McLeod, W. H. *Textual Sources for the Study of Sikhism*. Trans. W. H. McLeod. Manchester: Manchester University Press, 1984.

Mir, Farina. *The Social Space of Language: Vernacular Culture in British Colonial Punjab.* Berkeley: University of California Press, 2010.
Moon, Sir Penderel. *The British Conquest and Dominion of India*, 2nd ed. London: Duckworth Press, 1990.
Noor, Harbans Singh. *Connecting the Dots in Sikh History.* Chandigarh: Institute of Sikh Studies, 2004.
Panikkar, K. M. *The Founding of the Kashmir State – A Biography of Maharaja Gulab Singh (1792–1958)*, 2nd ed. London: George Allen & Unwin Ltd, 1953.
Pannu, Dalvir Singh. *The Sikh Heritage: Beyond Borders.* Lahore: Fiction House, 2019.
Pincott, Fredrick. *Sufi Influence on the Formation of Sikhism in the World of the Sufis.* London: Octagon Press, 1979.
Prasad, Bina. *Role of Maharaja Ranjit Singh in North Indian Politics.* New Delhi: Janki Prakashan, 2006.
Qaiser, Iqbal. *Historical Sikh Shrines in Pakistan.* Lahore: Punjab History Board, 1998.
Qanungo, S. N. 'Decline and Fall of the Maratha Power', in R. C. Majumdar (ed.), *The History and Culture of the Indian People: The Maratha Supremacy.* Bombay: 1971.
Ralhan, O. P. *The Great Gurus of the Sikhs: Banda Bahadur.* n.p: Anmol Publications Pvt Ltd, 1997.
Ranbir Singh. *Glimpses of the Divine Masters, Guru Nank – Guru Gobind Singh, 1469–1707.* New Delhi: International Traders Corporation, 1965.
Rawat, Ajay Singh. *Garhwal Himalaya: A Study in Historical Perspective.* n.p: Indus Publishing, 2002.
Rawlinson, H. G. *Buddha, Ashoka, Akbar, Shivaji and Ranjit Singh: A Study in Indian History.* New Delhi: Ess Ess Publications, 1913.
Rizvi, Syed Athar Abbas. *Muslim Revivalist Movements in Northern India in the Sixteenth and Seventeenth Century.* New Delhi: Munshiram Manoharlal, 1995.
Rose, H. A. *A Glossary of the Tribes and Castes of the Punjab and North West Frontier Provinces of India.* Patiala: Punjab Languages Department, 1970.
Roy, Olivier. *Islam and Resistance in Afghanistan.* Cambridge: Cambridge University Press, 1985.
Salahuddin, Iqbal. *Tareekh-e-Punjab.* Lahore: Aziz Publishers, 1974.
Sandhawalia, Preminder Singh. *Noblemen and Kinsmen: History of a Sikh Family.* New Delhi: Munshiram Manoharlal, 1999.
Sen, N. B. 'Marathas and the North Indian States', in R.C. Majumdar (ed.), *The History and the Culture of the Indian People, the Marathas Supremacy*, vol. 3. Bombay: 1977.
Sen, N. B. *Maharaja Ranjit Singh.* New Delhi: New Book Society India, 2001.
Shah, Waris. *Heer Waris.* Ed. Shamsher Singh Ashok. Patiala: Punjab Languages Department, 1976.
Sharma, Radha. *The Lahore Darbar.* Amritsar: Guru Nanak Dev University, 2001.
Sharma, T. R. *Maharaja Ranjit Singh, Ruler and Warrior.* Chandigarh: Punjab University, 2005.
Sheikh, Mohamed. *Emperor of the Five Rivers: The Life and Times of Maharajah Ranjit Singh.* London: I.B. Tauris, 2017.
Sidhu, Amarpal S. *The First Anglo-Sikh War.* London: Amberley, 2010.
Singh, Ajmer. *Maharaja Ranjit Singh Ate Punjabi Sahit* (Punjabi). Patiala: Publication Bureau, 1982.
Singh, Amarinder. *The Last Sunset – The Rise and Fall of the Lahore Durbar.* New Delhi: Roli Books, 2010.

Singh, Bawa Sitinder. *The Jammu Fox – A Biography of Maharaja Gulab Singh of Kashmir.* Carbondale, IL: Southern Illinois University Press, 1974.
Singh, Daljit. *Punjab Social and Economic Condition 1501–1700.* New Delhi: Commonwealth Publishers, 2004.
Singh, Dilip. *Guru Gobind Singh and Khalsa Discipline.* Amritsar: Singh Bros, 1992.
Singh, Dilip. *Life of Sri Gobind Singh Ji, Includes Clarifications on the Authenticity of Zafarnama, Fatehnama, Role of Banda Bairagi, Amarnama,and the Facts Connected with the Guru's Final Departure from Earth.* Amritser: B. Chatter Singh Jiwan, 2003.
Singh, Fauja. *Some Aspects of State and Society under Ranjit Singh.* Delhi: Master Publications, 1982.
Singh, Fauja, and A. C. Arora (eds). *Maharaja Ranjit Singh: Politics, Society, and Economy.* Patiala: Publication Bureau, Punjabi University, 1984.
Singh, Ganda. *Life of Banda Singh Bahadur: Based on Contemporary and Original Records.* Amritsar: Sikh History Research Department, 1935.
Singh, Gopal. *A History of the Sikh People, 1469–1978.* Delhi: World Sikh University Press, 1979.
Singh, Gulcharan. *Ranjit Singh and His Generals.* Jalandhar: n.p, 1949; Sujlana Publishers, 1978.
Singh, Gurbakhsh. *The Khalsa Generals.* n.p: Canadian Sikh Study & Teaching Society, 1927.
Singh, Gurbakhsh. *Sikhs under Brahmanical Siege.* n.p.: Canadian Sikh Study & Teaching Society, 2014.
Singh, Harbans, and Bilbir Singh. *Maharaja Ranjit Singh: Being Tribute to the Memory of the Great Monarch, Published on the Occasion of the First Death Century.* Lahore: the University Sikh Association, 1939.
Singh, Jaspal Kaur. *Violence and Resistance in Sikh Gendered Identity.* USA: Taylor & Francis Group, 2020.
Singh, Khushwant. *The Sikhs Today.* Calcutta: Orient Longmans, 1959.
Singh, Khushwant. *Ranjit Singh (1780–1839).* s.l: Allen & Unwin, 1962.
Singh, Khushwant. *A History of the Sikhs 1469–1839*, 2 vols. Delhi: Oxford University Press, 1977.
Singh, Kirpal. *The Partition of the Punjab, Revised by Sri Ram Sharma.* Patiala: Punjabi University, 1972.
Singh, Manmohan. *Tr Siri Guru Granth Sahib.* 4th ed., vol. 1. Amritsar: Golden Offset Press, 1993.
Singh, Pashaura. *Life and Work of Guru Arjan: History, Memory, and Biography in the Sikh Tradition.* New Delhi: Oxford University Press, 2006.
Singh, Patwant, and M. Rai Jyoti. *Empire of the Sihks: The Life and Times of Maharaja Ranjit Singh.* New Delhi: Hay House India, 2008.
Singh, Prithipal. *The History of Sikh Gurus.* n.p: Educa Books, 2007.
Singh, Prithipal Kapur, and Dharam Singh. *Maharaja Ranjit Singh: Commemoration Volume on the Bicentenary of His Coronation, 1801–2001.* Ed. Prithipal Singh Kapur. Patiala: Publication Bureau, Punjabi University, 2001.
Singh, Prithipal, and Mohinder Singh. *Guru Arjun's Contribution, Martyrdom,and Legacy.* Amritsar: Singh Brothers, 2009.
Singh, Rajinder. *The Secular Maharaja, Maharaja Ranjit Singh.* Delhi: Dynamic Publications, 2008.

Singh, S. P., and J. S. Sabar (eds). *Rule of Maharaja Ranjit Singh: Nature and Relevance*. Amritsar: Guru Nanak Dev University, 2001.
Singh, Sangat. *The Sikhs in History*, 2nd ed. New Delhi: Uncommon Books, 1996.
Singh, Sarbpreet. *The Camel Merchant of Philadelphia*. Chennai: Westland Publications, 2019.
Singh, Sardar Kapoor I. C. S. *Martyred by Shamanistic Laws in Guru Arjan Dev's Life, Martyrdom and Legacy*. Ed. Prithipal Singh Kapoor et al. New Delhi: Gurdawara Management Committee, 2006.
Singh, Sardar Ratnal. *The Khalsa*. Amritsar: Gurdawara Parbandhak Committee, 1979.
Singh, Teja. *A Short History of the Sikhs: 1469–1765*. Patiala: Publication Bureau, Punjabi University, 1999.
Singh, Teja, and Ganda Singh. *A Short History of the Sikhs*. Bombay: Orient Longmans, 1950.
Singha, H. S. *Sikh Studies, Book 6*. n.p: Hemkunt Press, 2005.
Sinha, Narendra Krishna. *Ranjit Singh*. Calcutta: University of Calcutta, 1933; Lahore: Nafees Printers, 1992.
Soundar, Chitra. *Gateway to Indian Culture*. n.p: Asia Pac Books (P) Ltd, n.d.
Sufi, G. M. D. *Kashmīr Being a History of Kashmīr from the Earliest Times to Our Own with a Bibliography and with Plates Including Maps*. Lahore: University of the Punjab, 1949.
Syan, Hardip Singh. *Sikh Militancy in the Seventeenth Century: Religous Violence in Mughal and Early Modern India*. New York: I.B. Tauris, 2013.

Dissertations

Bhatti, Inderyas. 'Nobility under Lahore Darbar'. MPhil diss., Guru Nanak Dev University, 1981.
Dar, Muhammad Bashir. 'Sikhoon Kay Ahad Main Muslimanoon Ki Saqafti Halat,1954'. MA diss., Punjab University, 1954.
Johal, Daljinder Singh. 'Society and Culture as Reflected in Punjabi Literature'. PhD diss., Guru Nanak Dev University, 1985.
Kaur, Barjinder. 'The Jats in the Punjab During the 19th Century'. MPhil diss., Guru Nanak Dev University, 1985.
Muhammed, Khan. 'Muslims in the Punjab under the Sikh Rule 1800–1849'. MA diss., Punjab University, 1964.
Sandhu, Kiranjeet. 'The Udasis in the Colonial Punjab 1849 AD–1947 AD'. PhD diss., Guru Nanak Dev University, 2011.

Encyclopedias and Dictionaries

Ahluwalia, M. L. (ed.). *Encyclopedia of Sikhism*. Faridabad: Common World, 1999.
Bhatia, H. S. and S. R. Bakshi. *Encyclopedic History of the Sikhs and Sikhism*, vol. 6. New Delhi: Deep&Deep Publications, 1999.
Bhatia, Sardar Singh. 'Vadda Ghallughara', *Encyclopedia of Sikhism*, vol. IV. Patiala: Punjabi University, 1998.
Chisholm, Hugh (ed.). *Encyclopedia Britannica*. 11th ed. Cambridge: Cambridge University Press, 1910–11.

Dogra, R.C. *The Sikh World; An Encyclopedic survey of Sikh Religion and Culture*. New Delhi: UBSPD, 2003.
Doniger, Wendy (ed.). *Encyclopedia Britannica*. Chicago, IL: Encyclopedia Britannica, Inc., 2006.
Hasrat, B. J. 'Sher Singh, Maharaja'. *Encyclopedia of Sikhism*. Patiala: Punjab University.
Honour, Hugh, and John Fleming. *A World History of Art*. London: Macmillan Reference Books, 1982.
Hughes, Thomas Patrick. *Dictionary of Islam*. London: W. H. Allen, 1885.
Jaques, Tony. *Dictionary of Battles and Sieges*. London: Greenwood Publishing Group, 2007.
Joshi, S. S., and Mukhtiar Singh Gill (eds). *The Punjabi–English Dictionary*. Patiala: Punjabi University Publication Bureau, 1994.
Ritter, R. M. (ed.). *New Oxford Dictionary for Writers and Editors – the Essential A–Z Guide to the Written Word*. Oxford: Oxford University Press, 2005.
Singh Bhagat, 'Mu'in ul-Mulk', *Encyclopedia of Sikhism*, vol. III. Patiala: Punjabi University, 1997.
Singh, Harbans (ed.). *Encyclopedia of Sikhism*. Patiala: Punjabi University, 1992.
Singh, Harbans (ed.). *Encyclopedia of Sikhism*. Patiala: Punjabi University, 1995.
Singh, Harbans (ed.). *Encyclopedia of Sikhism: A–D*. Patiala: Punjabi University, 1995.

Journals and Magazines

Chagtai, A. 'Lessons from the Zam Zamma Gun'. *Journal of the Research Society of Pakistan* 12 (1975): 17–44.
Chopra, R. M. 'Guru Nanak's Teachings'. *The Sikh Review* 44, no. 515 (1996): 19–22.
Datta, Vishwa N. 'Panjabi refugees and the urban development of Greater Delhi'. *Delhi Through the Ages. Essays in Urban History, Culture and Society*. Delhi: Oxford University Press, 1986, pp. 442–60.
Espiritu, Prof Henry Francis B. 'Dilip Singh on Muslim–Sikh Relations in Mogul India: A Pluralist Appraisal'. *Understanding Sikhism: The Research Journal* 12 (2010): 42–8.
Ganguli, Narendernath. 'The Koh-i-Noor'. *Past and Present* 73, no. 137 (July–December 1954): 91–103.
Harish, K. Puri, 'The Scheduled Castes in the Sikh Community – A Historical Perspective'. *Economic and Political Weekly* (2003): 2–3.
Kang, Jaswinder Singh. 'Shahada Deh Sartaj Guru Arjun Dev'. *Monthly Z-Premier Uk*, 2000.
Kohli, Sita Ram. 'Land Revenue Administration under Maharaja Ranjit Singh'. *Journal of the Punjab Historical Society* 7, no. 1 (1918): 85.
Kohli, Sita Ram. 'Land Revenue Administration under Maharaja Ranjit Singh'. *Punjab Past and Present*, vol. 2 (1971), 440–1.
Massey, Habil James. 'A Fresh Look at Sikh Religion'. *Studies in Sikhism and Comparative Religion* 6 (1985): 69–79.
Massey, Habil James. 'Guru Nanak Dev Ji's Teachings in the Context of Inter-Faith Dialogue'. *Sikh Review* 51, no. 5 (2013): 19–23.
Sikand, Yoginder. 'Building Bridges Between Sikhs and Muslims'. *Studies in Interreligious Dialogue* 9 (1999): 178–88.
Sikand, Yoginder. 'Sikh–Muslim Harmony, Contribution of Khawaja Hassan Nizami'. *Economic and Political Weekly* 31 (2004): 1113–16.
Yousaf, Sardar Shiakh Muhammad. 'Sikh Muslim Relation'. *Noor*, 1948.

Internet Sources

B. J. Hasrat, 'Sher Singh, Maharaja'. *Encyclopedia of Sikhism*. Patiala: Punjab University. https://archive.org/stream/TheEncyclopediaOfSikhism-VolumeIvS-z/TheEncyclopediaOfSikhism-VolumeIvS-z_djvu.txt.

Bhagat Singh. 'Chand Kaur'. *Encyclopedia of Sikhism*. Patiala: Punjabi University. http://www.guide2womenleaders.com/womeninpower/Womeninpower1840.htm: retrieved 05/09/2015.

C. A. Bayly, 'The Pre-History of "Communalism"? Religious Conflict in India, 1700–1860'. *Modern Asian Studies* 19, no. 2 (1985): 177–203. Cambridge University Press http://www.jstor.org/stable/312153: retrieved 23/05/2015.

Gurdashan Singh Dhillon. 'The Sikh Rule and Ranjit Singh'. https://www.allaboutsikhs.com/sikhism-articles/the-sikh-rule-and-ranjit-singh: retrieved 23/05/2014.

Guru Nanak's Understanding of God by Bipin Kujur. http://snphilosophers2005.tripod.com/bipin.pdf: retrieved 27/07/2015.

http://gurmatbibek.com/forum/read.php?3,11139,11139,quote=1#REPLY: retrieved 14/01/2015.

Great Seer and Philosopher Part II. http://www.dawn.com/news/794292/Guru-Nanak-a-Great-Seer-and-a-True-Son-of-Soil-part-ii: retrieved 11/10/2014.

http://searchsikhism.com/maharaja-ranjit-singh/financial-civil-and-military-administration-of-the-maharaja#sthash.kL4XknoA.dpuf: retrieved 14/05/2014.

http://sikhspectrum.com/2002/10/interview-makhdoom-syed-chan-pir-qadri-on-sikh-muslim-relations/#sthash.JO6VW4Iy.dpuf: retrieved 20/09/2014.

http://www.dawn.com/news/794292/guru-nanak-a-great-seer-and-a-true-son-of-soil-part-ii: retrieved 11/10/2014.

http://www.newsplus24.com/2011/10/28/ranjit-singh-as-observed-by-an-english-lady/: retrieved 15/07/2014.

http://www.nios.ac.in/media/documents/SecICHCour/English/CH.04.pdf: retrieved 22/02/2015.

https://www.allaboutsikhs.com/sikhism-articles/the-sikh-rule-and-ranjit-singh: retrieved 23/05/2014.

M. Abadullah Farooqi. 'Iqbal's Estimate of Guru Nanak'. http://www.allamaiqbal.com/publications/journals/review/oct62/8.htm: retrieved 16/03/2015.

Medieval Indian History and Culture Through the Ages. http://www.nios.ac.in/media/documents/SecICHCour/English/CH.04.pdf: retrieved 22/02/2015.

Sardar Singh Bhatia. 'Nau Nihal Singh Kanvar (1821–1840)'. *Encyclopedia of Sikhism*. https://archive.org/stream/TheEncyclopediaOfSikhism-VolumeIiiM-r/TheEncyclopediaOfSikhism-VolumeIiiM-r_djvu.txt: retrieved 23/05/2015.

'Women in Power (1840–1870)'. *Worldwide Guide to Women in Leadership*. http://www.guide2womenleaders.com/womeninpower/Womeninpower1840.htm: retrieved 06/02/2015.

Persian, Punjabi

Ali al-Din, Mufti. *Ibratnameh: Ba-ihtimam-i Muḥammad Baqir*. Lahore: The Panjabi Adabi Academy, 1961.

Bute Shah, Gulam Muhayy-ud-Din. *Tawarikh-i-Punjab*. Patiala: Punjabi University, n.d.

Jaggi, Rattan Singh. *Punjabi Sahit Da Srot – Mulak Itihas*, vol. 3. Patiala: Publication Bureau, 1999.

Urdu

Ahmad, Azizuddin. *Punjab or Bairuni Hamla Awar*. Lahore: Book Home, 2014.
Chishti, Noor Ahmad. *Tahqiqat e Chishti*. Lahore: Nashran Wa Tajran Jutab, 1867.
Griffin, Lepel. *Tazkara e Raosay Punjab, Hissa Dom*, vol. 1. Trans. Syed Nawazish Aliol. Lahore: Sang e Meel Publications, 1993.
Hali, Moulana Iltaf Hussain. *Hayat e Javaid*. n.p: National Book House, 1986.
Laal, Kanaya. *Tareekh-e-Punjab*. Lahore: Majlis-e-Tarakiay Adab, 1981.
Nizami, Khwaja Hasan. *Dai-i-Islam*. Amritsar: n.p, 1923.
Prasad, Debt. *Tarikh-i-Gulshan-i-Punjab*. Trans. Harminder Singh Kohli. Lucknow: 1872; Patiala: 2003.
Saeed, Mian Muhammed. *Ulema e Hind Ka Shandar Mazi, Hissa Dom*. Delhi: 1957.
Server, Mufti Ghulam. *Tarikh e Makhzan e Punjab*. n.p: Mnshi Nok Shor Man, 1859.
Singh, Ganda. *Aḥmad Shah Abdali*. Lahore: Takhliqat, 1993.
Tamimi, Mohammad Jahangir. *Sikh-Muslim Taluqaatek Tehkeeki Jayaiza*. Lahore: South Asian Study Center, Punjab University, 2007.

INDEX

aazan (Muslim's call for prayer) 64, 70
Abdul Samad Khan 35, 41
Abdullah Shah Qadri 66
Abu Ishaq 66
Abu-al-Muali 66
Abul Fazal 82
Adalatgarh 56
Afghanistan 3, 35, 36, 41, 44, 47, 48, 51, 58, 78, 81, 92, 98, 100, 112, 150, 158, 169, 173, 174, 178
Afghans 3, 41, 43, 48, 51–4, 58, 60, 61, 75, 90, 105, 123, 157, 172
Ahmad Khan 41, 46, 53, 82, 149
Ahmad Shah Abdali 9, 35, 36, 39, 40, 43, 47, 57, 71
Ahmad Yar 60, 82
Ahmed Khan 45
Ahmed Shah Rangila 57
Ajit Singh Sindhianwala 72, 118
Akal Takht 17, 23, 30, 139
Akali 5, 12, 48, 67, 70, 72, 73, 98, 112, 133
Akali Phoola Singh 12, 72
Akalis (Order of the Sikhs) 6, 70–3, 85, 88, 100, 128
Akbar 2, 15, 22, 23, 25–8, 36, 43, 70, 81, 89, 128, 133, 144, 165, 178
Akhvand Ali 82
alania 136
Aliabad 54
Aliwal 124
Amar Singh Kalan 53
Amar Singh Majithia 53
Amritsar 5, 7, 8, 17, 22, 23, 25, 36, 40, 42, 46, 55, 68, 69, 72, 75, 78, 81, 92, 94, 96, 104, 105, 107, 115, 119, 137–9, 141, 143–5, 147–50, 152–5, 158, 159, 162, 164, 167, 173–80, 183
Anand Pur 17, 23, 24, 30, 32, 33, 143
Anirudh 57, 106
Arain 64, 80
Armenian Jewish 99
Ata Muhammad Khan 52

Attar Singh Sandhiawalia 48, 119
Attock 41, 47, 48, 52–4, 60, 78, 100, 105, 106, 119, 120, 122
Attock Fort 41, 52, 105
Aurangzeb Alamgir 1, 17, 23, 24, 30–3, 37, 145
Awan 64, 80
Azim Khan 48, 54, 95

Baba Bakala 23, 143
Baba Farid 19–21, 66, 140
Babar 15, 18, 25, 26, 36
Badami Begum 68
Badozais 60
Badshahi Mosque 7, 66, 69
Baghel Singh 56
Bahadur Shah 24, 33–5, 38
Bahauddin Zakariya 45, 68
Baha-ul-Haq 68
Bahawal Khan 41, 47
Bahawalpur 41, 43–7, 49, 53, 60, 77, 106
Baisakhi (a festival celebrated for the start of new year) 24, 93, 142
Balakot 50
Bali Ram 92
Baluchistan 43, 53, 173
Banda Singh Bairagi 9, 34, 35, 37, 38, 147, 179
Bannu 41, 53, 68, 80, 151, 153, 155, 172, 173
Bara Mian 83
Bara Mullah 54
Barakzais 58
Bari Doab 80
Baron Hügel 70
Barr, William 67, 70, 71, 108, 155, 156, 166
basant (spring festival) 66
basanti (Orange colour) 66, 133
Basoli 57
Batala 56, 83–5, 119, 160, 176

Bedies 81
Bhagvan Singh 56
Bhai Buddha 23
Bhai Das 19, 140
Bhai Govind Ram 45, 80, 92, 113
Bhai Gurbukhsh Singh 42, 58
Bhai Mardana 25
Bhaia Ram Singh 58
Bhakhar 47
Bhakti 19, 20, 140
Bhandari family 84
Bhangi 40–3, 55, 70, 93, 106, 107
Bharwanas 46
Bhawani Das 90, 92, 93, 96
Bhima Singh Ardali 55
Bhimbhar 54
Bibi Bhani 22, 142
Bibi Pakdamen 66
Bokan Khan 69
Boostan 81
bowli (well) 22, 67, 133
Brahman 21
Brahmins 18, 26, 32, 85, 92, 134
Burnes, Alexander 8, 61, 72, 149, 150, 153, 157

Calcutta 49, 72, 137, 142, 143, 146, 151–4, 156, 159, 171, 172, 174, 175, 179, 180
calligrapher 65
Calvin, John 19, 140
capital punishment 84, 85, 128
Central Asia 3, 78
Chaks 75
Chamba 57
Chand Kaur 56, 93, 96, 113, 116–18, 168, 182
Chandu Lal 27, 29
Chat Singh 113, 114
Chattha chief 40
Chenab 64, 79
chiefs 6, 10, 33, 40, 47, 57, 59–62, 69, 90, 103, 135, 148, 149, 151–3, 162–4, 167–70, 176
Chiniot 55
chiraghan 66
Cis-Sutlej 5, 88, 93, 94
Colonel D. Ochterloney 58
Columbus 139
Court, Claude August 98

Dallevala *misl* 55, 56
Dara Shikoh 23, 69
Darbar Sahib 7, 25, 70–2, 133, 143
Dar-ul-Aman (abode of peace) 43, 133
daswandh (tithe) 83, 133
daswanth (charity) 37
Daud Potra 41
Deccan 3, 33, 34
Delhi 24, 25, 30–2, 35, 49, 57, 59, 75, 82, 96, 120, 137–41, 143–50, 152, 155–8, 162, 164–8, 170, 172, 173, 175–81, 183
Dera Ghazi Khan 41, 45, 47, 53, 60, 68, 78–80, 83, 112, 151, 155, 172
Dera Ismail Khan 41, 45, 47, 53, 79, 100, 151, 172
Desa Singh Majithia 56, 57
Dhamthor 52
dharamshala (a building devoted to religious or charitable purposes) 66, 81
Dhian Singh 51, 60, 67, 90, 97, 113–21, 161
dhimmis (non-Muslims living in Islamic state) 28
Dhinna Singh Malwai 48
dhora (Punjabi songs) 21, 136
Dhund 53
Di Avitabile, Paolo 98
diaspora 11
Dilip Singh 6, 25, 33, 34, 38, 96, 111, 118, 119, 121, 139, 143, 144, 146, 147, 168, 170, 181
Dina Beg 24
Din-i-Ilahi 28, 133, 144
Divali 36
Divan Singh 56
Diwan Ajudhia Parshad 92, 124
Diwan Amar Nath 44, 83
Diwan Bhawani Das 90, 92, 93, 96
Diwan Chand 45, 48, 54, 55, 92, 93, 95, 97, 163
Diwan Chunni 55, 77
Diwan Dena Nath 92
Diwan Devi Das 55, 90, 92
Diwan Ganga Ram 92, 93, 96
Diwan Karam Chand 90, 92
Diwan Kirpa Ram 48, 55, 94, 95, 106
Diwan Mohkam Chand 48, 53, 54, 58, 90, 92–4

Diwan Ram Dyal 94
Diwan Swan Mal 53, 60, 79, 80, 92, 93, 125
Dogra 12, 64, 90, 91, 97, 111–20, 123, 139, 142, 143, 168, 181
Dost Mohammad Khan 48, 51, 100, 105, 106, 158, 169, 174
Dr Murray 78, 99, 107, 164, 171
Dubir-ud-Doulah 82
Durrani rulers 71

East India Company 11, 41, 45–7, 49, 73, 111
Eid-ul-Azha (Muslim religious festival) 69
Eid-ul-Fitar (Muslim religious festival) 70, 156
Elahi Bukhsh 6, 79, 83, 90, 92, 100, 128
English 5, 8, 64, 72, 76, 82, 84, 93, 105, 106, 142, 153, 161, 172, 176, 182
English Coded Laws 84
European 5, 6, 8, 9, 19, 24, 33, 97–103, 109, 112, 122, 129, 139, 153, 161

Fakir Azizuddin 4, 6, 43, 51, 52, 54, 58, 65, 68, 70, 71, 74, 90, 92, 98, 105–7, 115, 116, 118, 121
Fakir Chiraghudin 121
Fakir Imamuddin 6, 94, 107, 121
Fakir Nuruddin 6, 73, 86, 87, 91, 107, 108, 121, 160
Fakir Shahdin 121
Fakir Tajuddin 121
Fakir Zahooruddin 121
Farrukh Siyar 35
Fateh Khan Barakzai 41, 46–8, 52–4, 58, 60, 80, 115–17, 119
Fatehjang 47
Fauj-e-Khas 98–100, 133
Fazal Shah 82
France 98–102
French 8, 12, 48, 53, 64, 75, 86, 97, 98, 100–2, 105, 106, 133, 134, 140, 152–4, 161, 164, 165, 177

Gakhakars 80
Ganga Ram 90, 92, 93, 96
Gardazis 60
Gardner, Alexander 120, 148, 163, 167, 169, 173, 174

General Avitabile 80
General Ventura 49, 53, 86, 101, 116
General Jean-François Allard 98
German 64, 140, 155, 173
Ghose Khan 69
Ghulam Rasool 82
Gilanis 60
Gobind Garh 107
Goindwal 22, 23, 27, 29, 81
Golden Temple 7, 17, 23, 65, 133, 134, 143
goldsmiths 85
Golkanda 57
Gujjars 80
Gujranwala 39, 69, 80, 95
Gujrat 40, 55, 69, 78, 93, 106, 153, 163, 172
Gujri 23
Gulab Singh 42, 55, 90, 96, 114–17, 119, 120, 123, 167, 169, 170, 178, 179
Gulab Singh Bhangi 42
Gulab Singh Dogra 90, 115, 117, 119
Gulabi Bagh 70
Gulistan 81
Gurbilas 10, 137
Gurdit Singh 55
Gurkhas of Nepal 57
Gurmukh Singh 77, 118
Gurmukhi (style of writing in Punjabi) 10, 22, 81, 159
Guru Amar Das 19, 22, 27, 28, 142
Guru Angad 19, 22, 26, 133, 142, 159
Guru Arjun 3, 19, 23–30, 37, 67, 70, 130, 140, 142, 144, 145, 179–81
Guru Gobind Singh 3, 9, 10, 16, 17, 24, 25, 30, 32–8, 72, 90, 130, 134, 141, 143, 145, 147, 148, 161, 177–9
Guru Har Gobind 3
Guru Har Krishen 23
Guru Har Rai 23, 30
Guru Nanak 6, 9, 10, 15, 16, 18–22, 25, 26, 137–42, 145, 152, 153, 158, 162, 164, 173–8, 180–2
Guru Ram Das 19, 22, 23, 25, 26, 142
Gurus 1, 8–10, 15, 17–20, 22, 24–6, 32, 37, 38, 119, 130, 131, 133, 137, 141, 143, 146, 156, 173, 178, 179
Gwalior Fort 28, 30

Hadi Abad 69
Hafizabad 80
hajj 49, 133
Hakam Hakim Rai 42
Hamilton, Walter 78
Haqiqat Singh 56
Harding, Henry 123
Hargobind Singh 17, 23, 25, 30
Hari Singh Nalwa 48, 49, 51, 53, 55, 68, 76, 90, 106, 107
Haripur 57
Harmandir Sahib 7, 23, 36, 38, 134, 139, 143
Hashim Shah 82
Hassan 5, 16, 68, 80, 141, 181
Hassan Abdal 80
Haughton, Alexander 148, 173
havali 67
Hazara 47, 53, 119, 161
Hazaras 53
Hazoori Bagh 71, 117
Hazrat Ali 68
Hazrat Data Ganj Bakhsh 3, 66
Hazrat Umar Sahib 68
Himachal Pradesh 57
Hindu *pandits* 18, 32, 37, 130
Hindus 3, 6, 7, 13, 16, 18, 20, 22, 25, 26, 30, 31, 36–8, 46, 55, 57, 59, 64, 65, 69, 70, 73, 74, 77, 80, 82, 85, 86, 89–92, 108, 109, 111–13, 120, 128, 129, 131, 136, 145, 154, 159
Holy Quran 3, 7, 19, 60, 65, 68, 69, 135
Holy Tank 22
Hoshiarpur 41, 69, 106, 151, 161, 163, 175, 177
Hukam Singh Attari 61
Hukma Singh Chimni 61, 90
Huldreich Zwingli 19, 140
Humayun 2, 26
Hussain 5, 66, 156, 159, 183
hymns 22, 25, 140

Ilmud Din 69
Imam Bukhsh 8, 82, 83, 92
Imam Hussain 156
Imam Nasiruddin 69
India 1, 3, 8, 9, 11, 17–19, 24, 26, 36, 40, 41, 45–7, 49, 50, 53, 57, 67, 73, 75, 77, 78, 87, 101, 111, 123, 127, 138–47, 149, 152–4, 156–8, 163–6, 169–82
Iran 3, 83, 98, 101
Islam 1–5, 15, 16, 18, 19, 27, 28, 30–2, 36–8, 48, 63, 82, 104, 106, 131, 136, 139, 141, 144, 150, 153, 175, 178, 181
Islamic Shariah Laws 84
Ismail Alias Wadda 67
Ismaili 19
Italian 64, 98, 101, 139, 140, 153, 161

jagirdars 10, 24, 69, 102
Jahandad Khan 41, 48, 105
Jahangir 2, 3, 23, 25–30, 37, 71, 144, 145, 183
Jai Singh 40, 56
Jaimal Singh 56
Jalandhar 69, 81, 95, 162, 163, 171, 179
Jalla 96, 119
Jamadar Khushal Singh 58, 71, 75, 101, 113, 115
Jamrud 51
Jasrota 57, 103
Jassa Singh Ram Garhia 42
Jaswan 57
Jats 49, 64, 91, 109, 122, 153, 180
Jawahir Mal Dogra 91
Jhang 5, 41, 45, 46, 60, 61, 69, 78–80, 90
jihad 48–51, 82, 100, 134
jizya (tax imposed on the non-Muslims) 134, 144
Jodh Singh 42, 56
jubbah (cloak) 68, 134
Julka 56
Junjuas 60, 80

kaafi (Sufi poetry) 21, 136
Kabir 19–21, 140
Kabul 3, 40, 42, 44, 47, 48, 51, 53, 54, 57–9, 78, 95, 100, 106, 123, 144, 148, 152, 155, 157, 164, 166, 172, 173
kacha (under garment) 17, 24, 135
kafirs (person who does not believe in God) 27, 105
kais (hair) 17, 24, 135
Kalanaur 56, 97
Kamboh 64, 80
Kanaya *misl* 40, 56

kanga (comb) 17, 24, 135
Kangra 41, 57, 100, 106
Kapurthala 41, 106
kara (bangle) 17, 24, 135
kardars 69, 79, 84, 92, 117, 124, 125
karpan (type of sword) 17, 24, 135
Kartar Pur 22
Kashmir 3, 26, 30, 31, 34, 48, 49, 51–5, 58, 60, 64, 68–70, 74–8, 86, 94–6, 100, 102, 107, 112, 123, 128, 152, 155, 158, 161, 163, 165–7, 169, 170, 173, 174, 178, 179
Kasur 41–4, 60, 61, 80, 90, 93, 96, 121
khanqah 66–9, 134
khans 5
Kharal 53, 64
Kharals 46, 80
Khatries 64, 85, 153
Khawaja Baki 27
Khawaja Bihari 67
Khawaja Suleiman 83
khojas 78, 81
khojis ((experts in tracing footprints of criminals) 84
Khokhar 66, 80
Khorasan 77, 83
Khosa 60
Khushhal Singh 71, 75, 90, 113, 115
Khusroo 3, 28, 29, 38
Khwaja Muhaiy-ud-din 77
Kirpa Ram 48, 55, 75, 92, 94, 95, 106
Koh-e-Noor 3, 6, 7, 57–9, 89, 152, 175–7, 181
Kotla 57
Kulu 57, 100

Ladakh 78, 123, 152, 155, 166, 173
Laghari 60
Lahna 21, 22
Lahore 3–6, 8–10, 12, 20, 22, 27, 29, 35, 36, 40–9, 53–7, 60–2, 64, 66–73, 75–9, 82, 83, 85, 86, 89, 90, 92–4, 96–104, 106–8, 115–26, 128, 130, 137, 138, 140, 141, 144, 146–54, 156–80, 182, 183
Lal Singh 90, 12
langar (free kitchen, food) 22, 134
Lehna Singh 72, 82, 90, 103, 118
Lehna Singh Majithia 72, 103
Leitner 82, 159, 160, 177
Leonardo 19, 140

Lodhi Dynasty 18
Lohanies 81
Lohgarh 23, 30, 35
loongi 75
Lord Auckland 70, 71, 106, 107, 171
Ludhiana 58, 64, 75, 99, 103, 118, 157, 172
Luther, Martin 19, 140

Macaulay, J. B 2, 137, 177
Madhu Lal Hussain 66, 67
madrassas 81
mafidars 69
Maha Singh 39, 40
Mahan Singh, Colonel 55, 75, 76
Maharani Jindan 118, 119
Maharani Mehtab Kaur 117
Mahtab Kaur 40, 56
Major Croft 119
Makhdooms 60
Makhowal 31
maktabs 82
Malik Fateh Khan Tiwana 115–17, 119
Malva 56
Mandi 57, 68, 100, 106
mango 71
Mankera 41, 46, 47, 53, 60, 79, 95
Mankot 57
Maratha 3, 96, 162, 178
Marhathas 49
Mata Sundari 33
Mecca 27, 49, 133
Metcalfe, Charles 56, 93
Mian Ashok Muhammed 42
Mian Fazal-ud-din 83
Mian Mir 19, 20, 23, 25, 30, 66, 69, 70, 140
Mian Qadir Bukhsh 73
Miani Sahib 66
Mianwali 46
Michelangelo 19, 139
minas 27
Mir Shadi 42
Mir Sher Muhammed Khan 68
Mirza Begun Baig 69
misls 6, 9, 10, 35, 39, 40, 148
Misr Beli Ram 92, 97, 113, 118
Misr Diwan Chand 48, 54, 55, 92, 93, 95, 97
Misr Ram Kishen 118
Misr Rup Lal 92, 93, 97, 103

Mit Singh Padania 61, 90
Moeenud Doula 41
Mohan Lal 78, 158, 159
Moj-e-Darya 3
Moorcroft, William 8, 57, 67, 76, 108, 152, 155, 157, 158, 166, 173
Moran 12, 68, 69, 83
Mosa Khokhar 66
mosque 5, 7, 8, 16, 52, 66–9, 71, 81, 83, 100
Moti Ram 55, 76, 90, 92–5, 106, 107
Moulvi Sheikh Ahmed 83
moulvis 82
Mubarak Haveli 58
Mudki 121, 123
Mufti Imam Bukhsh 83
Mufti Muhammad Shah 79, 104
Mufti Muhammed Mokarram 42
Mughal 1–4, 9, 11, 15, 17, 18, 23–5, 27–39, 47, 57, 59, 69, 70, 83, 89, 92, 130, 131, 143–7, 154, 156, 170, 176, 180
Muhammad Shah Nawaz Khan 41, 79, 104
Muhammed Shah Naqshbandi 68
Muharram 5, 7, 69, 70, 98, 156
Mujaddid Alf-e-Sani 27
mujawars 66, 67
Mukhdoom Shah Mahmood 68
Mul Raj 125
Multan 5, 6, 41–7, 60, 61, 64, 68, 69, 77–9, 81, 90, 94–6, 123, 125, 128
Munshi Sohan Lal 83
Muzaffar Khan Saddozai 43

Nadir Shah 39, 43, 47, 57, 59, 71, 147, 176
Nakai *misl* 56, 113
Namdev 19
Napoleon 6, 87, 98, 101, 123, 125
Naqshbandi *ulemas* 36
Nauroz 67
Naushehra 48, 95, 100
Nawab 5, 41–5, 47, 49, 53, 61, 67, 106
Nawab Bhikari Khan 67
Nawab Hafiz Ahmad Khan 53
Nawab Muzaffar Khan 5, 41, 44, 45, 61
Nawab Nizam-ud-din 42
nazims 79
Nihangs 72
Nizami 16, 18, 82, 139, 141, 181, 183
Nizam-ud-din Khan 5, 41–3, 104, 128

nobility 26, 36–8, 87, 90, 120, 131, 153, 180
Noorpur 57

Ochterloney, David 56, 105, 171
Osborne, W. G. 174

Painda Khan 24, 32
Pakhli 52
Pakpattan 66
panchayats 84, 119, 122
Pandit Birbel 76
Panj Pir 54, 135
Paper Mandi 68
parachas 78
Parthi Das 26, 27, 29
Pathan Kot 56
pathshala 20, 135
patkas 75
Peacock Throne 57
Persian 8, 10, 11, 20, 78, 81–4, 90, 105, 106, 134, 144, 160, 162, 165, 173–6, 182
Pertap Singh 118
Peshawar 3, 5, 41, 47–54, 64, 68, 77, 78, 80, 85, 86, 91, 99–102, 105, 106, 112, 122, 128, 152, 155, 159, 166, 172, 173
Pind Dadan Khan 69, 78
Pindi Bhattian 80
Pindigheb 47
Pir Makki 66
Pir Mittha 69
Pir Muhammad 40, 51
Poonch 54
Prachin Panth Parkas 83
Prince Dara Shikoh 23, 69
Prince Eugene 98
Prince Hira Singh 57
Prince Kharak Singh 54, 56, 57, 67, 69, 70, 89, 112
Prince Khusroo 3, 29
Prince Nau Nihal 51, 66, 114–16
Prince Peshawara Singh 119
Prinsep, Henry T. 74
Prophet Muhammad PBUH 27, 136, 156
pruhat 31, 135
Punjabi 8, 9, 11, 19, 21, 23, 60, 78, 83, 87, 90, 92, 99, 100, 102, 104, 136, 138, 141, 142, 146–9, 151, 154–6, 159–61, 163, 166, 170, 174–6, 178–82

Qadir Yar 82
Qaida Khan 73
Qazi Fakirullah 69
Qazi Nizam-ud-din 5, 79, 104, 128
qissas 82
Qutab-ud-Din 43

Rahitnamas 10
Rai Kesari Singh 119
Raj Kaur 28, 39, 56, 113
Raja Bhop Singh 57
Raja Dhian Singh 67, 90, 113, 161
Raja Sansar Chand 57, 106
Rajori 54
Rajputs 49, 61, 64, 90–2
Ram Deyal 53, 54
Ram Rai 23, 30–2
Ramananda 19, 20, 92, 140
Ramdaspur 30
Ramgarhia *misl* 56
Ran Singh 56, 163
Raphael 140
revenue 4, 8, 10, 13, 28, 43–5, 47, 52, 55, 59, 60, 66, 69, 74–7, 79, 80, 82–4, 91–3, 95, 109, 115, 121, 122, 124, 125, 129, 130, 134–6, 153, 158, 159, 161, 171, 174, 181
Rogers, Alexander 144, 173
Russia 98

Saadi 81
Sada Kaur 5, 12, 40, 55, 56
Sadiq Muhammad Khan 53
saffron 76, 78
Sahib Kaur 115, 116
Sahib Singh 42, 55, 93, 106
Sahib Singh Bhangi 42, 93, 106
Sahiwal 46, 60, 79, 80
sahukars 80
Saidan Shah 66
saint 3, 23, 67, 69, 133, 140, 144
sajda-e-ta'zeem 28, 135
sajjada nashins 66, 135
Sakhi Sarwar 66, 68
Sangatpura 56
Sansar Chand 41, 57, 106
Sanskrit 19, 22, 81
Sarayi Noor Mahel 69
Sarbat Khalsa 40, 148
Sardar Attar Singh Dhari 61, 90

Sardar Chattar Singh Attariwala 119
Sardar Desh Singh 160
Sardar Fateh Singh 61, 90
Sardar Gujjar Singh 107
Sardar Gulab Singh 123
Sardar Hari Singh 43, 51, 55, 106, 107
Sardar Jawahir Singh 119
Sardar Kapoor Singh 145
Sardar Ratnal Singh 145
Sardar Sham Singh 115
Sardar Sham Singh Attariwala 115
Sardar, Yar Muhammed 47
Sarfraz Khan 45, 60
shabat 21, 136
Shah Abdul Aziz 49
Shah Bilawal Qadri 67
Shah Ismail 49
Shah Jamaluddin Qadri 67
Shah Khairuddin 66
Shah Mahmood 47, 48, 68
Shah Malok 69
Shah Mirza Muhammad Ali 101
Shah Rukn-e-alam 68
Shah Shamas Tabriz 68
Shah Sharaf 5
Shah Shuja 3, 6, 7, 44, 45, 51, 58, 59, 88, 92, 99, 106, 123, 152, 164, 169, 172
Shahi Fort 71
Shahjahan 2
Shahla Bagh 70
Shahpur 57, 79, 80
Shalimar Gardens 55, 67, 70, 71
shalouks 19, 21, 22
Sham Singh 90, 115
shastars 86
shawls 50, 67, 75, 76, 78, 103, 105
Sheikh Ahmed Sirhindi 27–9, 31, 83
Sheikh Ghulam Muhaiy-ud-din 55
Sheikh Imamuddin 55
Sheikh Naimat Ullah Sirhindi 66
Sheikh Tahir Bandgi 66
Sher Singh 48–50, 53, 55, 56, 76, 85, 89, 96, 99, 101, 108, 111, 112, 114, 116–18, 121–3, 125, 160, 168, 181, 182
Shia 16, 19, 129
Shikarpuries 81
Shupiyan 76
Sialkot 54, 55, 57, 78, 83, 172
Sials 41, 46, 64, 80

Sikandar Nama 82
Sindh 8, 40, 41, 43, 44, 46, 47, 49, 77, 80, 98, 123, 150
Sindh Sagar Doab 80
Sirhind 24, 33–5, 37, 47, 143
smallpox 23, 40, 166
Sobraon 124
Sohan Lal Suri 4, 58, 137, 151, 162
Sonehri Masjid 3, 8, 67, 100
Sonipat 34, 146
Sri Guru Granth Sahib 18, 143
Sri Nagar 25, 26, 54
Subha Singh 91
Suchet Singh 90, 114, 116, 119, 120, 160
Sufi 19–21, 23, 27, 67–9, 75, 77, 106, 133, 139–41, 144–7, 150, 151, 157, 158, 163, 170, 178, 180
Sukarchakia *misl* 40
Suket 57
Sultan Muhammad Khan 47, 49–51, 61, 71, 74
Sunni 16, 19, 129
Surdas 140
Surjit Hans 5, 137
Sutlej 5, 8, 57, 61, 79, 88, 93, 94, 95, 100, 103, 105, 117, 120, 124, 133, 143, 175
suttee 22, 57, 136
Swar Khan Katti Khel 41
Syed Ahmad 48–50, 82, 100, 136
Syed Ali Shah 67

Taigh Bahadur 17
takiahas 69
Tamur Shah 42, 148
Tara Singh Ghaiba 55
Taran Sahib 142
Tarin 53
Tehrik-e-Mujahidin 48–50, 127, 136
Tej Singh 90, 115, 116, 120, 123, 124
Thomas, George 98
Tibet 8, 123, 154, 173

Tika Sahib Bahadur 113
Tiwanas 60, 80
tomb 5, 24, 66, 67, 71
topchi 69
toshakhana 68
tribute 9, 44–8, 50–3, 58, 67, 87, 106, 135, 151, 164, 179
Tulsi Das 20
Turkistan 158, 173
Tuzk-e-Jahangiri 26

Udassis 22
ulemas 26–9, 36, 50, 52, 59, 68, 91
Umdat-ut-Tawarikh 4, 80, 83, 102–3, 137, 148, 151, 154, 156, 159, 162–5, 168–9, 174
Urdu 81, 148, 174, 183
Ustad Pir Bukhsh 83

Vasco da Gama 19
Ventura, Jean-Baptiste 12, 98

Wade, C. M. 55, 76, 151, 155, 158, 164, 166, 171–2
Wafa Begum 58
Wahabi ulemas 50
Wazir Khan 24, 34, 35, 37, 41, 66, 67, 71
Wazir Khan Mosque 66, 71
Wazirabad 42, 69, 78, 101
Wyrowal 81

Yaqoob Zanjani 66
Yousafzai 48, 50

Zafar Jang 136
Zafar Nama 83
zakat 37, 136
Zaman Shah 40, 58
zamindars 28, 80, 103, 124, 125
Zamzama 55Abdel Haleem, Muhammad 65

www.ingramcontent.com/pod-product-compliance
Lightning Source LLC
Chambersburg PA
CBHW061832300426
44115CB00013B/2352